Crusader in Babylon

Crusader in Babylon

W.T. Stead and the Pall Mall Gazette

RAYMOND L. SCHULTS

UNIVERSITY OF NEBRASKA PRESS · LINCOLN

Publishers on the Plains

Copyright © 1972 by the University of Nebraska Press
All rights reserved
International Standard Book Number 0-8032-0760-3
Library of Congress Catalog Card Number 71-109603

Most recent printing shown by first digit below:

1   2   3   4   5   6   7   8   9   10

Manufactured in the United States of America

To Virginia, my wife

Contents

||||o||||o||||o||||o||||o||||o||||o||||o||||o||||o||||o||||o||||o||||o||||o||||o||||o||||o||||o||||o||||o||||o||||o||||o||||o||||o||||o||||o||||o||||o||||

A picture section follows page 142.

vii

Preface

A significant event in the development of the modern English press was the emergence, in the late Victorian era, of the "New Journalism." The term was used loosely, but in general it referred to the creation of a brighter, livelier, more readable newspaper. The important changes it introduced ultimately captured the fancy—and the pennies—of a reading public which had been vastly altered by the impact of the 1870 Education Act. The name of Alfred Harmsworth, founder of the *Daily Mail*, is that most often identified with the New Journalism; yet he was only reaping the harvest. The seeds had been sown earlier by such pioneers as George Newnes, T. P. O'Connor, and, above all, William T. Stead. The central theme of this book is the contribution of Stead, as editor of the *Pall Mall Gazette*, to this journalistic revolution.

Two existing studies deal in part with this subject: Frederic Whyte's *Life of W. T. Stead* (1925) and J. W. Robertson Scott's *Life and Death of a Newspaper* (1952). Whyte's two-volume work is the only full-scale biography of Stead, and Scott's book is a history of the *Pall Mall Gazette* with emphasis on its most important editors. In each instance Stead's contributions to the New Journalism are regarded as but one chapter in the stories of the man and the newspaper. The resulting treatment, although more than cursory, still is brief and incomplete.

Crusader in Babylon is neither a biography of Stead nor a history of the *Pall Mall Gazette;* yet it is something of both. The editor's background and character are considered in the context of what they produced in the way of journalistic innovation; and how these changes affected Stead's contemporaries also is considered. I have made extensive use of the files of the *Pall Mall Gazette* and of other London papers so that, as much as possible, Stead will speak through the pages of his newspaper, which for a time was the epitome of personalized journalism. Similarly, the reactions to Stead and the New Journalism have been drawn from the other journals of the day in the hope of recapturing something of the flavor and atmosphere of Fleet Street during a critical period in its history.

I would like to express my appreciation to the staffs of the British Museum Library and the Newspaper Library at Colindale for their courtesy and helpfulness; and to Eastern Washington State College for the financial assistance provided through its sabbatical leave program. My wife labored tirelessly in typing the manuscript and Mrs. Ninon Maxey was of inestimable help in doing the indexing. I am also grateful for the assistance given me in England by John Gough and Willoughby Smith.

RAYMOND L. SCHULTS

Eastern Washington State College

Introduction

For England the 1880s were years of transition as the nation began to shed the mantle of Victorianism and invest itself with the trappings of the modern age. It is true that the same statement could be made about other years, and the historian is sometimes tempted to exaggerate the significance of events which occur in the period of his interest, yet unquestionably from 1880 to 1890 English society was undergoing fundamental and far-reaching changes of degree and substance which would alter the traditional social, political, and economic structure of the nation.

It was in many ways a gray decade, and it opened in an appropriately gloomy atmosphere. Throughout the winter of 1879-80 an unusually persistent and heavy fog brooded over London, and to some it seemed to mirror the national mood.[1] To a large extent the despondency of the period was the product of economic depression; in 1878 England entered a long and disastrous period of agricultural decline, and the financial crisis and industrial slump of the mid-seventies was to be repeated in the eighties. Certainly the working classes, despite the improvement in their condition resulting from earlier factory legislation, had ample cause for discontent. Although real wages were increasing at a fairly steady pace (in fact, many members of the Establishment blamed recurring depressions on high pay), labor's share of England's growing wealth was still grossly disproportionate and inadequate. Unemployment was

1. R. H. Gretton, *A Modern History of the English People* (London: Martin Secker, 1930), p. 15.

an increasingly serious problem,[2] and many employed workers were exploited by low wages, dangerous or debilitating jobs, and appalling living conditions. Legislation had been passed to provide some measure of protection for women and children, but state intervention in business on behalf of adult males would mean defiance of the great Victorian gods Individualism and Laissez faire, and undoubtedly Thomas Escott was reflecting the views of the middle and upper classes when he applauded laboring men for not petitioning Parliament to take action about their working conditions. Escott evidently saw no contradiction between his advocacy of a "free contract" between employer and employee and his descriptions of the abuses and short life expectancy which prevailed in many industries.[3]

Compared to their Continental counterparts, British workingmen had been peaceful and patient, but during the 1880s their attempts to ameliorate their lot, whether expressed in trade unionism or political activities, tended to become more militant. Although it had had less impact in Britain than in the industrialized nations of Europe, socialism in the broadest sense of the term now began to appeal to many as the best way of ending the injustices of the existing system. Artisans living in parliamentary boroughs had been given virtual household suffrage by the franchise reform of 1867, and as a direct consequence had gained the opportunity for further social advancement through the Education Act of 1870.[4] The specific, tangible results of such legislation are difficult to tabulate, but it is generally agreed that by the 1880s these workers had become more articulate, more self-confident, and more conscious of their own strength than ever before.

The English governing classes also sensed the growing potential

2. The word *unemployed* first appeared as a noun in the *Oxford English Dictionary* of 1882.

3. T.H.S. Escott, *England: Its People, Polity, and Pursuits* (London: Cassell and Co., 1881), pp. 132, 146.

4. The Representation of the People Act of 1867 enfranchised adult males who occupied for a year, as either owners or tenants, houses on which rates (local taxes) had been paid, and those who had occupied for a year unfurnished lodgings worth ten pounds annually. The electorate was doubled by this bill, and in the towns the working classes now had a majority. The Education Act of 1870 was a giant first step in the direction of providing every Englishman with an elementary education. It created a national system of school districts, run by locally elected school boards, which could build schools where voluntary schools did not exist and require attendance of children between five and thirteen years of age. In 1876 elementary education was made compulsory, and in 1891 free.

power of the laboring man. Escott praised "the good sense, the good feeling, and the political docility" of the working classes, but he also noted that "a well-concerted uprising on their part in any of the great centers of manufacture and commerce would not merely terrorize a district but paralyze the trading system of the empire." [5] Some members of the hierarchy reacted to this threat, either individually or collectively in organizations such as the Liberty and Property Defence League, by opposing most social legislation under the banner of protecting England from socialism, radicalism, and revolution; others, whether from fear, pragmatism, or altruism, tried to come to terms with a changing society and ease some of the worst burdens borne by the lower orders. The festering growth of the slums, for example, was gradually recognized as a national evil, a problem which transcended party lines. It was felt that "the laws of economic liberalism should operate; grown men should make their own bargains; the state should refrain from grandmotherly legislation—but *people should not live like that.*" [6]

Even though the government already had shown its willingness to depart from the pure doctrine of laissez faire in the realm of health and housing, Edwin Chadwick's Public Health Act (1848), Richard Cross's Artisans' Dwelling Act (1875), and other such measures had scarcely begun to clean up the slum cesspools which soured the urban areas and mocked Britain's reputation as a prosperous, progressive nation. During the 1880s, however, as public concern and public protests mounted, men as far removed from the taint of radicalism as Lord Salisbury took up the cause of government health and housing legislation; and it became more difficult to defend repressive features of the existing social, political, and economic structure on the grounds of laissez faire or antisocialism.

On the broader scene of international relations the English nation seemed to be slowly emerging from the shell of "splendid isolationism." And although such developments cannot be pinpointed by dates, during the 1880s England was also experiencing that vague phenomenon known as the "New Imperialism." The greatest impetus to a revived sense of world responsibility was to come later in the century, but as early as 1881 Escott could write, "The popular veto upon an unqualified acceptance of the doctrine of non-

5. Escott, *England*, pp. 127-28.
6. Helen Merrell Lynd, *England in the Eighteen-Eighties* (London: Oxford University Press, 1945), p. 144.

intervention is said to have gone forth. We are . . . thirsting for the responsibilities of empire, and panting for the fresh and invigorating atmosphere which the periodical enlargement of our imperial boundaries brings with it." Escott also foretold the ensuing trouble between the advocates of imperial expansion and the Little Englanders, and saw it all as characteristic of the transitional nature of the age.[7]

It is against this socioeconomic background that another phenomenon of the 1880s must be considered—the emergence of what came to be called the New Journalism, which eventually was to transform the entire English press.

In the nineteenth century the English press was still primarily the London press, and the picture it presented at the opening of the eighties was both bright and dull. On the one hand, London journalism in all its forms was flourishing and expanding, notwithstanding the occasional failure of a newspaper or a periodical. It offered young men a reasonably profitable career, although of course one not as well paid as law or medicine. Moreover, technological developments were about to contribute to the improvement of the press. By 1880 the telegraph already was expediting the transmission of news, and soon electric power, the telephone, and the typewriter would greatly increase the efficiency of all phases of journalistic operations. On the other hand, London newspapers were drab in both form and content. Dreary columns of small type were unbroken by crossheads or, in many cases, even by paragraphs. Headlines, if any, were modest and unobtrusive, and the monotonous typography was unrelieved by illustrations. For most of the "respectable" press, political news was the great staple, and when Parliament was in session speeches were reported in overwhelming detail.

Newspapers were divided into categories at least as distinctly as the quality and popular journals of the present day. Some of the Sunday papers and certain specialty weeklies reveled in crime, scandal, sports, and other topics which a good many people considered frivolous if not debasing. These papers were bolder in make-up and format (as was, to a lesser degree, one evening paper, the halfpenny *Echo*),[9] but they were thought to be crude, plebeian,

7. Escott, *England*, pp. 4-5.
8. Ibid, p. 518.
9. Another evening halfpenny, the *Evening News*, was founded in 1881.

and tasteless. The only newspapers that counted with the people who counted were the morning dailies and the penny evenings. There were six of the former,[10] and they were dominated and influenced to a surprising degree by the stately, gray *Times*, the most prestigious newspaper in England—and, indeed, in the world. Under John Walter III it presented the news with a Conservative bias, solidly and exhaustively, and it was meant to be read word for word. No concessions were made to the reader's eyesight: long stories were unbroken by crossheads or paragraphs, the type size never varied, and the headlines were rare and unaggressive. The majesty of the *Times* was underlined by its price, which had stood at three pence since the repeal of the paper tax in 1861. Of the other mornings, three—the *Morning Post* (William Hardman),[11] the *Standard* (W. H. Mudford), and the *Daily Telegraph* (Sir Edward Arnold)—were Conservative, and two—the *Daily Chronicle* (R. W. Boyle) and the *Daily News* (F. H. Hill)—were Liberal. All five sold for a penny, but any other differences from the *Times* (except for political bias) were minor. Some had feature or editorial writers who imparted a note of individuality to their columns, but "all . . . maintained, even at a penny, the dignity in the presentation of the news characteristic of the old, pre-repeal, high-priced Press led by the Times."[12]

Apart from the Radical *Echo* (J. Passmore Edwards), there were four evening papers. The venerable *Globe* (Sir George C. H. Armstrong) and the *Evening Standard* (W. H. Mudford) were both Conservative and sold for a penny. The Liberal *Pall Mall Gazette* (John Morley) and its brand-new Conservative rival, the *St. James's Gazette* (Frederick Greenwood) were priced at two pence, but were soon to be reduced to the same price as their competitors. The evenings operated under somewhat more relaxed standards than the mornings. Their news stories were usually shorter and on more diverse subjects; their features, which were more numerous, were written more brightly; and their editorial matter was generally briefer and often less serious. Designed to be read at

10. This does not include the *Financial Times* or the *Morning Advertiser*, which were still primarily specialty papers. In appearance and style they were much like the other morning journals.

11. The names in parentheses are of the editors of the respective newspapers as of 1880.

12. [Stanley Morison], *The History of "The Times."* vol. 3, *The Twentieth Century Test, 1884-1912* (London: Times Publishing Company, 1947), pp. 91-92.

the end of the day, when presumably the reader had more leisure for reflection, the evening journals took on certain aspects of a daily review. This is not to suggest, however, that they resembled the more sensational newspapers of a later period or were fore-runners of the New Journalism. They were, as the *Times's* histor-ian has written, meant to be "cultivated" journals appealing to the "cultivated" middle- and upper-class reader.[13] If the editors of the respectable journals, evening and morning, in 1880 had discovered that the Education Act of a decade earlier had begun to create a vast potential readership with a different background and educa-tional level, they showed no signs of intending to capitalize on this new market.

Such, in brief, was the journalistic scene surveyed by William T. Stead when he took up his duties on the *Pall Mall Gazette* in 1880. When he resigned its editorship and left the field of daily journal-ism nine years later he had launched a revolution, the dimensions of which were not always appreciated in his own day. Although superficially the press may not have seemed much changed by 1889, the New Journalism had been born, and its effects were wide-ranging and permanent.

13. *The History of "The Times"* suggests that the pressure of competition created by four newspapers trying to appeal to one rather limited class was at least partially responsible for Stead's introducing the New Journalism in the *Pall Mall Gazette.*

Crusader in Babylon

CHAPTER ONE

A Journalist from the Provinces

It was on Saturday, August 25, 1883, that John Morley—journalist, man of letters, member of Parliament—wrote his last leader [1] as editor of the *Pall Mall Gazette*. He wrote it by hand in the newspaper's dingy, gaslit office on Northumberland Street: typewriters were still a novelty which few journalists had learned to use, and as yet only a few London buildings were illuminated by electricity. Morley had been editor of the *PMG*, as it was popularly known, since 1880, but now his parliamentary duties, added to the pressures of his other literary work, were forcing him out of journalism. [2] He was succeeded as editor by his hand-picked assistant, a young, brash, effervescent journalist who had descended upon London from the North Country in 1880. Full-bearded, with intense sparkling eyes that shine forth even in faded old photographs, William T. Stead looked like an Old Testament prophet and had some of the same qualities. He brought to his new position not only a decided journalistic flair, but a zeal, enthusiasm, and sense of righteousness that were to help him begin a revolution in his profession.

I

Stead was born on July 5, 1849, at Embleton, in Northumberland. The man who was frequently described as a latter-day Puritan

1. The leader, or leading article, is the English equivalent of the American editorial. In the *Pall Mall Gazette*, the follower was the article which came after the leader on the front page. A middle, or middle article, was most often nonpolitical and discussed a social or literary subject. It usually was placed somewhere between the leading articles and the reviews (see p. 45).

2. Morley was elected Liberal M.P. for Newcastle-on-Tyne, in February, 1883.

came by his convictions honestly enough through his father, the Reverend William Stead. In his memoirs, journals, later correspondence, and articles, William Stead the editor reiterated that he owed a great debt of intellect and character to William Stead the village Congregationalist pastor. His memory of both his parents was one of deep affection, and though his father's income was meager and the Victorian-sized family included six children, he recalled his childhood fondly.

Up to the time he was twelve years old, Stead received his only schooling from his father, whom he described as "my teacher, my storyteller, my universal encyclopaedia of knowledge and my greatest playmate." [3] Latin, French, and the Bible formed the core of his studies until 1861, when he entered Silcoates, a school for the sons of Congregational ministers. Soon after, a religious revival swept the school, and at about this time he formally joined the Congregational church and remained a member for the rest of his life. In school, he said, he acquired "three very important things" that were not in the curriculum—"Christianity, Cricket and Democracy." [4] He left Silcoates in 1863 and was apprenticed, at fourteen, as an office boy to a Newcastle merchant who was also the Russian vice-consul. Already he had become an inveterate book reader. Although he was familiar with the English classics, he remained unacquainted with much that was good in literature—Bernard Shaw later called him "an utter Philistine" [5]—and his tastes were not particularly catholic. The Bible, as might be expected, was a constant companion and in the realm of secular literature Carlyle's *Life of Cromwell* had the most profound effect on him. "The memory of Cromwell," he later wrote,

> has from my earliest boyhood been the inspiration of my life.
> . . . I can to this day remember the serious searchings of
> heart I experienced when I woke up to a consciousness of the
> fact that I felt a far keener and more passionate personal love
> for Oliver Cromwell, than I did even for the divine figure of

3. Frederic Whyte, *The Life of W. T. Stead*, 2 vols. (London: Jonathan Cape, 1925), 1:14. Unless otherwise indicated, all biographical information in this chapter is taken from Whyte's work, chapters I-IV. I have given page references for direct quotations only.
4. Ibid., 1:15.
5. J. W. Robertson Scott, *The Life and Death of a Newspaper* (London: Methuen, 1952), p. 85, reproduces a postcard in which Shaw made this statement to the author.

Jesus of Nazareth. Cromwell was so near, so human, and so real. And above all, he was still the mark for hatred, scoffing, and abuse.[6]

The *Poetical Works of James Russell Lowell* was another book which had a powerful influence on Stead. The volume came to him as part of a prize from *Boys' Own Magazine* for an essay on Oliver Cromwell written after he had left school. Stimulated by this success, for a time he dreamed of making a name by writing a history of the Puritan movement that would span the gap between the end of Froude's history and the beginning of Macaulay's, but eye trouble, which made him fear for his sight, temporarily put an end to his reading and eventually compelled him to abandon the grandiose project. He had two leading articles—on the assassination of President Lincoln in 1865, and on the disestablishment of the Irish church in 1868—accepted by provincial papers but wrote nothing more of note until 1870. By that time his eye condition, which he subsequently attributed to nervous exhaustion, apparently was cured.[7]

After he completed his apprenticeship during the 1860s and was taken on in the same office as junior clerk at £60 per annum, Stead's literary ambitions waned and his sights were set upon no loftier goal than perhaps a position as bank clerk at £150 per year, with evenings free. He had several adolescent "love affairs" during this period, which by his own admission tended to be one-sided. He twice fell in love, at ages thirteen and seventeen, with the young lady whom he later married (after falling in love with her a third time, in 1873). When Stead was eighteen he formed a romantic attachment for the sister of the village doctor; she was about ten years his senior and willing to encourage him one summer in lieu of anything more exciting to do. After her departure for Edinburgh, the temporarily miserable junior clerk wrote her long letters three times a week; later he often advised aspiring young writers "to fall in love with a clever woman a dozen years older than themselves, who . . . can only be communicated with by writing." [8] These innocent amorous adventures were symptomatic of Stead's lasting affection for women in general and of the tendency to form deep attachments which characterized his mature life and career.

6. Whyte, *Life,* 1:18.
7. Scott, *Life and Death,* pp. 91-92.
8. Ibid., pp. 93-94.

In 1869 or 1870 Stead's interest in journalism was renewed when he turned to the local press for help in a crusade. It was in February, 1870, that he wrote the first of the letters which led to his connection with the Darlington *Northern Echo,* but even before that date he had written to the local paper at Howden in an effort to put pressure on the local board to improve a slum in the town. According to Rev. W. C. Chisholm, an old friend who told the story in a 1904 article in the *Christian Realm,* Stead's "red-hot stinging letter" was printed as a leading article and aroused so much public indignation that the board was forced to act.[9] Stead also wrote a letter to the *Northern Daily Express* at Newcastle advocating the formation of a charity organization for vagrants. When someone wrote a reply, he responded with a longer letter, which appeared as a leading article. The result was a town meeting that led to the establishment of the Charity Organization Society of Newcastle.

The most important of Stead's communications to the local press was sent to the *Northern Echo,* England's first morning halfpenny. The *Echo* came into existence on January 1, 1870, under the proprietorship of J. Hyslop Bell, with John Copleston as editor.[10] On February 3 Stead contributed an article, published on February 7, on the subject of "Indiscriminate Alms-giving," in which he cited Newcastle's precedent of establishing the Charity Organization Society and urged Darlington to do likewise. Since Copleston expressed interest in further contributions, Stead continued to submit work and was soon corresponding directly with the editor, from whom he frequently received advice on newspaper writing and editing. Worried by deletions and alterations and by occasional rejections, Stead wrote in June asking if his style was "radically bad." Copleston reassured him with a discourse on the principles of editing and explanations of the various factors which might determine the fate of any manuscript submitted to a newspaper. He also praised Stead's work, and concluded, "If you do write again, and will allow me to *use your mind,* I shall be gratified." [11]

9. The article is quoted in Whyte, *Life,* 1:20. One suspects that Chisholm was being overly enthusiastic about the results of the article when he said that the slums were subsequently "reformed." Slum clearance usually takes more than a communication to a local newspaper.

10. An evening halfpenny, the *Echo,* had been established in London in 1868.

11. Whyte, *Life,* 1:23.

Stead did write again—and again. His brain teeming with
schemes, projects, and righteous causes, he was not about to abandon his new-found pulpit. In September he was rewarded with
his first formal assignment for the *Northern Echo*: to cover, as
special correspondent, a social science congress being held in Newcastle. As with his other journalistic endeavors, Stead completed
the assignment without taking any time from his job, but it occurred to him that writing for newspapers would be even more
enjoyable if he were paid for it. He had not received a penny
for some eighteen leaders, a review, a sketch, assigned reports, and
other notes submitted to the *Northern Echo*, and as Christmas
approached he was looking for ways to supplement the seventy-
five-pound annual wage he was now earning at the merchant's
office. But when he asked Copleston if it would be possible to
arrange for "some remuneration, however slight," for future work,
he was told that the paper was in no financial position to pay for
any contributions. Although Stead thanked the editor for his
candor, there is an aggrieved tone to part of his letter: "I have
also to thank you heartily for the assurance that although my
articles are very convenient as a gift they are not worth buying
at any price. I have been mistaken, I admit, in thinking otherwise."
Nonetheless, he continued to submit his contributions without pay,
and Copleston continued to offer encouragement and advice.
Despite the blue penciling that still was necessary, Copleston
undoubtedly recognized his pupil's inherent talent. "I am glad
that you have taken my blunt remarks in good part," he wrote
early in 1871, "and I sincerely hope that you will have the strength
and health to persevere; for I do *not* flatter you when I say you
have a brilliant future before you. Would I could change talents
with you." [12]

Stead later stated that at this time he still had no intention of
becoming a journalist, [13] but in a letter to Copleston early in 1871
he specifically discussed the possibility. Citing his many current
activities—Sunday school, Young Man's Mutual Improvement Society, Newcastle Mendicity Society, etc.—he wondered if he could
not help to benefit his fellow man to an even greater extent through
a career in journalism. But, he wanted to know, could he really
hope for success in this field? Copleston's reply was succinct.

12. Ibid., 1:26, 27-28.
13. Scott, *Life and Death*, p. 95.

"Success," he said, "is certain." [14] At this point, Copleston, who was dissatisfied with his position on the *Northern Echo,* decided to try his hand at journalism in America. Presumably acting on his advice, and also impressed with the work of the young unpaid contributor, the proprietor of the *Echo,* Mr. Bell, in April, 1871, offered Stead the chance to succeed to the editorial chair. Stead first made sure that his predecessor was determined to leave in any event, and then, even though conscious of his limitations and inexperience, took his first paid (£150 a year) newspaper job—as editor of a daily paper—in July, 1871.[15]

Before accepting the job Stead had acted on Bell's suggestion that he seek some advice from Wemyss Reid, then the editor of the *Leeds Mercury* and later a considerable figure in the world of journalism and letters. Reid has left an amusing and revealing account of the interview held in his office; it ended with Stead doing a good deal of the talking. Inexperienced as he was, he had his own ideas of how a newspaper should be written and edited. While Reid agreed with his assessment of the potential power of the press over public opinion, he was staggered by the audacious schemes for improving the press which Stead poured out on this, his first visit to a newspaper office. As the hours passed the veteran found himself in the role of pupil, listening to the dicta of a brash young teacher who "lectured me for my own good on questions of journalistic usage which I thought I had settled for myself a dozen years before I met him." The discussion went on until dawn, and Reid recalled it many times afterward, particularly when he "recognized in some daring development of modern journalism one of the many schemes which Stead had flashed before my eyes." There were many times when he thought Stead mad, but "I recognized my visitor from the first as a man with remarkable gifts, of something that came near to genius. I recognized, too, his honesty and sincerity, though I had, even then, forebodings as to what might be the consequences of his impetuous ardour and reckless defiance of old customs and conventions." [16]

Despite the limitations of Darlington, Stead plunged directly

14. Whyte, *Life,* 1:28.
15. After working for some years in America, at least part of the time on the *New York Herald,* Copleston returned to England and in 1893 became editor of the London *Evening News* (Whyte, *Life,* 1:30).
16. T. Wemyss Reid, *Memoirs,* ed. Stuart J. Reid (London: Cassell, 1905), pp. 309-11.

into the task of preaching to the world. He had a pulpit now, and his sermons were soon forthcoming. Many of them were of chiefly local interest; others were to be repeated later before the much larger audience commanded by a London editor. His crusades and campaigns on such issues as imperialism, more positive relations with Russia, and the Contagious Diseases Acts helped to bring him to the attention of well-known and public-spirited men and women, a process which he expedited by regularly sending marked copies of articles to the individuals mentioned in them. Reid, self-proclaimed disciple of the old journalism, disapproved of this tactic, which he regarded as "an attempt to force oneself upon the notice of public men in a way which was not consistent with an editor's independence, to say nothing of his dignity." [17] It brought results, however, and by the time Stead left the *Northern Echo* his correspondents and friends included an impressive number of political, religious, and literary personalities, among them John Bright (who, according to Reid, was one of the first to be impressed by and call attention to Stead's articles); Gladstone; Albert Henry George (later fourth Earl Grey); Josephine Butler, champion of reform and long admired by Stead; the historians Edward Freeman and James Froude; Dean Church; Canon Henry Liddon; William E. Forster; Thomas Carlyle; and Mme Olga Novikoff, the self-appointed ambassadress of good will for Russia in English society. [18] Earl Grey later said, with some exaggeration, that "this provincial editor of an obscure paper was corresponding with kings

17. Ibid., p. 312.
18. Albert Grey (1851-1917) was the grandson of Charles, Second Earl Grey, famous for passing the 1832 Reform Bill. A Liberal imperialist, he served as administrator of Rhodesia after the Jameson Raid (1896-1897), and was a successful governor general of Canada (1904-11). He succeeded his uncle as fourth Earl Grey in 1894. Richard William Church (1815-90) was a disciple of Newman—although he never wavered from his loyalty to the Church of England—and helped found the *Guardian* in 1846 as the organ of the High Church party. As Dean of St. Paul's (1871-90) he helped revive it as the spiritual center of London; Henry Parry Liddon (1829-90) achieved a national reputation as a dynamic preacher and after he became canon of St. Paul's in 1870 his sermons there became famous. Although he was a political liberal with deep sympathy for the poor, the Bulgarian atrocity agitation of 1876 was one of the few occasions when he used the pulpit for political purposes. William E. Forster (1818-86) was early in his career considered to be of the more advanced wing of the Liberal party, and during Gladstone's great reform ministry (1868-74) was largely responsible for carrying the Education Act of 1870. During Gladstone's second ministry (1880-85) Forster, as Chief Secretary for Ireland, became identified with the Coercion Bill of 1881, and resigned over the government's "Kilmainham Treaty" with Parnell in 1882.

and emperors all over the world and receiving long letters from statesmen of every nation." [19] All in all, Stead was a solid success at his new job and he had an effective and characteristic way of making sure that his employer was aware of it. At the end of his first year he asked Reid for a written opinion of his work. The response was favorable, as Stead undoubtedly anticipated, and he used it to get a salary increase, a gambit he repeated for the next two years.[20]

In June, 1873, Stead married Emma Lucy Wilson, who was to bear him three boys and three girls; and by his twenty-fifth birthday, on July 5, 1874, he had reason for the self-satisfaction that exudes from the entry in his personal journal for that date. He was pleased with his "position on the platform of the world," which he attributed to God's favor, as well as with his personal and material well-being. He felt, however, that he must achieve his life's work before another twenty-five years passed ("After fifty there is not much for a man to do"), and he dreaded the possibility that his complacency might lead him to miss his call of duty as "a God-sent messenger to the age in which I live." This expression of contentment, a little unusual from a man earning three hundred pounds a year, was followed by ruminations on journalism, its pitfalls and responsibilities, and by certain modifications of personal opinion which might seem to give substance to charges of inconsistency in his political philosophy. From his youth he had been committed to radicalism in politics, but he now believed himself to be "less of a prophet and more of a journalist than in 1871," and "not by any means so ardent a Radical or as ardent in anything as I was." He no longer felt certain of anything and was not "so enthusiastic as some are about remodelling the Universe." Strange words, indeed, from William T. Stead. He ticked off the various areas in which his opinions had been altered: Disestablishment of the Anglican Church no longer seemed so clear-cut an issue; his faith in "the people" had been shaken by the Paris Commune; he felt considerably less zeal on behalf of the poor; he now had strong doubts about the efficacy of land laws in emancipating England; he felt a "distrust of uneducated majorities," but he had lost faith in the regenerative powers of education; and even international arbitration and disarmament seemed like hopeless causes. He acknowledged that he still held to one fixed principle: "the duty of

19. Quoted in Whyte, *Life,* 1:39.
20. Reid, *Memoirs,* p. 311.

England as a civilising power among the weaker and more de-
graded nations of the earth. The Anglo-Saxon idea has gained
possession of my brain." [21] Such near-racist, chauvinistic imperialism was typical of the times, and the "Anglo-Saxon idea" remained
an article of faith for Stead throughout his career, his later opposition to the Boer War notwithstanding.

Making a success of the *Northern Echo* required hard work from
the young editor. He reckoned that during his first three years
on the job, in addition to administrative duties, he had written
more than one thousand leaders, three thousand notes, and various
other articles. The drain on his strength no doubt accounted in
great part for a slightly different attitude toward life in 1875 than
that expressed in his journal the previous year. His July 4 notes
began by lamenting that he was only three years away from thirty
(actually, he was just twenty-six), had been in ill health, and was
subject to fits of despondency which had even led to thoughts of
suicide. Although his health had been improving, he felt that he
must find a way to get more sleep "on the penalty of death." Stead
also mulled over the possibility of a change of locale. Apparently
he had been sending out feelers to other papers, for he had turned
down a job in Cornwall that paid a salary of £250.[22] Perhaps it
was at this time that he wrote to the proprietor of the *Newcastle
Chronicle* guaranteeing that if he became editor he would increase
the paper's importance. Although the proprietor laughed at Stead's
cheek, Aaron Watson, who related the incident, noted that he "had
the excuse of having worked real wonders with his little halfpenny
newspaper." [23]

In the same journal entry Stead recorded his reluctance to work
on the metropolitan press: "I have been to London and have no
wish to go again. If the Lord wishes me to go He will have to
drive me thither with whips." Despite his disturbed state and un-
characteristic despondency, he seemed reasonably pleased with
Northumberland ("a healthier spot could not be found") and almost smugly content with his work on the *Northern Echo*, through
which he was reaching some thirteen thousand people:

> There is no paper now in existence which can be to me what
> the *Echo* is. I have given it its character, its existence, its

21. Scott, *Life and Death*, pp. 99-102.
22. Ibid., pp. 102-3.
23. Aaron Watson, *A Newspaper Man's Memories* (London: Hutchinson,
[1925]), p. 64.

circulation. It is myself. Other papers could not bear my image and superscription so distinctly. I have more power and more influence here than on almost any other paper, for I work according to my inclinations and bias. In money of course it is not much, but it is enough to keep me comfortable, and Bell has promised me a share in profit hereafter. I think I shall stop here. All signs are for it.

If this sounds more like the Stead the world came to know, so too did his acknowledgment of a "rekindling of the ideal," a return of "a sense of my prophethood," and a conviction that his mission was to promote "the social regeneration of the people of the world." Still, Stead had reservations about one of the popular reforms of the day. He said that he was doubtful about the extension of the suffrage. "I fear that we shall yet suffer evil results from the extension of the franchise to ignorant men." [24]

The next year, 1876, saw Stead's greatest journalistic achievement in Darlington: the role he played in the "Bulgarian Atrocity" campaign, which was another chapter in the perennial Eastern Question. Turkish exploitation and mistreatment of the Christian minorities in the Balkans disturbed Gladstone, and the massacre of the Bulgars in May and June gave him and his Liberal party followers a potent moral weapon to use against the prime minister, Lord Beaconsfield.[25] For a season the traditional English Russophobia was washed away by a tide of popular indignation against the Turks, particularly in the Nonconformist North. The first of a number of mass meetings protesting the government's apparent support of Turkey was held in Darlington on August 25, with Gladstone playing the major role in its organization. On September 6 Gladstone published his emotion-charged pamphlet *The Bulgarian Horrors and the Question of the East,* which launched "the most famous political campaign ever waged by a popular leader in the annals of English democracy." [26] The pamphlet had sold forty thousand copies within a few days, and two hundred thousand by the end of the month. On September 9, at a great open-air public meeting at Blackheath, attended by Stead, Gladstone declared that the issue transcended party differences and was based on the ground

24. Scott, *Life and Death,* p. 103.

25. Gladstone's great opponent, Benjamin Disraeli, who was prime minister from 1874 to 1880, had accepted a peerage in 1876 and became the first Earl of Beaconsfield.

26. R.C.K. Ensor, *England, 1870-1914* (London: Oxford University Press, 1963), p. 45.

of "our common humanity." On November 9 Lord Beaconsfield caused further consternation among the Liberals—and many others —with provocative statements in a speech at the Guildhall. He attacked Serbia and Montenegro, which had declared war on Turkey, and threatened to take military action against Russia unless she stopped sending so-called volunteers to aid the smaller Balkan states. But Beaconsfield's actions did not match his threatening words, and he put pressure on Constantinople to concede an armistice to the Serbians. There followed the abortive Constantinople Conference of the Great Powers (December, 1876-January, 1877) and the proposal of a series of reforms, which Turkey promised to undertake but ultimately failed to institute. The Russo-Turkish War broke out in April, 1877, and was ended the following January, chiefly by the sheer numbers of the Russian hordes. The Treaty of San Stefano, whose terms included the creation of a large state of Bulgaria as a Russian satellite, was drawn up in March, but when both England and Austria-Hungary objected, Russia was forced to agree to its revision at the Congress of Berlin (June-July, 1878).

The months between the arrival of the news of the massacre in 1876 and the convening of the Conference of Constantinople at the end of the year marked the important phase of the controversy for Stead. Through his leaders and his letters to statesmen and other public figures, he put the *Northern Echo* in the vanguard of the relatively few English newspapers to defend Russia and attack Beaconsfield's ostensibly pro-Turkish policy. It was during this period that Stead made the acquaintance of a number of political and intellectual leaders, including Gladstone and Mme Novikoff, a woman who was to play an important role in his personal life and career. His own account of those days is typically Steadian in its animation, its sense of dramatic mission, and its exaggeration of his admittedly important role in the general excitement. On January 14, 1877, while the Constantinople Conference was still in session, Stead wrote in his notebook that the "Bulgarian Atrocity" agitation had shown his usefulness, and he proudly enumerated the public figures, Gladstone among them, who had commended his efforts. He exulted that

> new possibilities of usefulness open out. Life is once more brilliant as in the heroic days. Our time is as capable of Divine service as Puritan times. The agitation of this Recess had rekindled my faith in Liberalism, strengthened by trust in

God. For the Bulgarian agitation was due to a Divine voice.
I felt the clear call of God's voice, "Arouse the nation or be
damned." If I did not do *all* I could, I would deserve damnation.

This exercise in hyperbole was followed by a melodramatic description of the events of the summer and autumn of 1876. Because
Bell, the proprietor, was vacationing in Switzerland, Stead had
been able to commit the *Northern Echo* "heart and soul" to the
movement. His journalistic work, along with organizing the Darlington meeting and writing "dozens of letters a day" until he had
"roused the north," had brought him to a point where he feared
he "might perish by overstrained excitement." But it was all worth-
while because, he was convinced, he had succeeded. He had written to Gladstone the night of the Darlington meeting voicing his
hopes for leadership, and the *Bulgarian Horrors* pamphlet seemed
to him an answer to the letter. He had been roused to action again
by Beaconsfield's Guildhall speech, but by this time Bell was back
from his vacation and his more cautious view about attacking the
government led to a "great row" with Stead.

As a result of the Guildhall speech, Stead had had visions of war,
slaughter of his fellow men, and of himself mobbed and murdered
if he persisted in opposing the policy of a war against Russia. In
his broodings he had wondered how much the sale of his possessions would bring in to help support his widow and children,
but had consoled himself by reading the Bible and thinking of "the
Father of the fatherless and these poor noble Russian volunteers."
Now, viewing the crisis in retrospect, Stead could see that it had
helped to develop or crystallize in him certain attitudes and convictions, including a renewed spiritual faith and a belief in the
need to encourage it. He was convinced that "the keen sense of
female honour is a more potent force to arouse men to generous
action than any mere massacre"—this referred to the reaction in
England to stories of the rape of Bulgarian women—and that "the
honour of Bulgarian virgins is in the custody of the English voter."
Finally, he felt a "more earnest desire to make the profession of
the Press the worthy leader of a regimented people. At present
it does not lead, it follows, reluctantly. The higher element in the
nation is badly represented in the Press."[27] Unquestionably, the

27. Scott, *Life and Death*, pp. 104-6.

"Bulgarian Atrocity" agitation was a decisive event in Stead's career. Although he may have exaggerated his own importance in the campaign, nevertheless he played a significant role[28] which made him known to important politicians and journalists.

For the rest of his tenure at the *Northern Echo*, Stead kept his name to the fore with his leaders and articles on such matters of moment as the Far Eastern Question, the Afghan War, the annexation of the Transvaal, and the growing concern over economic problems at home. Indeed, there were causes enough to keep his editorial sword sharply honed, and his private journal for the period frequently refers to fatigue from overwork and the need to spend more time with his growing family, although it was not always journalistic activity that kept him from home. He had been swept off his feet by Olga Novikoff, the charming Russian "ambassadress" whose salon attracted some of the most noted men of politics and letters of the day. She was particularly close to Gladstone, who may have been influenced by her to some degree in his stand against the Turks in Bulgaria. Thought by some to be an agent of her country, Mme Novikoff was simply an intensely patriotic woman who devoted much of her life to fostering better Anglo-Russian relations. Stead became so devoted to her that for a time he feared the "shipwreck of what I had fondly, passionately hoped would be a Christian home." Eventually his ardor cooled, and although she remained a friend and political confidante, and he helped to prepare—in fact, according to his own statement, almost completely wrote—her book, *Russia and England* (1880),[29] he noted in his journal entry for January 11, 1880, "I sin no more in relation to her. I am still deeply attached to her and would do anything for her, but I no longer love her with that sinful passion the memory of which covers me with loathing, remorse and humili-

28. A.J.P. Taylor is overstating the case when he says, "It was Stead, too, who got hold of Gladstone and persuaded him to write his famous pamphlet" (*The Trouble Makers: Dissent over Foreign Policy* [London: Hamish Hamilton, 1957], p. 80). The most comprehensive study of the "Bulgarian Atrocity" campaign is by Richard Thomas Shannon, *Gladstone and the Bulgarian Agitation, 1876* (London: Thomas Nelson and Sons, 1963). He says of Stead's role in the agitation that he was the "principal agent" in converting public excitement into a campaign of public meetings, and that although he did not start the movement, "it was Stead more than any other who supplied [it] . . . in the last days of August with a voice, a method, and a direction" (pp. 49-50).

29. Scott mistakenly identifies this as *M.P. for Russia*, which Stead edited, but which was not published until 1909 (*Life and Death*, p. 111).

ation." But despite his "passionate hope" for a "Christian home,"
the preceding summer of 1879, while his wife was pregnant, Stead
had carried on a brief flirtation with a visitor from Scotland; later
he naively remarked, "I had no idea my wife was so grieved about
it till long after the girl had returned to Scotland and the baby
was born."

This same journal entry exhibits an example of the prescience
which often startled his friends, but which Stead himself took for
granted. He wrote that his wife, who was "suffering from nervous
depression and the like" (understandably, in view of his suscepti-
bility), refused to live out another winter in the country, and this,
he felt, presaged a change of jobs. "About the direction in which
God may lead me," he continued,

> my own secret premonition is that I shall be summoned to
> edit a London daily, possibly the London *Echo* or the *Daily
> Chronicle.* [Both of these papers supported the Liberal Cause.]
> The great lack of the London Press is absence of enthusiasm.
> If God need an editor of enthusiasm in London I will serve
> His turn best. He will send for me and make it clear beyond
> all doubt that I must go. One of the signs should be giving
> me a free hand as I have here to control and to speak as
> seemeth good to my own conscience." [30]

Although he did not guess the right newspaper, Stead received
what he interpreted as a sign before the year was out. And when
it came, his earlier assertion to the contrary, the Lord did not
have to drive him to London with whips.

II

The paper that Stead was destined to join, the *Pall Mall Gazette,*
had been founded in 1865 during the period of newspaper expansion following the repeal of the "taxes on knowledge"—the newspaper stamp tax in 1855 and the tax on paper in 1861. The proprietor, George Murray Smith, was also the founder of the *Cornhill Magazine* and the *Dictionary of National Biography,* and the
PMG's first editor was Frederick Greenwood. It was he who had
conceived the idea for an evening journal while he was editor of
the *Cornhill* and had won Smith over to the project. Greenwood
had intended to call the paper the *Evening Review,* but to Smith
this seemed too colorless and he borrowed the name of the news-

30. Ibid., pp. 108, 111, 110.

paper in Thackeray's *Pendennis*.[31] The purpose of the *Pall Mall Gazette*, according to Greenwood, was "to bring into daily journalism . . . the full measure of thought and culture which was then found only in the reviews."[32] It not only would report the news, but, like an earlier weekly, the *Anti-Jacobin*, would also cover the arts and important political and social questions. Greenwood had not planned to edit the *PMG* himself, but when no satisfactory man could be found, he was persuaded to stay on the job and continued to occupy the editorial chair until 1880.

During its early weeks the new venture came close to foundering—for a time its circulation remained below one thousand—but Greenwood was a competent writer and had a knack for attracting talented contributors. Under his guidance the *PMG* weathered its start and attained a circulation of more than two thousand by the end of its first year. In the second year the paper's finances received a fillip from a series of articles entitled "The Amateur Casual," written by Greenwood's brother James, who spent a night in the casual ward of the Lambeth Workhouse and recorded his impressions and experiences. In the context of the tradition-bound press of 1866, this modest venture into journalistic innovation won the *PMG* an undeserved reputation for sensationalism; more importantly, it nearly doubled the paper's circulation, and much of the increase was permanent.[33] Thanks in great part to Greenwood —who, according to Stead, put in a sixteen-hour day—the sales continued to rise, reaching the neighborhood of nine thousand in 1880. The *Pall Mall Gazette* became, in Stead's words, "the paper which was read by the political and literary classes,"[34] but the ordinary citizens, of whom there were so many more, preferred the evening papers specializing in sports and crime. One of the more popular features inaugurated during Greenwood's regime was "Occasional Notes," paragraphs which covered a wide spectrum of political, social, and literary topics. Stead himself contributed to them while still editing the *Northern Echo*. However, as he ob-

31. William T. Stead, "The 'Pall Mall Gazette': Character Sketch," *Review of Reviews*, February 1893, pp. 139-40.
32. Harold Herd, *The March of Journalism* (London: Allen and Unwin, 1952), pp. 225-26.
33. Ibid., p. 266. According to J. W. Robertson Scott, *The Story of the Pall Mall Gazette* (London: Oxford University Press, 1950), p. 169: "In plain figures, 1,500 copies extra were sold on the three days the articles appeared and there was a permanently increased circulation of 1,200."
34. Stead, "The 'Pall Mall Gazette,'" p. 146.

served, in the Greenwood era they were longer and heavier than "the notes which subsequently did so much to give smartness and life to the *Pall Mall Gazette*." [35]

Perhaps the best-known incident involving Greenwood during his editorship did not benefit the newspaper. In 1875 he was given secret information that the khedive of Egypt was preparing to sell to the French his nation's shares in the Suez Canal. He passed this information along to the government, and Disraeli persuaded the cabinet to approve purchase of the shares for England. Disraeli never acknowledged the source of his information; furthermore, Greenwood did not make use of his knowledge to scoop his competitors, nor did he ever try to capitalize on the episode.[36] At this same time, Stead was consternating his proprietor by his support for Disraeli's purchase of the shares, thus staining the "Radical purity of the columns of the *Northern Echo*." As Stead saw it, the Suez Canal purchase was "the first of a series of measures which led some observers to declare that the destinies of Egypt were not decided at Downing Street but at Northumberland Street" [37] in the offices of the *PMG*.

Partisan politics precipitated the first of several editorial and staff shakeups at the paper. Although Smith and Greenwood leaned toward liberalism, the *PMG* was supposedly independent politically. As time went by, Greenwood became a steadfast anti-Gladstonian and a supporter of Disraeli's imperialism, and by 1880, when he was about to leave the *PMG*, Leslie Stephen wrote to an American friend, "The *Pall Mall Gazette* has been the incarnation of Greenwood, and, as you know, the most thoroughgoing of Jingo newspapers." [38] The editor's Toryism, Gladstone's triumphs in the 1880 general election, and the paper's continuing financial losses[39] combined to disenchant Smith with the *PMG* and in April, 1880, he presented it as a gift to his wealthy son-in-law, Henry Yates Thompson. Since Thompson was an orthodox Liberal and proposed to reshape the paper's policies accordingly, on May 1 Greenwood became the first—but not last—editor to leave the *PMG* because of

35. Ibid., p. 143.
36. Herd, *March of Journalism*, p. 227.
37. Stead, "The 'Pall Mall Gazette,'" p. 147.
38. F. W. Hirst, *Early Life and Letters of John Morley*, 2 vols. (London: Macmillan, 1927), 2:91.
39. According to [Morison], *History of the Times*, 3:92, these amounted to some twenty-five thousand pounds by 1880. A brief attempt to conduct a morning *PMG* as a rival to the *Times* had been a costly failure.

political differences with the proprietor. Backed by H. H. Gibbs (later Lord Aldenham), he founded another evening journal, the *St. James's Gazette*, as a Tory competitor to the *Pall Mall Gazette*, and took many *PMG* staff members with him to the new paper. Thompson, with no journalistic experience, managed to keep the *PMG* afloat for a week until he was able to persuade John Morley, an ardent Gladstonian and editor of the *Fortnightly Review*, to assume the editorship. Morley agreed to take on the task on May 8, and the first issue under his direction was that of Monday, May 10.[40]

At forty-one, John Morley was a craggy intellectual already well known as a man of letters. In appearance and conduct, he was somber, austere, and forbidding, although intimates claimed that his coldness was merely a façade. Regarded by some as an agnostic, even atheistic, Radical, he was conservative in many respects and, in his own estimate, temperamentally a Whig. Stead saw him as a "cautious man with strong conservative instincts," whose love for tradition was manifested by his admiring Burke far more than Cromwell. "Mr. Morley does not like new-fangled notions," Stead wrote. "He shrinks from leaps in the dark, and venturesome experiments. . . . He is repelled rather than attracted by the men whose heroic or venturesome career makes them stand out from the canvas like scarlet figures in a great painting. 'I like drab men best,' he used to say. And the vein of serious, sober sedateness is very characteristic of his politics." [41]

Born in 1838, the son of a Blackburn physician, Morley was educated at Cheltenham College and Lincoln College, Oxford. His funds from home were cut off when he refused to enter the Methodist ministry, and he turned to writing to supplement his small income; although called to the bar, Morley never practiced law. Soon he was contributing reviews, essays, and articles to a variety

40. Stead, "The 'Pall Mall Gazette,' " pp. 147-50. During the first week in May a lively—and frequently bitter—correspondence involving Greenwood, Thompson, and Smith appeared in several London newspapers. Greenwood felt obliged to publicize his reasons for leaving; Smith and Thompson claimed his version, including a statement that he had been told to take the Liberal position on certain specific issues, was inaccurate. In another letter Smith also denied a statement made in the *Manchester Guardian* (April 30) and reprinted in the *Observer* (May 2) that the *PMG* would "henceforth be a Ministerial journal" (*Daily Chronicle*, May 3).

41. William T. Stead, "Character Sketch: The Right Hon. John Morley, M.P.," *Review of Reviews*, November 1890, p. 428.

of periodicals, and for a brief time he edited a short-lived weekly, the *Literary Gazette.* His greatest literary and journalistic renown came to him after he had assumed the editorship of the *Fortnightly Review* in 1867. Over the next decade and a half he transformed this struggling periodical into a prosperous, influential organ, attaining in its pages what has been called the high-water mark of nineteenth-century reviews.[42] A roster of the contributors reads like a British *Who's Who* of literature, art, and politics, and during these years Morley became a friend and confidant of many leading politicians. In 1869 he took on additional responsibilities as editor of the *Morning Star.* This paper and its companion, the *Evening Star,* had been founded in 1856 by Richard Cobden and John Bright to support Radical interests. Its funds and circulations were dwindling when Morley was called in, and it proved to be a journalistic property that he could not salvage. Within four months of his advent, it was absorbed by the *Daily News.*[43]

Perhaps the memory of the *Morning Star* made Morley reluctant to take the editorial reins at the *Pall Mall Gazette* even at a high yearly salary of two thousand pounds. The demands of daily journalism were quite different from those of a periodical review, as were the requisite editorial skills, and Morley's experience on the *Fortnightly* was no guarantee that he would succeed on the *PMG.* According to Stead, "No one was less of a journalist by instinct or training,"[44] and another able contemporary, H. W. Massingham, agreed that Morley never had the "journalist's flair for news."[45] Aaron Watson, who worked for a time on the *PMG,* reached a similar conclusion. "John Morley always had a scarcely concealed contempt for journalism," he wrote. "The news in which he was alone interested was that which was concerned with great affairs. He carried a certain dry austerity into everything, and would have made the *Pall Mall Gazette* into a daily *Fortnightly Review.*"[46] In a character sketch of Morley written in 1890, Stead made a more concrete analysis of Morley's shortcomings as the editor of a daily, attributing them as much to personal and intellectual qualities as to lack of experience. Stead stressed that Morley's mind

42. Ensor, *England,* p. 145.
43. Scott, *Life and Death,* pp. 25-26.
44. Stead, "The 'Pall Mall Gazette,' "p. 150.
45. H. W. Massingham, "The Great London Dailies: The Penny Evening Papers.—The 'Pall Mall Gazette,' " *Leisure Hour,* July 1892, p. 607.
46. Watson, *Memories,* p. 68.

was one of solidity rather than agility. He was an intellectual aristocrat whose limited range of sympathies made him indifferent to much of the matter that usually fills a newspaper; and without journalistic instinct, he was contemptuous of the trivia that interested the general reader. To Morley as to Stead a newspaper was a pulpit, but Morley's sermons were often monotonous.[47] Nonetheless, as Stead recognized, "from the political point of view Mr. Morley made the *Pall Mall Gazette* once more a power in the land."[48]

When he took over the editorship in the midst of the confusion following Greenwood's departure, Morley's immediate task was to rebuild the depleted staff. Most of the occasional writers who had contributed to the *PMG* were still available, and, as on the *Fortnightly Review*, he was able to attract distinguished new contributors. But in addition to his duties on the *PMG* and the *Fortnightly* Morley was writing a biography of Cobden in his "English Men of Letters" series and he needed a capable assistant if he and the paper were to survive. It is not certain how he happened to think of Stead for the post. Possibly, as has been suggested, Gladstone gave him the idea,[49] and certainly Morley was aware of Stead's considerable reputation.

Stead was genuinely hesitant about making the move, but both Morley and Thompson stressed to him the element of public service. In the journal entry for his thirty-first birthday, Stead related that in his reply to Thompson's invitation he had written that although he hated London, he felt he could not turn down a chance to be at the center of power, and an interview was arranged for the following Monday. (Sunday originally had been suggested by Morley and Thompson, but Stead "would have felt wicked going to discuss a business engagement on that day.")[50] Negotiations continued during the summer of 1880, for a number of matters had

47. Stead, "Character Sketch: Morley," pp. 430-31.
48. Stead, "The 'Pall Mall Gazette,'" p. 150.
49. Scott, *Life and Death*, p. 72.
50. There is a dating problem here. A thirty-first birthday entry would indicate that Stead had heard from Morley and Thompson prior to July 5, but according to Whyte the negotiations began with a letter sent by Thompson on July 24, 1880 (*Life*, 1:71). Whyte may simply have overlooked the earlier communications or have misdated the letter; there are several dating errors in his book. Another journal entry by Stead, dated August 23, tells of having received Thompson's *formal* offer the previous week (Scott, *Life and Death*, p. 116).

to be worked out. There were some difficulties over salary and added pay for specific contributions; Stead regretted having to give up country life in the North and opined that his children, of whom there were now four, "must not be reared in Babylon"; and Morley's presumed atheism worried the latter-day Puritan. Also, Stead wanted to be sure that he could enjoy the "luxury of silence" on issues over which he and Morley were in disagreement; and while he liked Morley at once, he did not quickly take to Thompson. He sought advice from a number of people, including W. E. Forster (who thought Stead would do better to become editor of the *Daily Chronicle* instead of being second to Morley), and it was natural that with his pervading sense of divine mission he should seek help from spiritual leaders. The "Bulgarian Atrocity" campaign had brought him close to Dean Church of St. Paul's and Canon Henry Liddon, then at Oxford, and he consulted both. Morley's irreligion made Stead ponder the biblical text "Be not unequally yoked with unbelievers," but the clerics advised him to take the position if his other difficulties could be settled. (Dean Church envied—and at the same time did not quite believe in— Stead's confidence that when the time came God would clearly show him the proper path to take.) An important factor in Stead's decision to make the move was his belief that as "the lieutenant of a chief who will probably often be absent, I would have more power in driving the machine of State" and that increasingly Morley would become merely the nominal editor of the *PMG*. Thus Stead would be one of the handful of men whose advice was listened to by England's rulers. He was serenely convinced that this was God's mission for him, and was sure that with God's help he could take a "full slap at the Devil." [51]

Ultimately, the doubts and disputes were resolved and Stead agreed to a salary of seven hundred pounds, with a stipulated number of weekly columns which figured to bring his annual income up to eight hundred pounds. The salary was to begin in mid-October of 1880, and would be raised to one thousand pounds the second year. [52]

He came down to London in early October but did not wish to bring the rest of the family with him until he could "surround the children with the simple natural life to which they had become

51. Scott, *Life and Death*, pp. 113-15.
52. He was also to continue to write a weekly leader, and occasionally a note or letter, for the *Northern Echo* until July, 1881, and to receive a month's annual holiday (Whyte, *Life*, 1:72-73).

accustomed." [53] This requirement was fulfilled when he found a house in Wimbledon Park, and he moved his wife and children down in January, 1881.[54] On October 12, 1880, Morley wrote his sister that his new assistant had arrived. He described him as "a queer child of virtue, but a nice and good fellow" who would be most useful in lightening the editorial burden.[55] As his assistant Stead was to give him some uncomfortable moments, but despite stories to the contrary, Morley never seems to have doubted Stead's journalistic abilities or the wisdom of his choice. As he later wrote,

> He was invaluable, abounding in journalistic resource, eager in convictions, infinitely bold, candid, laborious in surefooted mastery of all the facts, and bright with a cheerfulness and geniality that no difference of opinion between us and none of the passing embarrassments of the day could ever for a moment damp. His extraordinary vigour and spirit made other people seem wet blankets, sluggish, creatures of moral *défaillance*.[56]

The striking contrast between Stead and his new chief was often noted by their friends and colleagues; their relationship has been called "a union of classical severity with the rude vigor of a Goth." [57] And yet it is equally plain that the two men liked, admired, and respected each other. On the paper their duties and relative spheres were clearly defined. Morley was the political editor, writing most of the leading articles, and Stead was responsible for other editing. When Morley was away from the Northumberland Street offices, Stead was in sole charge and had a relatively free hand. When both were in town, their working day began with a conference, which was frequently spirited.

> Every morning [Stead later wrote] we used to discuss the world, and all the things therein, for half an hour, the range being as wide as the universe, while the immediate objective point was narrowed down to the practical duty of bringing out the *Pall Mall Gazette*. We differed about everything from the Providential government of the world to the best way of displaying the latest news in an "Extra Special"; and the

53. William T. Stead, "Character Sketch: My Father and My Son," *Review of Reviews,* January 1908, p. 25.

54. Estelle Stead, *My Father* (London: Wm. Heinemann, 1913) p. 91.

55. Hirst, *Early Life,* p. 98.

56. John Viscount Morley, *Recollections,* vol. 1 (London: Macmillan, 1917), p. 169.

57. Stead's obituary, *Times,* April 18, 1912.

strenuous conflict of opinion with which the day began led
Mr. Morley at one time to postpone the talk until the paper
was out. It took more out of him, that half hour, he said, "than
all the rest of the day's work." [58]

One important difference in point of view involved the basic
character of the newspaper and journalism in general. "Mr. Morley,"
said Stead, "was as studious of decorum as Mr. Greenwood, if not
more so. He abhorred sensationalism and if he satisfied his own
public he cared for nothing else." [59] Stead, on the other hand, was
a sensational journalist, although the term needs to be used
cautiously. J. Saxon Mills put it too strongly when he asserted that
sensationalism "was the breath of Mr. Stead's nostrils." [60] Massingham was more nearly right when he wrote that Stead, in contrast to
the cold, formal, and conservative Morley, was "flamboyant,
expansive, full of ideas transmuted by the rough and ready alchemy
of an impressionable nature, a born sub-editor, a brilliant, incisive,
though not faultless writer, and a man of impetuously daring
temperament." [61]

Another major difference between them concerned the function
and responsibilities of an editor. It was Morley's custom "to choose
a number of experts and get them to write articles when their
subjects turned up," a practice which had served him well on the
Fortnightly Review. But Stead believed that it was the duty of the
journalist—particularly the editor—"to interpret the knowledge of
the few to the understanding of the many." With his weakness for
overstatement, he went so far as to say that Morley's willingness
to be guided by others was a cause of England's involvement in
Egypt. Instead of investigating the Egyptian situation himself and
using his editorial power to try to prevent war—which he loathed—
Morley was content to rely on the dispatches from his Cairo correspondent. Thus, as Stead saw it, "The *Pall Mall Gazette* by its
negative, rather than by its positive, policy paved the way to the
occupation of Egypt." [62]

Writing style was another point of contention. In his leading
articles—and he wrote most of them during this period—Morley was
careful to avoid anything savoring even remotely of Telegraphese;

58. Stead, "Character Sketch: Morley," p. 424.
59. Stead, "The 'Pall Mall Gazette,'" p. 150.
60. J. Saxon Mills, *Sir Edward Cook, K.B.E.* (London: Constable, 1921),
p. 48.
61. Massingham, "The 'Pall Mall Gazette,'" p. 607.
62. Stead, "The 'Pall Mall Gazette,'" pp. 151-152.

in Stead's words, "he would have no purple patches in his leaders."[63] Not surprisingly, then, as Stead confessed, "[Morley] was no doubt very often a chilly frost on the exuberance of my youthful enthusiasm. 'No Dithyrambs *s'il vous plait,*' he would remark drily, as he returned to me my article with all the most telling passages struck out. He was a great stickler for severity of style, and restraint and sobriety of expression. He was always down upon my besetting temptation to bawl when a word in an ordinary tone would be sufficient."[64]

There were also policy differences which cropped up occasionally. For example, Stead was less enthusiastic about Joseph Chamberlain than his chief (Morley was one of the first to recognize and publicize the talents of the then obscure Chamberlain, and to a lesser degree, of Arthur Balfour), and Morley was considerably less of a Russophile than Stead. Apparently, also, Stead and Morley had at least one disagreement over religion in the first months after Stead joined the paper. But when Stead threatened to resign if the *PMG* carried what he regarded as a piece of atheistic propaganda, Morley backed down and the article was not run.[65] When he was out of town, Morley often felt the need to constrain or advise his assistant. In addition to criticisms, his letters included warnings against his overworking and praise for the overall job the younger man was doing. One letter criticized the *PMG* for being too full of politics; others complained of a pro-Russian bias in certain articles; still others mentioned the use of inflated language; and one, provoked by a leader expressing the hope that England and America might be united "by a supreme tribunal," stated starkly, "Your article tonight turned my hair grey."[66]

For all these differences of opinion the men seem to have stayed on friendly, if not intimate, terms until the day of Stead's death. "Of Mr. Morley, as editor, in his personal relations I cannot speak too enthusiastically," Stead declared in his character sketch. And further on: "For my part I had never worked with anyone before with whom comradeship was at once such a pleasure and a stimulant."[67] Some writers have recalled—and perhaps exaggerated—Morley's displeasure with Stead after the former left the *PMG.*

---

63. Ibid., p. 150. *Telegraphese* referred to a flamboyant style as popularized by George A. Sala after he joined the *Daily Telegraph* in 1857.

64. Stead, "Character Sketch: Morley," pp. 431-32.

65. Scott, *Life and Death,* p. 70.

66. Ibid., p. 68.

67. Stead, "Character Sketch: Morley," p. 431.

Wilfrid Scawen Blunt published an entry from his diary dated
June 5, 1884, relating a conversation with Morley that morning in
which Morley allegedly characterized his successor as a political
quack and said he no longer had any use for his old newspaper.[68]
Aaron Watson wrote that Morley could not have had "more than
a suspicion of the fiery character of the steed that he was harness-
ing in front of his team," and that he referred to Stead as "that
cockatrice" when "The Maiden Tribute" appeared in 1885.[69] But
it must be borne in mind that Blunt was not overly fond of Stead,
and that Watson, in many of his Fleet Street anecdotes, seems ad-
dicted to the apocryphal story. At any rate, it is certain that when
Stead went to trial over the "Maiden Tribute" series, Morley came
to his defense, and Morley's reminiscences of Stead in his *Recollections* are cordial and appreciative.

One aspect of their relationship is fairly well established: although Morley undoubtedly found his assistant a trial at times and
spoke of him as "irrepressible," there was no dispute as to who
was the editor. Stead had some grandiose visions of the *PMG's*
future while he worked under Morley and he was able to introduce
some of his journalistic innovations, but it was always understood
between them that, in the editorial sense, the *Pall Mall Gazette*
was Morley's newspaper. So long as both men were on the paper
Morley's influence predominated—"so much so indeed that Mr.
Stead is understood to have painfully acquired 'Morleyese' and to
have written it with submission and docility."[70] And Stead himself attested to his subordinate role: "[Morley] believed in authority and I believed as implicitly in obedience. No one ever took
liberties with Mr. Morley."[71]

However, acceptance of Morley's authority did not preclude
Stead's making his presence felt on the paper, and some of his
less spectacular and less controversial ideas were incorporated into
the *PMG* while he was still the editor's assistant. In part, the
changes he wrought were a matter of style and approach. He expanded and enlivened the "Epitome," a summary of news and
opinions presented by the morning and provincial papers, a solid
asset for the *PMG*. He also brought a livelier style to the Occas-

68. Wilfrid Scawen Blunt, *Gordon at Khartoum* (London: Stephen Swift,
1911), p. 253. Whyte records that Lord Morley, when he read this account,
"wrote an emphatic NO in red ink" against it (*Life*, 1:80n.).
    69. Watson, *Memories*, p. 65.
    70. Mills, *Edward Cook*, p. 48.
    71. Stead, "Character Sketch: Morley," p. 431.

sional Notes, though apparently not always with the approbation of the editor, who was dubious about Stead's ability to write breezy prose. On December 31, 1880, after confiding to his private journal that he felt he had "more go, more drive, more journalistic capacity" than Morley, Stead added:

> But in regard to literature I feel rather depressed. I used to think I could write Occ. Notes. I thought he liked my middle articles, but he has dropped these. I think for a solid, forcible, telling leader I can beat most people. It is well I should learn my forte and stick to it. But I feel rather crestfallen at my evident incapacity to write light articles to please Morley's taste. But as yet I have not had my swing. When Morley is away I shall see how I get along.[72]

A typographical innovation which Stead sponsored was the use of informative crossheads to break up the longer articles. As Stanley Morison notes in his excellent survey of the typographical and mechanical developments of the English newspaper, "The reader of the London morning newspaper had never seen that humble but vital aid to quick reading, the 'cross-head,' until Stead used it in the *Pall Mall Gazette* during the year 1881."[73] Paradoxically, the need for crossheads in the *PMG*, with its small format and shorter articles, was not as great as in the interminable stories of such morning papers as the *Times*, which refused to follow Stead's lead for many years. Still more noteworthy, perhaps, and more in advance of the times was the introduction of illustrations as a regular feature of daily journalism. There had long been illustrated weeklies, including the venerable *Illustrated London News*, and as early as January, 1871, the *Times* published maps of the war zone and of Paris during the last stages of the Franco-Prussian War. However, in the next decade it repeated this experiment only rarely, and other London papers did not follow its lead.[74]

72. Scott, *Life and Death*, p. 121.
73. Stanley Morison, *The English Newspaper* (Cambridge: Cambridge University Press, 1932), p. 284.
74. Joseph Pennell later claimed that the real pioneer of illustrated daily journalism had been the *Daily Chronicle*, which in the 1890s printed a series of his drawings to illustrate the various works and departments of the County Council. He rejected the *PMG's* claim to the honor, apparently on the grounds that its drawings were not of sufficient size or quality. ("Art and the Daily Paper," *Nineteenth Century*, October 1897, p. 654.) Another candidate was advanced by Henry Blackburn, who cited the weather chart which first appeared in the *Times* in 1875, because it appeared every day ("The Illustration of Books and Newspapers," *Nineteenth Century*, February 1890, p. 214).

Thus, although the innovative nature of Stead's use of illustrations in the *PMG* is sometimes exaggerated, he was the first editor to use them on a regular basis, and he went beyond just maps. Stead himself considered this one of the more important journalistic contributions for which he was responsible.[75]

The earliest efforts at pictorial representation of the news in the *PMG* were still in the form of maps and diagrams, which were pretty crudely done. Mr. Hunt, the foreman in the composing room, bent and cut metal rolls into the required shapes, put them on galleys with the proper names set up in type, and filled up the whole with plaster of Paris. According to Stead, "The most daring attempt of this description was a not unsuccessful representation of the scene of the explosion of dynamite at the Local Government Offices. I made a very rough drawing of the scene on the back of an envelope, which I reduced to shape on reaching the office." Mr. Hunt then proceeded not only to diagram the scene, but to construct a crude picture "with his rules, his quads, and his turned type," which, if not artistic, did make the story clearer to the reader. And, as Stead pointed out, "The fact of making the thing clear to the reader is the one object of illustrated journalism." [76] In later years the *PMG* produced blocks by much more efficient methods, and before Stead left the paper illustrations of reasonably good quality, as well as editorial cartoons, were a staple of its news presentation.

Such changes as he was able to bring about were only a small part of Stead's dreams and plans. In the private journal which he began after his arrival in London in 1880, Stead set down his thoughts about the paper, its mission and future. On October 22, in a lengthy entry, he defined the purpose of the *PMG* in a way that foreshadowed the ambitious pattern he would attempt to follow when he was its master. It should "lead the leaders of public opinion" and combine literary distinction with good journalism; it should interpret the aspirations of the lower, inarticulate classes to those in power; it should "combine the function of Hebrew prophet and Roman tribune with that of Greek teacher"; and while keeping the public informed about everything that needed improvement it should be at once "lively, amusing and newsy." He listed what he considered to be the paper's political

75. Stead, "The 'Pall Mall Gazette,'" p. 153.
76. Ibid. The sketch appeared in the *PMG* of March 15, 1883.

aims—they included greater unity among European and English-speaking nations, improvement and reform in imperial policy, and educational and land reform—and cited improvements which could be made in the *PMG* office, along with noting features of the paper that he felt should be added or changed.[77]

In later journal entries Stead occasionally betrayed impatience with his subordinate position and disappointment at some of Morley's criticisms of his work, but he also recorded his gratitude for the valuable training he was receiving. In the entry for December 31, 1880, after speaking of his secondary role, Stead foretold his own accession to power and the changes he would introduce in the *PMG*. He wrote that he had had a premonition that Morley would leave the paper by April, and then he, as autocrat of the *PMG*, would "revolutionise everything, sink or swim." Because the competiton was so feeble, he confidently expected to become the most powerful man in England. As he often did, he lamented that this would entail the sacrifice of a normal home life, but he once more invoked the image of God leading him along the chosen path, of his being God's instrument of righteousness and enlightenment. "I shall be not only a centre of life and love and power in my paper," he wrote, "but the whole idea of newspapers will be so raised that my own paper will be but as one among many." For all his frequent protestations of humility, Stead had no doubts about his qualifications to edit a daily paper—and not only as compared to Morley's. He believed there were few men in England who had his combination of journalistic skill and fervor. "In such a lazy world," he mused, "there is no saying how far an industrious man may go. I feel ashamed of myself being so far up until I see those who are further up and then I am not surprised."[78]

In August, 1883, Stead's prophecy came true and John Morley resigned the editorship of the *Pall Mall Gazette*. The year before, he had given up his position on the *Fortnightly Review* but then had taken a similar position on *Macmillan's*, and the journalistic load, along with his political activities, had become too heavy.[79] Undoubtedly Morley's most celebrated achievement during his tenure on the *Pall Mall* was his successful campaign in 1882 to

77. Scott, *Life and Death,* pp. 117-19.
78. Ibid., pp. 119-22.
79. One source states that Morley resigned because he foresaw "unwelcome changes" in the *PMG's* struggle for survival among other penny evening papers ([Morison], *History of the Times,* 3:93).

have W. E. Forster deposed as Irish Secretary. Ireland had been
Morley's abiding interest during these years; in fact, Stead complained that "sometimes he bored me to death with Ireland." [80]
From 1880 to 1883 the tone of the paper had faithfully reflected
the personality of its editor. Edward Tyas Cook, who succeeded
Stead in 1890, has described how the *PMG* appeared to a faithful
reader and incipient journalist: "It delighted us at Oxford, with
its grave philosophical radicalism, its deliberate and weighty reviews, and its subdued style. It dealt with practical politics, and
as we know, influenced them deeply. But it did so . . . without
any striving or crying or bustling, by mere force of the application
of general doctrines, philosophically arrived at, to particular questions." [81] But the New Journalism was about to open its assault
on the old. Although technically Thompson became editor when
Morley resigned, for all practical purposes William T. Stead moved
into the editorial chair and the new era of English journalism began.

80. Stead, "Character Sketch: Morley," p. 429.
81. Quoted in Stead, "The 'Pall Mall Gazette,'" p. 155.

CHAPTER TWO

The New Journalism

The term *New Journalism* was coined by Matthew Arnold in a
May, 1887, article for *Nineteenth Century* on the issue of granting
home rule to Ireland. Attacking Gladstone's "dangerous plan,"
Arnold wrote:

> I have said that no reasonable man, who thinks fairly and
> seriously, can doubt that to gratify these aspirations by re-
> constituting Ireland as a nation politically, is full of dangers.
> But we have to consider the new voters, the *democracy*, as
> people are fond of calling them. They have many merits, but
> among them is not that of being, in general, reasonable per-
> sons who think fairly and seriously. We have had opportu-
> nities of observing a New Journalism which a clever and ener-
> getic man has lately invented. It has much to recommend it;
> it is full of ability, novelty, variety, sensation, sympathy, gen-
> erous instincts; its one great fault is that it is featherbrained.
> It throws out assertions at a venture because it wishes them
> true, does not correct either them or itself, if they are false;
> and to get at the state of things as they truly are seems to feel
> no concern whatever.

Just as the upper class was disposed to be selfish and the middle
class narrow, said Arnold, so "the *democracy*," like the New Journalism, was disposed to be featherbrained, and he went on to castigate
those who would stir it up.[1] Although neither Stead nor the *Pall*

---

1. Matthew Arnold, "Up to Easter," *Nineteenth Century*, May 1887, pp.
638-39. The thinly veiled distrust of the unintelligent masses which shows
through Arnold's analysis was the basis of much of the future criticism of the
New Journalism.

Mall Gazette was mentioned by name, it was obvious that they were the target of the allusion. Since everyone read Matthew Arnold, "the virtues and vices of the New Journalism were, for many weeks to follow, the topic of the town," [2] and thus a new term was born.

I

As promulgated by Stead, his contemporaries, and his successors, the New Journalism came to connote a good deal more than the rather general attributes Arnold ascribed to it. Variety and sensation, yes, but also new techniques and new features, a new style and a new format, and, above all, a fresh approach to the news. Because it was constantly evolving, it was hard to find a satisfactory, all-embracing definition, but in 1889 J. W. Robertson Scott, who had worked for Stead and went on to a distinguished career as a journalist and newspaper historian, attempted the task in *Sell's Dictionary of the World's Press.*

Replying both directly and by inference to Arnold's criticisms, he stressed the increased influence and responsibilities of the press that came with the New Journalism, which he defined as journalism with a mission—"'the Journalism of the Ideal.' The high mission of the journalist and the great possibilities of journalism are always within its remembrance." Factual accuracy—the endeavor "to get to the bottom of things before dogmatically and didactically pronouncing upon them"—was another admirable characteristic of the New Journalism, and Scott also had praise for its new methods and techniques, deploring that they had not been more widely adopted. But journalism "is full of conventionalities, is choked with prejudices and conservatisms"; thus interviews, signed articles, crossheads, and other innovations pioneered by Stead were regarded in many quarters as "incompatible with the 'dignity of the press' and respectable journalism." As for illustrations, "the very suggestion of even an occasional illustration makes some daily newspaper conductor's hair almost stand on end—[but] why persistently and crassly fill up space with half a column of dry laboured description, when a small block . . . would make everything as clear as possible in a moment?"

Sensationalism in a pejorative sense was the epithet most often applied to the New Journalism by its critics. Scott quoted Stead, who said their use of it "covers a wonderful lack of thinking.

2. Whyte, *Life,* 1:237.

They denounce the novel, the startling, the unexpected; the presentation of facts with such vividness and graphic force as to make a distinct, even though temporary impact on the mind. . . . When the public is short-sighted—and on many subjects it is a blear-eyed public, short-sighted to the point of blindness—you need to print in capitals." Sensationalism could be justified, Scott believed, when it was a means toward achieving a worthy end; it "must be judged impartially upon its merits, first by its intentions, and second, and much more, by its results." As examples of justifiable sensationalism, he cited *Uncle Tom's Cabin*, Samuel Plimsoll's outburst in the House of Commons which eventually led to the passage of the Merchant Shipping Act, and some of Stead's successful crusades on the *PMG*. Scott also discriminated between the men concerned solely with profit making and the men with a mission. The former published "newspapers which were no newspapers" and aimed "to sweat dividends, however earned, out of their properties. . . . . A newspaper conducted in such circumstances may be 'magnifique' in its way, but it is not journalism, let alone the 'New Journalism,'" for it was a tenet of the New Journalism that newspaper directors could not profit at the expense of their workmen. They were invested with high moral obligations; since they had a great power for good or evil they also had great responsibilities. There was an overriding need, Scott believed, for "journalism with a mission" to work for social and political reform in aid of the masses. "Leaving our manner of government completely alone," he wrote, "the famous 'condition of England' question is still unsolved," and in the New Journalism lay a hope for its solution. Young journalists with high ideals were flocking to the newspapers that practiced it, and while it would be difficult for veterans of the old school to accept them, these young enthusiasts "with new principles . . . will do a good work in the world in the coming years."[3]

Because of his personal knowledge of Stead and because the article was written while Stead was in command at Northumberland Street, Scott's comments are of particular interest. Since he wished to show the continuity and evolutionary nature of the press's development, he minimized to some degree Stead's role as an innovator, seeing him as a prophet and disciple of the move-

3. J. W. Robertson Scott, "The 'New Journalism,'" *Sell's Dictionary of the World's Press, 1889* (London: Sell's Advertising Offices, 1889), pp. 48-59.

ment rather than its founder. He conceded that the *PMG* was the most important example of the New Journalism but maintained that it would have developed, though not so soon, "if the *Pall Mall Gazette* had never existed; and Mr. Stead had never left the office of the Russian merchant in Northumberland."

Later commentators offered more limited definitions than Scott's, from which idealism was conspicuously absent. "By the New Journalism," Evelyn March Phillips stated in 1895, "I take it we mean that easy personal style, that wealth of intimate and picturesque detail, and that determination to arrest, amuse or startle, which has transformed the press during the last fifteen years." [4] And in 1915 men were still groping for the meaning when Malcolm Stark wrote that "the modern demand for excitement in every sphere has had a response in what is called the 'new journalism,' a phrase that is interpreted in various ways. Sometimes it is used in a derisive sense, at others to indicate a more admirable and especially a brighter style, with increased efficiency." [5]

Not all of the techniques of the New Journalism were invented or even pioneered by Stead. Before Victorian respectability stifled unorthodoxy, there had existed in England brash, highly personal, sensational newspapers,[6] and in Stead's own time such an approach and tone was characteristic of the "unrespectable" section of the British press: some of the Sunday newspapers and certain weekly gossip magazines. Even Stead's crusading was reminiscent in some respects of the *Times's* "thundering" under Delane.[7] Moreover, he was familiar with the methods of the American press, and many facets of England's New Journalism were already in evidence across the Atlantic. Indeed, this was precisely the basis of some

4. Evelyn March Phillips, "The New Journalism," *New Review*, August 1895, p. 182.
5. Malcolm Stark, *The Pulse of the World: Fleet Street Memories* (London: Skeffington and Son, 1915), p. 184.
6. See Francis Williams, *Dangerous Estate* (London: Longmans, Green, 1957), pp. 102-5. Actually, the tradition of sensational, personalized journalism goes back as far as the beginnings of the English press, with the Civil War newsbooks.
7. John Thaddeus Delane (1817-79) was perhaps the greatest and most famous of *Times* editors (1841-77). The *Times* acquired the nickname "The Thunderer" under Delane's predecessor, Edward Sterling (1812-40); under Delane, the tradition of "thundering forth" on all sorts of issues was continued and strengthened. Delane had many friends among influential ministers, and while he was editor of the *Times* his paper was noted for the remarkably close knowledge it had of governmental matters.

of the criticism of the *PMG*: Andrew Lang, for example, regarded it as "an Americanized sensational product," at about the level of what later came to be called the tabloids.[8]

Whatever the influence of other journals on Stead, it was he who combined the elements of a newer or revived journalism and introduced them into England at the "respectable" level. Directly or indirectly, sooner or later, despite indifference and outright hostility, his innovations permeated the English press. And though there have been other claimants, no man did more than Stead to launch the phenomenon known as the New Journalism. Reflecting on the revolution English journalism had undergone during the past decade, Henry Cust, one of the important journalists of the period, wrote in 1893: "It would be difficult to put one's finger on the beginning of the change; but the *Pall Mall Gazette* under Mr. Stead first brought home to our doors the change that was passing over journalistic methods; since then witnesses have come in clouds."[9] And nearly twenty years later, Edward T. Cook, a friend and admirer of Stead but no uncritical sycophant, expressed his belief that Stead was "the most creative and invigorating force in modern English journalism" and that "there are few, if any, laudable features in 'the new journalism' which the historian will not have to trace back to the *Pall Mall Gazette* and *Budget* and *Extras* of Mr. Stead's time."[10]

II

Even as he had hoped and prophesied, the *Pall Mall Gazette* after August, 1883, did express the personality, the ideas, the aspi-

8. Morison, *The English Newspaper*, p. 293. The British view of the American press is suggested by the remarks of an 1892 observer who wrote that "every Englishman who travels in the United States . . . will feel much thankfulness for the general sobriety and dignity of our great London and Provincial papers, and for the sense of responsibility with which they are conducted. Those who have not crossed the Atlantic can have no conception of the miserable petty personalities, the shameless straining after sensation, the impertinent invasion of individual privacy of the popular Press in America." (S. C., "A Few Remarks on the 'Fourth Estate,'" *Welsh Review*, July 1892, p. 932.)

9. FitzRoy Gardner, Henry Cust, Walter Herries Pollock, W. E. Henley, and Sidney J. Low, "The Tory Press and the Tory Party," *National Review*, May 1893, p. 363.

10. Edward T. Cook, in Millicent Garrett Fawcett, Henry Scott Holland, and E. T. Cook, "W. T. Stead," *Contemporary Review*, May 1912, p. 614. The *Budget* was a weekly digest of *PMG* news and features; the *Extras* were pamphletlike issues devoted to a single topic.

rations of William T. Stead. Like his predecessors, he was able
to attract first-rate contributors, and he had the assistance of such
staff members as Alfred Milner, Edmund Garrett, Edward T.
Cook, and Charles Morley, among others, who performed their tasks dili-
gently and well. But now that he had the opportunity he had
been dreaming of since his *Northern Echo* days, Stead was not
about to dilute the influence of his voice by sharing his pulpit.
Seldom has the term *personal journalism* been more aptly used
than to describe the *PMG* from 1883 to 1890. As Massingham put
it, "Mr. Stead carried the defiant ideal of self-expression not merely
to its perfection, but to its extravagance of completeness. His fads
and his personal admirations, his policies and his whims, his moral
enthusiasms and his intellectual vagaries, were all printed equally
large in the 'Pall Mall Gazette.'" He found English journalism "a
thing of conventions and respectabilities, buried in anonymity, and
fettered by party ties"; he succeeded in making the *PMG* "the instrument of one intensely individual mind." [11]

Stead had boasted to Aaron Watson of doing the work of six
men while still under Morley;[12] once in charge, his insistence on
having his finger in every pie at Northumberland Street brought
him close to making the boast the simple truth. According to Cook,
who took over the direction of the *PMG* when Stead left,

> The amount of personal work in execution which Mr. Stead
> threw into the paper would be incredible if one had not wit-
> nessed it. He would think nothing of writing the leading
> article, half-a-dozen "Occasional Notes," a special article or
> an interview, and a column of "exclusive information," all in
> one day's paper. The personal and confidential talks which
> lay behind such information were innumerable. The great
> Delane himself was not acquainted with more important per-
> sonages, and Mr. Stead's range of curiosity was far wider.[13]

Alfred Milner (later Lord Milner), who had joined the *PMG* staff
in 1881 and became Stead's chief assistant in 1883, wrote to Stead's

11. [H. W. Massingham], "A Great Journalist," *Nation,* April 20, 1912,
p. 83.
12. Watson, *Memories,* p. 67.
13. Cook, "W. T. Stead," pp. 614-15. Stead's connection with "important
personages" was on a different basis than Delane's. The *Times's* editor mixed
with them socially, dined with them, belonged to the same clubs, and visited
them at their country homes; Stead rarely dined out, had still never attended
the theater at the time he left the *PMG,* and, according to E. H. Stout, never
joined a club. (Whyte, *Life,* 1:97).

daughter that "as far as actual work was concerned, my duties were almost a farce. No power on earth could have prevented your father from doing all the work himself—not only writing almost the whole of the literary matter in the paper, but inspiring and controlling every part of it." [14]

Stead's complete domination of the *PMG* did not mean that Milner was a servile subordinate. Their relationship was analogous to that which had existed between Stead and Morley: Stead was the unquestioned chief, but Milner was permitted full freedom to express his ideas and often to implement them. Once Stead was convinced of the righteousness of a cause, he would unsheath his sword and charge unswervingly into battle, but, as Massingham has noted, he had an essentially uncritical mind which was open to all sorts of ideas and influences.[15] Stead's own account of his relationship with Milner, in one of his character sketches for the *Review of Reviews*, was written in 1899, at a time when he was very critical of his former assistant's suggestions for English policy toward the Boers. Disturbed by Milner's language in a dispatch which played up the Uitlanders' grievances and the need for a firm British stand against them, Stead began by recalling that one of Milner's daily tasks, as his assistant, was to tone down the leading articles, killing adjectives, deflating superlatives, and in general modulating the lion's roar. "He was always," wrote Stead, "putting water in my wine." Now the tables were turned, and it was Milner who was guilty of extravagances—"But, Alas! there was no Milner to revise Milner, and the result is before us." When Stead had begun assisting Morley in the autumn of 1880 Milner already was an outside contributor, sending in two or three Occasional Notes a day. Stead's first impression of him was not favorable: his handwriting was poor, his copy was not neat, and his prose colorless. "In those days," wrote Stead, "Milner was still in the chrysalis stage, and it needed a great deal to rouse him." But despite, or perhaps because of, Milner's placid personality—according to Stead, he was never known to say a harsh word—Stead made him his right-hand man after becoming defacto editor in 1883. In addition to acting as editor in Stead's absence, Milner wrote Occasional Notes every day, leaders about once a week, and middles

14. Alfred Milner, in "The World Pays Its Tribute," *Review of Reviews*, May 1912, p. 477.
15. [Massingham], "A Great Journalist," p. 83.

and reviews on occasion. Their association was a happy one on a personal as well as a professional level, and Milner was often a guest in the Stead household at Wimbledon. Stead recalled that they laughed together "to an extent not very usual in newspaper offices before or since. . . . We were almost schoolboys together, having, to use his old phrase, 'great larks' every day." A further bond between the two men was their shared belief in England's imperial destiny. Milner was perhaps more of a jingo and Stead was certainly more enthusiastic than he about Gladstone, but this was their common cause, and Stead, with his usual extravagance, claimed for them a major role in converting a nation of Little Englanders into a people devoted to the cause of Empire. "We founded in those days, Milner and I, a veritable school of political thought." [16]

Milner, too, recalled with fondness the exciting years when "the 'new journalism,' in full blast, first burst upon an astonished London." Although he and his chief were frequently "at friendly loggerheads" over style and method, they were in general agreement on principle and policy. However, Milner denied that he had ever been able to act as a check on the sometimes intemperate Stead: "The real truth was that he loved to develop his ideas dialectically, in discussion with somebody personally congenial to him, but whose habit of mind was as dissimilar as possible to his own." He found Stead courageous, sympathetic, kind, and genial, an assessment which his fellow workers apparently shared. "I don't suppose any editor was ever so beloved by his staff, from the first lieutenant down to the office boy," Milner wrote. "It was such fun to work for him." [17]

Milner was one of a number of Oxbridge graduates who were beginning to invade London journalism at this time. Stead's attitude toward these "University Tips," as he called them, was sometimes one of good-natured condescension (he explained to one of them that he himself had "the good fortune" never to have attended a university),[18] but his closest associates on the *PMG* had, like Milner, come down from Oxford. The most important of these was Edward T. Cook, the Ruskin scholar, who ultimately succeeded

16. William T. Stead, "Character Sketch: Sir Alfred Milner," *Review of Reviews*, July 1899, pp. 19-27.
17. Milner, in "The World Pays Its Tribute," pp. 477-78.
18. J. W. Robertson Scott, *'We' and Me* (London: W. H. Allen, 1956), p. 93.

Stead as editor. Cook, who had begun developing his political liberalism while still at Winchester, was a great admirer of Morley's journalism while a student at New College. By the time he left Oxford in December, 1881, he had contributed pieces to a few periodicals and at least one Occasional Note to the *PMG*. Early in 1882, after an interview with Morley, he was given a general invitation to contribute to the *PMG* and over the next year and a half his contributions increased until in August, 1883, Milner, at Stead's instigation, invited him to come to the paper on a regular, salaried basis. As a staff member he showed typical *PMG* versatility, writing Occasional Notes, middles, descriptive articles, and much of the theater, art, and literary criticism. He was also responsible for many of the *Pall Mall Extras*, including a guide to the members of the House of Commons which went through many editions. In April, 1884, he wrote to a friend that the paper had already changed much since Morley's time, and was now an interesting mixture of bad and good. "You never know," he said, "whether you will hear the voice of culture (that's me, you know, and Milner), or the blatantest vulgarity." [19]

Like Milner, Cook was a diffident man of placid temperament. However, he and Stead shared liberal political convictions, enthusiasm for imperialism, and belief in a higher purpose for journalism. When Milner left the *PMG* in the summer of 1885 there seems to have been no question that Cook would succeed him as assistant editor.

Charles Morley, John Morley's nephew, was another valuable colleague. He became secretary to his uncle in 1880 and a full-fledged writer for the paper when Stead took over as editor in 1883. An ardent supporter of Stead's brand of New Journalism, he soon showed his "mettle for description and inquiry," [20] and along with Cook he became involved in the world of art and drama. He was a meticulous writer who rewrote his stories over and over—not a common trait among journalists. In 1888 he introduced a good-natured gossip column in the *PMG*, but probably his most significant contribution was as editor of the *Pall Mall Budget*.

Yet another young Oxonian to work for Stead was Edmund F. Garrett, who joined the *PMG* in 1887. One of his early articles, a feature on the Salvation Army which appeared on July 19, 1887,

19. Mills, *Edward Cook*, p. 59.
20. Charles Morley, *Travels in London* (London: Smith, Elder, 1916), p. 9.

attracted some attention and led Milner to proclaim, "Behold the new Stead, with all of his virtues and none of his faults."[21] Garrett developed a special skill at interviewing and Cook later said of him that he and Stead ranked as the "ablest interviewers I have known."[22] Like many *PMG* staff members, Garrett was a journalistic jack-of-all-trades, and he wrote news paragraphs, leaders, parodies, verse, criticism, and special correspondence, as well as, in his own words, "turning a ready hand to any trivial, dull little piece of drudgery which happens to need doing."[23]

Other notable staff members during Stead's years as editor of the *PMG* included Henry Norman, who with his leaders, notes, reviews, and special correspondence made "some very brilliant contributions"[24] to the paper; the great political cartoonist Frank Carruthers Gould, whose first work for the *PMG* appeared in 1886; William Hill, an important sub-editor who liked to call himself "news editor"—a term imported from American journalism; J. W. Robertson Scott, "the best sub" Stead had ever known;[25] and Hulda Friedrichs, "the first woman in journalism paid and treated (more or less) as a man."[26] For a time Miss Friedrichs was Stead's private secretary, and he worried that having a female in this post might cause further domestic problems. To Scott she was a "Prussian governess," and although she came to be respected as a journalist he indicates that she never won the complete admiration of either Stead or her colleagues.

In addition to regular and part-time staff members Stead also made use, as Greenwood and Morley had done, of noted outside contributors. Among those who wrote articles or reviews for the *PMG* during Stead's time were Oscar Wilde; Matthew Arnold; Dean Church; Bernard Shaw; Mme Novikoff; Reginald Brett (later Lord Esher); Leslie Stephen, a man of letters and first editor of the *Dictionary of National Biography;* Henry Fawcett, political economist and reformer; Grant Allen, novelist and philosopher; the Earl of Shaftesbury, philanthropist and social reformer; Charles

21. Edward T. Cook, *Edmund Garrett, a Memoir* (London: Edward Arnold, 1909), p. 17.
22. Sir Edward T. Cook, *Literary Recreations* (London: Macmillan, 1918), p. 4.
23. Cook, *Edmund Garrett*, p. 19.
24. Massingham, "The 'Pall Mall Gazette,' " p. 610.
25. Scott, *'We' and Me*, p. 128.
26. Ibid., p. 123. Miss Friedrichs was not, however, the first woman journalist in England; she had many predecessors, including some editors of periodicals.

Bradlaugh, free-thought advocate whose refusal to take the customary oath in 1880 touched off a five-year constitutional struggle before he was allowed to take his seat in the House of Commons; Octavia Hill, crusader for reform of working-class housing; Sir Walter Besant, scholar, literary critic, and moving spirit behind the People's Palace for the recreation and education of the poor in London's East End; and other writers, politicians, and professors who were relatively well known at the time, if not today.

The man most responsible for guiding and directing these—and other—diverse talents in the task of putting out six editions of a newspaper six evenings a week was, of course, William Stead. The editor of any London newspaper of the 1880s was powerful because he had to "rule the tone of the paper and direct the line of policy it will take on all questions, whether Political, Literary, Social or Dramatic."[27] The limits to his power were fixed by his own ability and personality, or, in some cases, by a proprietor who insisted on exercising his authority. Ironically, Stead, who did not officially bear the title, was a more dominant figure than most of his fellow editors. Editing an evening paper meant arriving at the office between seven-thirty and eight o'clock in the morning; before noon[28] mastering the news and opinion presented in the morning papers and deciding what line to take on these matters; making assignments for leaders, special articles, reviews, news reports, etc.; dealing with a large stack of letters and correspondents' reports; and,

27. John Dawson, *Practical Journalism* (London: L. Upcott Gill, 1885), p. 31. The technical information about the publication of newspapers in the 1880s is drawn from Dawson and the following additional sources: H. A. B., *About Newspapers* (Edinburgh: St. Giles, 1888); Conservative Journalist, "The Establishment of Newspapers," *National Review*, August 1885, pp. 818-28; "Contemporary Literature: VIII. Newspaper Offices," *Blackwood's Magazine*, October 1879, pp. 472-93; A London Sub-Editor, "Sub-Editing a London Newspaper," *Chambers's Journal*, October 18, 1879, pp. 663-64; Massingham, "The 'Pall Mall Gazette,'" pp. 607-10; "The Modern Newspaper," *British Quarterly Review*, April 1872, pp. 348-80; John Pendleton, *Newspaper Reporting* (London: Elliot Stock, 1890); Arnot Reid, "Twenty-Four Hours in a Newspaper Office," *Nineteenth Century*, March 1887, pp. 452-59; J. W. Robertson Scott, "Newspaper Head-lines," *Journalist*, June 24, 1887, pp. 173-74; idem, *'We' and Me*; idem, "Some Newspaper Men," *Sell's Dictionary of the World's Press, 1888* (London: Sell's Advertising Offices, 1888), pp. 118-27; Edwin H. Stout, "How an Evening Newspaper Is Produced," *Young Man*, November 1893, pp. 373-74; H. Yeo, *Newspaper Management* (Manchester: John Heywood, 1891).

28. The press time of the evening papers varied somewhat. The first editions of most of them came out at about eleven-thirty, but the halfpennies usually came out at ten o'clock. For some reason the first editions to be actually sold in the streets were called the second editions.

if the editor was like Stead, doing a considerable amount of original writing. These tasks were carried on in an atmosphere of extreme pressure, of haste bordering on confusion.

Apart from the editor, the most vital position on a newspaper—evening or morning—was that of the chief sub-editor, who would usually have from three to six assistant "subs." One newspaperman of the day claimed that while weaknesses in reporters, editors, leader writers, and correspondents might be covered up, no one was as essential to the making of a good newspaper as a sub-editor. On a typical working day the chief sub-editor of an evening newspaper would arrive at the office at the same time as the editor and begin distributing assignments to his assistants. The immediate job was to decide which news items to use from the morning papers, and whether to cut them down, expand them, or completely rewrite them. Other duties might include writing a news summary of the past twenty-four hours, summarizing foreign intelligence, combing provincial papers for newsworthy items, or researching an obituary and making it the proper length. The London evening sub-editor of the 1880s was more than a scissors-and-paste worker. In editing and arranging the news he had to be aware not only of his editor's views, but also of what would appeal to the constituency served by that particular journal. He often gave assignments to reporters and late in the morning he began to receive the latest news, including the first reports from the law and police courts. These arrived in the form of "undigested flimsies" and telegrams which had to be rewritten into intelligible stories. Again, all of this had to be done in the face of a menacing first-editon deadline. Once that crisis was past the pace slowed down, but a great deal of hard work remained. For each new edition the latest reports and telegrams were put in type as quickly as possible, with a corresponding amount of copy marked out from the earlier editions. This process continued until the final edition went to press at 5:30 or 6:00 P.M.

One other significant editorial post was that of city editor. His chief concern was the business and financial news of the day—the main attraction for many middle-class readers—but he also had to know how politics, science, agriculture, and even the weather might affect this news. His copy was rarely altered, for "in his domain" he was "king-emperor." [29]

As with the other newspapers of the day, reporters on the *PMG*

29. Dawson, *Practical Journalism*, p. 84.

could be placed in two broad categories: regular staff members and free-lance contributors. Evening papers had smaller staffs, in part because they used the reports from the mornings for much of their first-edition news. When Parliament was in session it was the most important news beat, but most significant Parliamentary debates took place after the evening newspapers' deadline. Thus, whereas the morning papers had teams of six or more reporters in the gallery, taking down debates verbatim, most evening papers would have no more than one or two men regularly at Westminster. It is true that during the day—usually between 10:00 A.M. and 4:00 P.M.—numerous Parliamentary committees sat, and had their deliberations reported, but this work was mostly handled by the press associations. Another important staple of news in the 1880s was provided by the police and higher courts of justice. These were generally covered by reporters who attached themselves to one court the year round and sent copies of their stories to numerous papers, at a fixed rate per line or for a small regular salary. During the 1880s all newspapers were hiring larger staffs of regulars whose work might include covering accidents, speeches, fires, sports events, trade shows, inquests, etc., but a large portion of news paragraphs, particularly in the evening papers, were still supplied by free-lance reporters, or "liners."

All London newspapers also made use of correspondents, but this term was not a precise one. In the by-line to a story, "Our Special Correspondent" usually meant one sent out by the paper to cover a special story, while "Our Own Correspondent" generally resided in the city from which the story came. He was often a regular staff member of some provincial organ, and his articles might appear in several metropolitan papers simultaneously. All London newspapers had arrangements with such correspondents, and the quality papers, such as the *Times*, had many scattered throughout the United Kingdom. The same general situation prevailed in the realm of foreign news, with the *Times*, as usual, setting the pace in terms of regular correspondents stationed abroad. Less exalted morning newspapers had foreign correspondents in key locations and sent out "specials" upon occasion, but they often shared the services of these men with their rivals. The *PMG* and other evening papers had still smaller rosters of correspondents—even on a shared basis—and made frequent use of the morning newspaper foreign correspondence.

A major source of news was the material supplied by the news

services. Easily the most famous of these in the 1880s was that
founded by the Prussian Julius Reuter at Aix-la-Chapelle in 1848.
Reuter's set up a London office in October, 1851, one month before the completion of the telegraph line between England and the
Continent, but it was not until 1858 that it really established itself
with the metropolitan press, when the *Times* began to accept and
print its telegrams. Soon after, a number of English news services
were organized, and at the time Stead succeeded Morley as editor
the most important of these were the Central Press (founded in
1863), Press Association (1868), Central News (1870), and Exchange Telegraph (1872). The *PMG* used mostly Reuter's and
Exchange Telegraph services.

An important, if unpublicized, position on any newspaper was
that of business manager. The proprietor, of course, paid the bills,
but the manager was supposed to see to it that there were profits
as well. As a rule he would keep accounts, purchase supplies, supervise day-to-day expenditures, and seek ways to lower costs. It
was generally agreed that the positions of editor and manager
should be kept quite separate, and attempts to combine the two
often had unhappy results. On the *PMG* Morley and Thompson
were fortunate at the outset to obtain the services of Horace
Voules, who had founded London's first halfpenny, the *Echo*, in
1865. In 1880 Voules was working for Henry Labouchere's successful *Truth* magazine, and agreed to work for Thompson only on the
condition that he would not have to come to the office on Mondays
or Tuesdays—the days he was busy helping to get out *Truth*.
Greenwood had been extremely casual about the business side of
his paper, but now the *PMG* was for the first time to be truly
managed. Voules soon hired as his assistant Henry Leslie, who in
1883 succeeded him as manager with equal success.

One matter over which business managers might well be at odds
with editors—and sub-editors—was the limiting of space for the
literary content of the paper to meet the demands of advertising.
By the 1880s revenue from ads had already become the main
financial prop for the metropolitan press. Indeed, an article published in 1879 on the difficulties of starting a newspaper pointed
out that the established papers "have practically the monopoly of
advertisements; and in this advertising age, that advantage is in-
calculable." [30] Six years later another journalist discussing the
problems of launching a metropolitan daily claimed that many

30. "Contemporary Literature," p. 473.

successful newspapers owed their position not to their political content or the genius of their editors, but to their tradition of attracting many advertisers. However, the same writer also felt that managers too often gave in to advertisers, and that if a newspaper was made so good that people flocked to buy it, advertisements would follow.[31] And this was the factor that made the role of the advertiser less omnipotent than it might appear: a circulation large enough to attract advertisers depended ultimately on the labors of editors, sub-editors, feature writers, and reporters— the journalists, not the businessmen.

Once the day's news had been gathered, written, edited, and printed, together with leaders, features, and advertisements, the problem of circulation remained. Distribution and sales were primarily the job of the publisher, whose title had a different meaning than in American journalism. In England he oversaw the activities in the publishing room, where the printed papers were gathered for distribution, and decided how many copies to print of each edition. The contents bills—large sheets bearing bold headlines of the day's top stories—were a useful guide; a good publisher could base his estimate of how many papers to send out on the news value of these posters. This decision was particularly important to the helfpenny evening papers, for whom too many returns, with their small margin of profit, could be disastrous.

The building in which all of this activity was transmuted into issues of the *Pall Mall Gazette* was unimposing compared to some of those of its Fleet Street rivals. In 1867 the paper had moved into its quarters in Northumberland Street, which runs for a single block from the Strand to Northumberland Avenue. Aaron Watson described the street as "a rather mean-looking thoroughfare which was more like a passage than a street."[32] Of the four-story brick structure that housed the newspaper, Scott said, "There may have been less convenient, darker and grubbier daily paper offices in London but I never heard of them."[33] Inside, a flight of dark, narrow stairs led to a passageway with three offices opening off it. Stead's was the first—and largest—of them; the sub-editors, city editor, and reporters worked in the other two. Stead's quarters were roomy enough, and included, in addition to a table, a desk and a highboy topped with a rack of pigeon holes, and an

31. Conservative Journalist, "The Establishment of Newspapers," pp. 825-26.
32. Watson, *Memories,* p. 66.
33. Scott, *Life and Death,* p. 47.

overstuffed chair in front of a fireplace.[34] However, the stack of newspapers and other clutter which surounded the editor made it seem cramped, and its two small windows admitted little light. Above the editorial offices were the business offices, which housed the manager, a clerk, and an advertising canvasser. The paper was made up on the top floor, where the compositors were, in Scott's time, "aghast at the introduction of one pioneer linotype." [35] The printing of the *PMG* was done in the basement on two small Marinoni presses. From there the papers were sent by elevator to the publishing room counter on the ground floor, to be picked up by newsboys and runners or loaded on horse-drawn carts for distribution to news agents throughout London. The final edition of the evening paper, usually called the Extra Special, reached the street vendors and newsstands at about 6:00 P.M. and almost always had the heaviest sale.

It is difficult to determine circulation figures, except in general terms, for the 1880s, since most newspapers did not divulge them. *Deacon's Newspaper Handbook,* aware that it was "treading upon delicate ground," but believing, with logic, that such information would be valuable to advertisers, tried with scant success throughout the decade to persuade proprietors to reveal their circulations.[36] The morning papers had the highest circulation, led by the *Daily Telegraph,* which in 1883 sold close to 250,000 copies a day. The *Times's* circulation was but 50,000; yet it was considered a more important paper because it was read by the most important people. The *Echo* set the pace among the evenings in 1883 with sales of over 100,000, while among the penny papers the *Globe's* figure of 60,000 was easily the highest. In comparison, papers like the *PMG* and the *St. James's Gazette,* with their more selective appeal, had a relatively low circulation. Stead told Aaron Watson that although sales doubled after the price was reduced to a penny in 1882, the circulation of the *PMG* rarely exceeded 13,000 under Morley. However, like the *Times* in the morning field, the *PMG* was considered to have much greater influence than implied by such statistics.

34. There is a photograph of the office as it looked in Morley's day in Stead, "Character Sketch: Morley," p. 430.
35. Scott, 'We' and Me, p. 16.
36. "Newspaper Circulations," *Deacon's Newspaper Handbook, 1883* (London: Samuel Deacon, 1883), p. 29. It was able to list circulation figures for only three London newspapers in 1883, and for only five, ten years later.

III

The newspapers which came over the counter at Northumberland Street in 1883 were, at 14½" x 10", substantially smaller than any other London newspaper except the *St. James's Gazette,* which Greenwood had consciously patterned after the *PMG.* Among the evening papers the *Evening Standard* (26½" x 17½"), the *Evening News* (24" x 18"), and the *Echo* (24" x 17½"), were roughly equal in size to the morning papers, and the *Globe* (20" x 13") was somewhere in between. However, these four gave their readers only four- or eight-page issues, while both the *Pall Mall Gazette* and the *St. James's Gazette* had sixteen pages.[37] Except for some of those given over to advertising, the pages of the *PMG* were divided into two columns, each four inches wide, of eight- or ten-point type. Headlines and crossheads were ten-, twelve-, or fourteen-point. When Stead took over, crossheads were used only infrequently, as were illustrations.

There were, of course, variations from day to day, but during the first months of Stead's editorship advertisements took up slightly more than a quarter of each issue, mostly on pages 13 through 16. Of the literary matter, usually five to six pages were straight news; the rest, leaders, followers, and other special features. On the front page was a headed leader, about a column and a half in length, and a headed follower, or "turnover," which would be continued on page 2. Once Stead had established himself, an increasing number of these followers would be signed. Their subject matter was quite diverse, and except during Stead's crusades they usually did not follow any theme set by the leader. Most of the letters to the editor were printed on the second page and at times the Occasional Notes also began there. Under Stead this long-popular feature invariably ran two columns, and often three or more. On pages 4 and 5 would be found theatrical and literary criticism, vital statistics, a few ads, a business column headed "City Notes," and a middle. Middles were feature articles on varied topics; for example, the one for August 27, 1883, dealt with the question of whether or not cremation could help check the spread of cholera, which was then ravaging Egypt. Under the general heading "This Evening's News" pages 6 and 7 contained short, headed paragraphs, mostly of the older news items.

37. The *Times* (23½" x 16½") was slightly smaller in page size than the rest of the morning papers but had sixteen or twenty pages while the others had eight.

The main news section, with fresher stories, began on page 8, with the number of that particular edition printed at the top of column one.[38] This section usually ran about four pages, and included the weather report, an article entitled "This Day's Money Market" when appropriate, with share prices listed, and an occasional feature article. The news stories ranged in length from a column or more under several headlines to a series of unheaded items of a few lines each. The ratio of foreign to domestic news fluctuated, of course, under the pressure of events, but as a rule the United Kingdom, and London in particular, was given more extensive coverage than the rest of the world. During the first week of Stead's editorship, for example, there were approximately thirty-seven columns of domestic news and twenty-three columns of overseas stories. On the national scene the space given to political news was considerable over the course of a year, but it varied more or less seasonally. Thus, during the week after Stead took over the *PMG* there were only a few stories of a purely political nature, for Parliament was not sitting and its members had scattered for their holidays.[39] Later, after the summer doldrums had ended, their were enough banquets, meetings, and other excuses for speechmaking to swell the proportion of political to other domestic news. When Parliament was in session its deliberations were given a column or more in addition to individual stories on debates or events of special interest. Sports news, so important to many of the London evening papers, appeared only sporadically in the *PMG* until later in the decade. Certain county or university cricket matches or a major horse race might merit a paragraph or two, and an occasional middle might deal with some aspect of sport, but, except for the annual Oxford-Cambridge boat race, this was not an important part of the *Pall Mall's* world.

The principal feature of page 12 was the "Epitome" of opinions from the other newspapers in England, which often took up both columns. On Saturday there were usually excerpts from the weekly reviews, and once a month the significant articles in the monthly magazines were briefly summarized—either on page 12 or as one of the features of pages 4 and 5.

A look at some of the stories which appeared in the news, leader,

38. The files of the *PMG* are mostly 4th edition.
39. The August 31 issue was an exception; it devoted three columns to "Members of Commons and Their Votes in 1883," which listed how many times each member had voted during the past session.

and feature columns of the *Pall Mall Gazette* in the late summer and autumn of 1883 will perhaps suggest the direction of Stead's interests as well as conveying something of the flavor of the times. The leader for August 29, the third of the Stead regime, was a portent of the future and of his first major crusade on the *PMG*. Headed "The Criminal Breeders of Croydon," it derived from a story about a Croydon slum dweller named Cole who had brutally murdered his own child. Was Cole the real criminal, Stead asked, and would society by executing him be discharging its responsibilities? There followed a bitter denunciation of the overcrowding, the wretched moral and sanitary conditions, and the lack of educational opportunity for children which characterized the slum environment, and Stead scored not only the local authorities and get-rich landlords for permitting these horrors, but also the general public for its apathy. In the same issue an Occasional Note warned, "If Messieurs the burglars will persist in using revolvers we shall not be able to postpone much longer the arming of our police"—a perennial issue to this day.

A news story on August 30 reminds us that Stead, like the later popular journalist Alfred Harmsworth, was early interested in the possibility of man's flight. It described an experimental flying machine, powered by steam, with sails and a nine-bladed propeller, which would, so it was claimed, lift a four-wheeled car a mile in the air. The inventor, one H. C. Linfield, conducted experiments with his contraption on a section of the Great Western line and "expressed himself fully satisfied" with the result of the trial. An Occasional Note in this issue, although expressing skepticism about Linfield's efforts, did state, "We shall all fly some time."

Other leaders and stories dealt with such matters as the need for railways in India (September 1); the decision of Pope Leo XIII to open up the Vatican archives (September 21); plans for introducing electricity into private homes (September 25); the problem of sewage disposal in the lower Thames Valley (October 13 and 16); the death from an "inflamed brain" of a girl of seven who had been given too much homework at school (November 29); the threat of strikes in the Yorkshire coal fields (November 29); the arrest, for trying to stage a prize fight in a wood near Barnet, of the two boxers, the referee, and some spectators (December 5); the extension of the telephone exchange system in London (December 6); and the declaration by Charles Bradlaugh of his in-

tention to present himself once more for his seat in the House
when Commons convened again in February (December 29).

The *PMG* frequently carried news from the United States. These
stories—such as the account of the attempt to stamp out polygamy
in Utah (August 30) or of the holdup of a train in Kansas by a
"gang of cowboys" (October 1)—were usually more likely to startle
or amuse than instruct. However, to a story of some political importance, a Reuter's account of President Arthur's State of the
Union Message (December 4), Stead gave more than a full page,
with thirteen crossheads.

There were a number of running news stories which kept crop-
ping up in the pages of the *PMG* during these last months of 1883.
The account of a serious volcanic eruption in Java (September 1),
which was illustrated with a map made by Mr. Hunt's brass-rule
technique, was one of many on this subject; the threat of war between France and China was an almost daily feature, and brought
forth a number of maps; England's difficulties in Egypt and the
Sudan were highlighted by the smashing of an English-led Egyptian
army; the return, trial, and execution of Patrick O'Donnell for the
murder of James Carey, who had informed on the Irish "Invinci-
bles," was a recurring story. The violence of the age is brought
home by surprisingly numerous accounts of explosions, steamship
and rail disasters, bombings, murders, and suicides.

A reader searching the advertising columns during the last
months of 1883 would find the Victorian craze for patent medicines
catered to by such products as Eno's Fruit Salt, which was good
for excessive drinking, gout, rheumatism, blood poison, pimples,
and sour stomach, among other things; Holloway's Ointment, to
be applied externally on any "agonizing pains"; and the most famous of all, Beecham's Pills, which claimed to have the "largest
sale of any patent medicine in the world." Of course, purchasers
from the working classes might be interested in these remedies, as
well as in fountain pens, automatic pencils, hair dye, whiskey, magazines, Lea and Perrins Worcestershire sauce, soap, tinned fruit,
exhibitions, furniture, insurance, or the pamphlet on curing stutter-
ing offered for thirteen stamps. However, the middle- and upper-
class appeal of the *PMG* was reflected in ads for such things as
yacht engines, private schools, tutors and governesses, electric
dynamos, cruises, singing lessons, French wines, opera glasses, and
at least one £25 adult tricycle on sale for £15/15s. The prospective
world traveler might be attracted by a first-class steamship ticket

to Australia which could be had for 45 guineas, a two-month Mediterranean luxury cruise from 120 guineas, or a ticket on the Atchison, Topeka and Santa Fe, which could be purchased at the railway's London offices.

The reader with a need for housing could pick from, among others, a seven-bedroom house in Oxford, with a tennis court, stable, and large garden, which could be purchased for 1,500 guineas or rented for £100 per year; a furnished nine-room house near Clapham junction which could be rented for 2 guineas per week; or a furnished apartment near the Victoria Station for 12s. weekly. Carpeting was offered at sixpence a square foot and pianos could be bought for as little as £14. For the large-sized Victorian family, special arrangements could be made with the Belgrave Laundry, which was fortunate in being able to secure the services of some experienced "French ironers." For holidays there was the Grand Hotel in Paris, where three meals and service cost 18 francs a day, or a furnished two-bedroom cottage at Margate at 11 guineas for two months. Those with more specialized requirements might even be interested in a private "Asylum for Idiots" at Surrey.

For amusement there was a wide selection of drama, comedy, operetta, and farce to choose from at London theaters, with Gilbert and Sullivan's *Iolanthe* enjoying an extended run at the Savoy. There were also numerous museums, galleries, and more or less specialized exhibitions to attend. Book and magazine advertisements were abundant, and 6s. would buy most volumes, whether the reader was interested in Thomas Hardy's *The Return of the Native*, Matthew Arnold's *Literature and Dogma*, an abridged version of Justin M'Carthy's *A History of Our Own Times*, or one of the numerous popular Victorian novels which strike no responsive chord in the reader of today.

This was the *Pall Mall Gazette*, and the view of the world it presented to its mostly middle-class readers at the end of 1883. As Stead settled down in the editorial chair, the newspaper was going to change, and the horizons of its world broaden perceptibly.

IV

If a date can be singled out for the inception of Stead's brand of New Journalism, perhaps it was Tuesday, October 16, 1883, the tion for this first tilt against the forces of darkness was Andrew Mearns's recently published pamphlet, *The Bitter Outcry of Out-*

cast London. It was fitting that Stead's opening campaign should attack the horrors of the slums, for the New Journalism was strongly identified with radical democratic movements. The leader which fired the opening shot, "Is It Not Time?," occupied most of the first page. Noting that the "bitter cry" had often been heard, Stead proclaimed that the problem of the slums should now be brought to the public's attention, "not with a view to the generation of profitless emotion, but with a view to its solution." It might be audacious to suggest that slum problems had a solution, but

> if the heart and intellect of mankind alike revolt against the fatalism of despair, then indeed it is time . . . that the question of the homes of the poor be faced . . . with a resolute determination to make an end of the crying scandal of our age. It is true that that is much easier said than done. But at the present who can even be got to say it, much less to set about doing it? Yet it is the one great domestic problem which the religion, the humanity, and the statesmanship of England are imperatively summoned to solve.

He wrote with passion of the filth, immorality, and brutality of slum life. In a passage which even today sounds all too familiar, he pointed out that the feeble slum-clearance programs up to that time had tended only to make matters worse by replacing slum housing with dwellings too expensive for the poor to rent. Among those responsible were first and foremost the tenement owners: "These fever dens are said to be the best-paying property in London, and owners who, if justice were done, would be on the treadmill, are drawing 50 to 60 per cent on investments in tenement property in the slums." But the landlords were not alone to blame: there were the churches, which did nothing to abate the evil, but rather spent their time engaged in petty quarrels, thus making a mockery of Christianity. And outside the Church there were many qualified individuals—wealthy men, intellectuals, politicians—who had done little or nothing about "the one great domestic problem." Now, Stead concluded, "it is high time to make the attempt." Reinforcing Stead's leader, the *PMG* printed a condensed version of Mearns's pamphlet, with its telling descriptions of disease, prostitution, high rents, and sweated labor in the London slums.

Such a presentation by a newspaper would seem routine today; in 1883 it was a surprising departure from traditional journalism. True enough, reformers, philanthropists, and churchmen had long concerned themselves with the "condition of England" question;

the problems of health and housing were coming more and more
to public notice; many groups and individuals were willing to
abandon their policy of laissez faire in respect to social questions;
and a number of groups had concerned themselves specifically
with the slum problem.[40] But respectable newspapers were not
given to offending the Victorian Establishment by calling for better
conditions for the lower classes. And now here was the *Pall Mall
Gazette* not merely deploring an evil, but scolding the Establishment for neglecting its responsibilities.

The "Bitter Cry" crusade followed a pattern which was to become a familiar one. Leaders and signed articles on various phases
of the problem appeared; relevant articles in other periodicals were
publicized and often excerpted; speeches of key figures in the ensuing debates were reported; scores of letters were printed; frequently, straight news stories on slum evils were run; and, as public
interest increased, related accounts from the London and provincial press were quoted and summarized. From October 16 through
November 7 every issue of the *PMG* included at least one "Bitter
Cry" item; from the latter date until December 4 the number gradually diminished; and from December 4 until the first of the year
the references were sporadic. After the beginning of the new year,
when Parliament reconvened, the campaign was revived in a more
modest fashion—by that time Stead had other irons in the fire—
and it continued until the formation of a Royal Commission to deal
with slum housing in late February, 1884.

On Wednesday, October 17, the day after the campaign was
launched, the *PMG* printed four letters on the "Bitter Cry"; on the
following Monday, October 22, the correspondence column was
headed with a notice that the paper had been "inundated with
correspondence" from all over England and that only a few of the
letters could be printed. Eight followed, including one from
"General" William Booth of the Salvation Army.[41] The schemes
and suggestions for ameliorating the lot of the London poor which

40. On August 20, 1883, the *PMG* printed a small news item about a
resolution which had been forwarded to Gladstone by the Metropolitan lodges
of the Labourer's Union, urging the appointment of a Royal Commission to
inquire into the housing of the laboring classes. This seems to have had no
significant influence on government policy, and the *PMG* offered no editorial
comment on the subject at this time.

41. There are numerous stories during this period of physical attacks and
other outrages against the Salvation Army, which people of all classes looked
upon as a very questionable organization. The *PMG* under Stead, however, was
a staunch supporter and defender of the organization and its work.

now began to flow into the *PMG* office ranged from the picayune
to the grandiose, from the practical to the visionary. They included
proposals for setting up a new form of government for London,
amending the Artisans' Dwelling Act, and keeping the birth rate
down. One correspondent, willing to do more than merely expound
his views, offered to donate thirty acres of open country for a
farm for the poor (October 22).[42] The *PMG* itself, when it came
down to specifics, tended to be vague, and disappointing to any
reformer expecting radical proposals for slum abolition. On October 23 the paper ran a full-page leader, "'Outcast London'—
Where to Begin," which pointed out that this was the real problem. After surveying the weaknesses of existing legislation, the
writer (probably Milner) suggested that local governmental bodies
should be goaded into greater action—he failed to say how—and
that Sanitary Boards should be strengthened. The limits of the
paper's radicalism were indicated by the statement that "it is certainly putting the cart before the horse to cry out for more State
interference while the stringent laws already existing . . . remain
a dead letter. . . . If [practical reformers] strike now, while the
iron is hot, the 'bitter cry' will not die away for a season, and leave
no practical good behind it as the outcome of all our sympathy
and all our remorse." In fact, the most specific suggestion the
PMG ever put forward was that a Royal Commission should be
appointed to study the question (November 9).

In late October, the leader of the Conservative party, Lord Salisbury, who had for some time been concerned with the problem of
housing for the poor, entered the lists with a *National Review*
article on "Labourers' and Artisans' Dwellings."[43] Although he
ventured no revolutionary proposals, it gave a great boost to the
crusade that a man of Salisbury's stature, so clearly untainted by
radicalism, should reject the principles of laissez faire in this area.
The publication of the article was noted in the *PMG* news pages
on October 25, and on October 27 a leader, "Lord Salisbury's Omission," delineated certain reservations about his ideas, notably that
he had not dealt with the vexing problem of compensating present
property owners. But on balance Stead and Milner were pleased,
for Salisbury had "once and for all definitely emancipated himself

42. Dates given in parentheses refer to the date on which an item appeared
in the *Pall Mall Gazette*.
43. Lord Salisbury, "Labourers' and Artisans' Dwellings," *National Review*,
November 1883, pp. 301-16.

from the dismal pedantry of the Liberty and Property Defense
League, and cast his lot with the advocates of further action on
the part of the State. That decision . . . marks a turning point in
the history of the question." Still, the reservations were there, and
on November 9 an Occasional Note announced that Joseph Chamberlain would reply in the *Fortnightly Review* to "Lord Salisbury's
well meaning but inadequate article." On November 23, the *PMG*
printed more than three columns extracted from the reply, in which
Chamberlain accused the Tory party of using Salisbury's article for
political advantage. He declared that Salisbury's proposals did not
go far enough and did not come to grips with such basic problems
as the need for better education and more effective trade unions,
and that Salisbury himself was too apprehensive of state action
when it was required in the public interest. Chamberlain's own
proposal was to increase the power of local authorities to punish
slum landlords and to acquire property.[44]

The metropolitan and provincial papers reported on and discussed slum housing from the beginning of the campaign, although
none of them bore down so heavily on the issue as did the *PMG*.
If the London press's concern with the issue was influenced by
the *PMG*, which was the first to publicize Mearn's's pamphlet, they
failed to acknowledge it (one of Stead's recurring laments was that
the London newspapers refused to recognize the contributions, or
even the existence, of their competitors); however, several provincial papers did mention the *PMG* and its part in the agitation,
and even certain London journals commented on ideas expressed
by correspondents to the *PMG*. In its "Epitome" section, the *PMG*
dutifully chronicled the reaction of the rest of the London press
and the provincial press to the "Bitter Cry." It varied, of course,
according to the political stance of the particular journal, but party
lines tended to be blurred on this issue and almost every paper at
least admitted the existence of the problem and the necessity for
action. In the provinces, party confusion was even more noticeable: the Liberal *Birmingham Post*, for example, worried about
the dangers of state interference, while the Conservative *Western
Mail* thought it did not matter if the proposals were socialistic,
since socialism already existed and in many cases was needed
(October 29).

44. Joseph Chamberlain, "Labourers' and Artisans' Dwellings," *Fortnightly
Review,* December 1, 1883, pp. 761-76.

Among the London papers, the Liberal *Daily News* was, next
to the *PMG*, the most vociferous and the most interested in fairly
sweeping reforms; at the other end of the spectrum was the Conservative *Morning Advertiser*. The respective positions taken by
these two papers are illustrated by their reaction to the Salisbury
and Chamberlain articles. The *Daily News* declared that Salisbury
had not sufficiently considered the miserable realties of slum life
or gone far enough with his proposals; the *Morning Advertiser*, on
the other hand, despite the mounting outcry and piling up of convincing evidence, was still "disposed to doubt whether the evils
resulting from overcrowding, in London at least, are as great as
they are commonly represented, and as Lord Salisbury represents
them" (October 25). Two days later, the *Morning Advertiser*
opined that Salisbury had ventured onto "delicate ground" by hint-
ing that Parliament might involve itself in the slum problem, "for
he is nearing the boundary line which divides public policy from
mere socialism. Directly the state devotes the money derived from
one class to the material aid of other classes it lends countenance
to Socialistic ideas" (October 27). When Chamberlain replied to
Salisbury, the *Daily News* praised his article to the skies, while
the *Morning Advertiser* condemned it out of hand for being an
attack on property as "wild" and "unjust" as any promulgated by
Henry George (November 26). As for the stately *Times*—still the
most prestigious paper in London, though no longer the "Thunderer" and in circulation second by a wide margin to the *Telegraph*
—its attitude toward better housing for the poor was one of cautious concurrence. Although the *Times* accused Chamberlain of
an assault on one segment of society and of appealing to "larger"
principles than was necessary, in the main it agreed with his proposals (November 26). And when, on December 19, it advocated
the establishment of a Royal Commission, the *PMG* noted with
satisfaction that "the *Times* this morning strongly supports the
plea which we have been urging for so long for a Royal Commission on the question of housing the poor." There might be some
doubt about whether this was solely and precisely what the *PMG*
had been urging, but at least these rather disparate political journals were in general agreement.

The entire "Bitter Cry" crusade reflects some of the major
politico-economic questions of the late Victorian period. How
valid were the principles of classical economics in modern industrial

society? To what degree, if at all, should the doctrine of laissez
faire be modified in the interests of society as a whole? How much
socialism, if any, was acceptable to solve a pressing social problem? What, indeed, was socialism? These were broad philosophical issues which some newspapers, Liberal as well as Conservative,
preferred to avoid. While not really providing answers, the *Pall
Mall Gazette* under Stead did not hesitate to bring them to the
fore in the context of the "Bitter Cry" campaign, and not only did
it indicate its own position but it also provided a forum for other
views.

On October 19, three days after its first leading article of the
crusade, the *PMG* reported on a *Daily News* article which cited
the "evidence recently afforded of a 'widespread feeling of sullen
discontent' among the London poor" and averred that bolder, more
comprehensive legislation was needed. The *PMG* commented that
"this, of course, we shall be told is revolutionary Socialism. It may
be Socialistic, but it is not revolutionary. . . . Socialism, like Imperialism, is a very good thing within the limits of sanity and the
Ten Commandments. It is only when they are pushed beyond
these limits that either of them become mischievous." A much
stronger defense of socialism appeared on October 29 in a two-
column follower written by H. M. Hyndman, founder and chairman of the Marxist Social Democratic Federation. The miserable
condition of the London poor had long been known, said Hyndman, and public attention had again recently been drawn to it,
but little was to be hoped, "so far as the well-to-do are concerned,
from the present excitement." At the invitation of the *PMG* editor,
he was going to present the Democratic Federation's views on the
problem; the existing parties, controlled by the middle and upper
classes, could not deal with it. What followed, however, offered
virtually nothing in the way of concrete proposals; it was largely a
bitter, heartfelt attack on the capitalist system. According to an
Occasional Note in the same issue, "State Socialism is the order
of the day," and the writer of the paragraph went on to speak
approvingly of Bismarck's social legislation in Germany and on
recent Danish activity in the realm of state welfare.

On November 5 the *PMG* devoted a leader to collectivism and
individualism. Entitled "Socialism and Freedom," it began: "State-
help versus self-help is a very old controversy. The antithesis may
indeed turn out to be a false one. To help a man help himself is

not an absurd idea; and why should not this be after all the duty
of the community to its members?" The leader writer agreed with
George Goschen, who in a recent speech had referred to the dangers of state interference in social and economic matters; however,
the leader emphasized that worse dangers might arise from reliance on a pure laissez-faire philosophy. Two days later another
leading article, "The Housing of Outcast Liverpool," referred with
approval to the remarks of Arthur Forwood, a Conservative candidate for Parliament from that city, who had pointed out the
progress toward better housing in Liverpool since 1847, when it
had abandoned the theories of pure laissez faire.

The balance in *PMG* exposition between state socialism and
classical economics was redressed to some extent by a November
12 follower, "A Word for Laissez-Faire," signed "By a Political
Economist." It maintained that the principle was still valid, and,
as redefined by John Stuart Mill, left room for state control in
certain areas which would cover the current demands for reform.
By this time the "Bitter Cry" crusade was slacking off, but on
November 20 there appeared another follower on the subject, "The
Housing of London," by Dr. J. H. Bridges. The article was primarily a laudatory discussion of Henry George's *Progress and
Poverty*, which Bridges saw as one of the forces that had created
so much public interest in slum housing, and a plea for the establishment of a London town council. An Occasional Note on the
same day asserted that Dr. Bridges was more socialistic in his
approach than any others who had addressed themselves to the
problem except Hyndman, and readers were reminded that Bridges
was no visionary, but "one of the ablest and most experienced in-
spectors of the Local Government Board, who may or may not be
mistaken—on that we pronounce no opinion—but who is eminently
qualified to speak on the subject."

Articles, features, and correspondence on slum housing continued
to decrease until January, 1884, when, after Parliament reconvened,
the crusade picked up momentum, particularly late in the month
and through the first week in February. On January 2 the leading
article proclaimed as "the First Fruits of the Bitter Cry" two recent
circulars issued by the Local Government Board, the first administrative steps toward finding a solution for slum housing. For a
time the *PMG* became so engrossed in the Sudan question and the
dispatch of Chinese Gordon to that troubled land that the cause

of housing was almost neglected;[45] then, on January 31, the crusade
was resumed with a new twist. A leader, "Under the Microscope,"
reported that since the publication of Mearns's pamphlet the *PMG*
had been conducting its own investigation of the conditions of London's working-class dwellings. Stead and Milner had sent observers
armed with questionnaires to a corner of St. James's Parish, Westminster (the area between the angle of Oxford and Regent streets).
They had deliberately chosen a district which was not classified as
a slum area, and they did not seek out "fearful examples" to support
a thesis. "What is wanted now," the article said, "is not more sensation but more light. It is for this reason that we have always
advocated a Royal Commission." And one of the commission's
duties should be to inspect a wide area with the same thorough-
ness with which the *PMG* investigators had surveyed the chosen
section of St. James's Parish. The first of a four-part series, "The
Housing of London Workmen—Not in the Slums," appeared in the
same issue; it ran more than a full page and was accompanied by
a map of the area investigated. The other installments, each also
running more than a page, appeared on February 4, 5, and 11.
There was nothing very startling or bloodcurdling in the reports,
which may have made them all the more effective. It was patent
that grim, drab, unsanitary, and frequently dangerous living conditions obtained among the working-class families in a district that
by no means represented the depths of London slums.

On February 22 Lord Salisbury moved in the Commons the
establishment of a Royal Commission, and on the next day the
PMG leader exulted, "Amid a perfect chorus of approval in Parliament and the press, the Royal Commission on the Dwellings of
the Poor has at length become a certainty." For all practical purposes this article marked the termination of the crusade. The problem of housing the poor did reappear in the pages of the *PMG*—
indeed, it would be making news for years to come—but the *PMG*'s
concentration on the matter ended with the appointment of the
Royal Commission. In writing of the crusade later in his career,
Stead exhibited his tendency to overestimate the results of his work.
He credited the *PMG* articles with bringing about the appointment
of the Royal Commission, and—blithely disregarding all govern-

45. Currently the *PMG* was also devoting space to such matters as a
circular which it had sent to Liberal M.P.'s (see p. 87); the growing dilemma
involving Boer, Bantu, and gold in South Africa; Henry George's speaking
tour of Britain; and the imminence of franchise reform.

ment action from the Factory Acts through the program of Richard Cross as home secretary under Disraeli—asserted that "modern social legislation may almost be said to date" from the formation of the commission. It is pleasant to report, however, that he gave Milner full credit for his contributions, noting that after the movement had been launched Milner was put in charge of the "Housing Question" and in the following weeks "became more than ever indispensable." [46]

While it is difficult to measure the amount of influence exercised by the *PMG* in stimulating public interest and ultimately bringing about the appointment of the Royal Commission, the paper was given at least some indirect recognition for its part in the campaign. On October 26, 1883, at a meeting of the London Board of Works, one member, Mr. Selway, denied that the board had been negligent with regard to slum clearance and held that "the facts of the case were sufficiently grave, without resort being had to exaggerated statements and sensational writing such as had lately appeared, of which no good would come." It is not clear what "exaggerated statements" he referred to, but he did commend the *PMG* for a "very interesting article," which advocated the view more than once expressed by the Board of Works that it should have the power to remove unfit houses by "paying compensation solely for land and material" to the Home Secretary. He also agreed with the M.P. for Brighton, Mr. Holland, who opined in a letter to the *PMG* that local boards already possessed valuable powers (October 27). The Earl of Shaftesbury, known for his efforts on behalf of the working classes, praised the paper for its crusade in a follower, "The Housing of the London Poor," in the November 6 issue. And, as previously noted, several provincial papers credited the *PMG* for the "Bitter Cry" campaign. Mearns's pamphlet must, of course, be considered as primarily responsible for the action that was taken, and the other members of the London press contributed in various ways to stimulating public interest. However, the *PMG* was the first to call attention to Mearns's effort, and certainly its trumpeting was heard by many. Since its readers included other journalists as well as the paper's usual upper-middle-class, politically oriented audience, it reached some people who counted.

During the heat of battle the *PMG* was less effusive in self-

46. Stead, "Character Sketch: Milner," p. 21.

praise than during later crusades. The leader on October 31 noted with satisfaction the interest in slum-housing problems and stated: "We need go no further than this day's paper to see what progress the question has made during the past fortnight, since we published the substance of the little pamphlet 'The Bitter Cry of Outcast London.'" And in the leader on January 2, 1884, it was remarked that the interest in the cause had been substantial and long-lasting, and Mearns's pamphlet would have gone unheeded had not the "bitter cry" been taken up by the press—which was undoubtedly correct. The same leader voiced some of Stead's convictions, as yet still cast in rough form, on the social responsibility of the press: "As for that still more important factor, the maintenance of a lively public interest, it is the business of the preachers and the press. With the immense start which the recent agitaton has given them it will be little to their credit indeed, if they cannot keep the politicians up to the mark in respect of this vital question." [47]

If the success of the "Bitter Cry" campaign is measured in terms of what it actually accomplished, the objective answer must be "very little." Stead might attempt to claim in 1899 that modern social legislation dated from the appointment of the Royal Commission on Housing, but he could not point to much in the way of tangible gains in the war against slums. In September, 1884, when the *PMG* was in the midst of another campaign, the *Spectator* was moved to remark:

> The *Pall Mall Gazette*—whose general service to Liberalism we heartily acknowledge—spoils its "finds," often hunted up with great cleverness, by screaming so loud over them. Nothing practical has been done to remedy the evils described in "Outcast London," or will be done until sense supersedes sensation, and the reformers, recognizing the limits of the possible and admitting that in crowded cities the residuum will never be well-housed, confine their demand to sewerage, ventilation, and light, which can after a year or two of severe and irritating compulsion be served. [48]

Without commenting on either the justice of the indictment of the *PMG* or the worth of the prescription for future legislation, one

47. There was, perhaps, an important literary consequence of the agitation. Bernard Shaw, who knew Stead well and followed his crusades with interest, may have drawn from the "Bitter Cry" campaign the inspiration for his play *Widowers' Houses* (1898).

48. "The Condition of the Navy," *Spectator*, September 27, 1884, p. 1260.

may still acknowledge the truth of the *Spectator's* claim that nothing practical had been done to eradicate the problem of slum housing in London. In the summer of 1885, the same periodical, in the course of belittling the effectiveness of still another *PMG* crusade, again reminded its readers that after the furor over the living conditions of the poor and the appointment of a Royal Commission to report on the problem, the excitement had soon died down and the "Blue-books went the way and shared the fate of other Blue-books." The current Housing of the Poor Bill, said the *Spectator*, had not been introduced by popular demand; and whereas it would have passed by acclamation at the time of the "Bitter Cry" agitation, in the recent debate all sorts of reasons had been put forward to delay its passage. The bill did pass in the end because the Opposition did not want to be blamed for throwing it out, "but the contrast between the reception it actually met with, and that which would have been confidently predicted some twenty months ago, is marked and instructive." [49]

Its limited practical effectiveness does not lessen the importance of the "Bitter Cry" campaign to the history of modern journalism. It was a demonstration of how a newspaper could create and for at least a brief time sustain interest in a cause. In future agitations it would be shown that a newspaper crusade with popular appeal could significantly increase circulation, and the technique of employing a newspaper's own staff to conduct an investigation also would be more fully developed by the *PMG* and its successors. Finally, this particular campaign was the first to demonstrate the connection between the New Journalism and late Victorian radicalism.

The need for better housing for the poor was not the most important of Stead's causes; it did not win him the fame of later campaigns; and its success was debatable. But it is of particular significance in any account of Stead because it was typical and symbolic of his concept of the responsibility of the press. Under later practitioners of popular journalism, the crusade in some instances degenerated into a circulation-raising gimmick, but when Stead showed the way he was genuinely a journalist with a mission, plunging into combat against social and political evils. Although his motives and objectives have been questioned and impugned by a number of journalists, social critics, and historians, the weight of the evidence is on the side of those who see him as a selfless, if

49. "The Housing of the Poor," *Spectator*, August 15, 1885, p. 1066.

self-satisfied, crusader. Hugh Kingsmill, no great admirer of Stead, believed that "his daily paper was, beyond everything else, the means by which he could unremittingly assuage, though never satiate, his passion for creating an emotional situation between himself and the public." [50] Stead's crusades were not, however, planned to make money; the most famous of them cost the *PMG* more than was ever realized by the spectacular but brief jump in circulation. Granted that Stead's campaigns were "essential devices to kindle the passion of his readers," they nonetheless were aimed to achieve what he believed were worthy and necessary goals.

V

During his first months as de facto editor of the *Pall Mall Gazette*, Stead, along with launching the "Bitter Cry" crusade, introduced or refined a number of practices which came to characterize the New Journalism. The signed article began to appear almost every day, usually as a follower. On the typographical side, multiline heads became more common, and crossheads were used more frequently to break up the longer pieces. Beginning in November, maps and diagrams appeared almost every day to illustrate news stories and woodcut drawings or portraits to supplement feature or special articles. And it was during these early months that Stead shocked the traditionalists by beginning to run interviews, an innovation he considered one of his three most important contributions to the *PMG* and to journalism. [51]

It is difficult to appreciate, at this distance in time, how controversial the interview seemed to the England of the 1880s. Stead himself wrote in 1893, "The interview is now so much at home with us that it seems incredible that its adoption should have been opposed by any sane body of persons." [52] But Sir Wemyss Reid, for example, regarded Stead's interviews with "the foremost men of the time" as a startling enough departure from orthodox practice to mark the birth of the New Journalism. [53] One aspect of in-

50. Hugh Kingsmill, *After Puritanism* (London: Duckworth, 1929), p. 180.
51. Stead, "The 'Pall Mall Gazette,'" p. 153. The other two main contributions were illustrations and indexing.
52. Ibid.
53. Reid, *Memoirs*, p. 313. Unlike many other orthodox journalists, Reid was willing to give the New Journalism its due: "To me, as an old journalist, it is not a thing with which I can pretend to have much sympathy, but I must acknowledge its brightness, its alertness, its close grip of actualities, and its rapid and remarkable success."

terviewing which distressed traditionalists was that it seemed to
be another step in the dreaded Americanization of the British press.
In a history of English newspapers, written in 1887, Henry Fox
Bourne pointed out that Stead's views "as to the proper functions and
methods of journalism in dealing with political matters, . . . hitherto
more approved in the United States than England, were promptly
introduced into 'The Pall Mall' as soon as he had full control over
it." Interviewing, which had long been common with foreign
correspondents and "cautiously adopted nearer home in such series
as 'Celebrities at Home,' " was now

> freely resorted to in the case of any politician, religionist,
> social reformer, man of science, artist, tradesman, rogue, mad-
> man, or any one else, who cared to advertise himself or his
> projects or pursuits, and in whom the public could be ex-
> pected to take an interest. The skill in what at first they
> called "the Americanization of English journalism," but what
> they afterward designated as "the new journalism" was the
> boast of both the editor and the proprietor of "The Pall Mall,"
> and they boldly applied it alike to national and individual,
> political and social ends, dressing out their interviews with
> dramatic or melodramatic, minutely accurate or judiciously
> imagined details.[54]

A later historian of the British press, J. D. Symon, had some reflections on the long-range implications of this innovation:

> The new journalism under Mr. Stead in the *Pall Mall Gazette*
> introduced what is known as the "personal note." . . . It began
> with the interview and the personal paragraph. It remained
> in its fullest expression chiefly in the signed authoritative
> article. In the introduction of the personal note is Nemesis:
> insidiously, implicitly, it exposed the impersonality of the
> newspaper *qua* newspaper. The impersonal view was seen
> to be relatively impotent, hence the change that has made
> the daily press an open and avowed reflection of the passing
> thought more than an attempt to impress impersonal thought
> upon the masses.[55]

54. Henry Fox Bourne, *English Newspapers*, 2 vols. (London: Chatto and
Windus, 1887), 2:343. Bourne did concede grudgingly that interviews, which
he called a "lower level" of personal journalism, "may be interesting and, to
those who might read them, not uninstructive" (p. 381).

55. J. D. Symon, *The Press and Its Story* (London: Seeley, Service, 1914),
p. 106.

Before Stead became its editor, the *PMG* occasionally had commented in a semijocular vein on the American practice of interviewing. On November 15, 1880, for example, under the head "Interviewing Mdlle Sarah Bernhardt," it was noted that the "victim" of an interview could benefit from self-advertising, which in Bernhardt's hand was "almost one of the fine arts." On December 8 of the same year, in an article on two interviews with President-elect Garfield which had appeared in the American press, the *Pall Mall* remarked, "It seems the President Elect made it a rule 'not to be interviewed;' but who can escape the ubiquitous inquisition of the American reporter?"

When the *PMG* published its first interview, on October 31, 1883,[56] an Occasional Note called attention to the new feature:

> We publish in another column a report of the impressions which appear to have been made on Mr. [W. E.] Forster by his recent journey through the Balkan Peninsula. The form is perhaps a slight departure from the conventionalities of English journalism, but its convenience is indisputable and its utility obvious. Mr. Forster, it may be remarked, has come back with deepened convictions as to the progress and development of the emancipated provinces, and as to the irremediable decay of the Ottoman system. The whole of his remarks, however, will be read with interest both at home and abroad.

The interview, which ran about a page and a half, was broken up by five crossheads and was illustrated by a crudely reproduced map of "The New Bulgaria."

The *Spectator* lost no time in disparaging this innovation. Mr. Forster, it feared, would learn "a disagreeable lesson from the result of his interview on Wednesday with the Agent of the *Pall Mall Gazette*." His remarks were "excellently reported, with his permission," and if given in a speech would have attracted worldwide attention and provided a trustworthy contribution to Western knowledge of the Russo-Turkish war. But the interview "nearly fell dead. Even the *Pall Mall Gazette* had no leader on the statement, and, so far as we know, no London journal either reproduced it or commented on it, or attacked it"—not because of lack of interest, but because of the lowly form in which it was presented.

56. Stead might actually have claimed an even earlier introduction of this feature with certain news stories which had an element of an interview in them. A good example was a September 1 follower about a visit to the actress Mary Anderson by "A Special Correspondent."

"One-half, we believe, even of the readers of the *Pall Mall Gazette* either never saw the statement, or glanced at it without a notion of its importance." [57] Stead quickly retorted that the London newspapers, obeying their unwritten code, would not deign to take notice of "exclusive information" published by a competitor, but "in the provinces, where the press is less hidebound by tradition and formalism, Mr. Forster's remarks received the attention they deserved" (November 3, 1883). Sir Wemyss Reid later recalled that Forster was the first public man in England to be interviewed (he gave the date erroneously as 1880 or 1881), and that he had reproached Forster "for having countenanced such an abominable innovation from America." After much discussion they had agreed that although "the ordinary interview was not a thing to be encouraged," if a man stated his views on "some great topic of interest" it might be useful to the public. "All the same," Reid added, "Mr. Forster was much blamed at the time for having submitted to being interviewed." [58]

The second interview published by the *PMG* was with H. C. Linfield, whose steam-powered flying machine had previously been good for a paragraph in Occasional Notes (August 30). It was run as a middle, entitled "How to Fly," of more than a column in length, and included two small sketches (1¼" and 3" high; one column wide) of the inventor's designs. The article opened with the explanation that "Mr. Linfield, who recently made an attempt to fly in a machine which he had invented, had been interviewed by a representative of the *Pall Mall Gazette*, to whom he gave some interesting particulars on the problems of aerial navigation." In a short time, according to Linfield, air travel would be as commonplace as travel by rail or ship, and planes would go sixty miles an hour, regardless of the wind. Carrying passengers would present no problem because "the more you carry the easier it is to lift." He had done everything but fly his machine, and this he considered "only a detail" (November 28, 1883). The *PMG*, it should be noted, did not scoff at Linfield's plans and predictions.

Despite the reservations of Reid and many others, Stead, needless to say, continued to run interviews, and in time they became a regular and popular feature in the *Pall Mall Gazette*, with some

57. "Mr. Forster on European Turkey," *Spectator*, November 3, 1883, pp. 1402-03.

58. Raymond Blathwayt, "Literature in Journalism: A Talk with Sir Wemyss Reid," *Great Thoughts*, April 5, 1902, p. 218.

137 appearing in the year after he had broken the ice with Forster. Gradually and grudgingly this form of reporting was accepted by the British press, and other papers followed Stead's lead. Writing in *Sell's Dictionary* in 1888, J. W. Robertson Scott listed the interviewer as one of the regular staff positions for a journalist. The interview, he said, provided information in a succinct form, and "many newspapers up and down the country . . . bring out few issues without an interesting contribution of this sort." [59] Members of the old guard took what comfort they could from assuring themselves that the methods of the English interviewer were "a vast improvement over those of America" and that "leading Americans" confessed that "as a rule, the English interviewer is far superior to the American." [60]

59. Scott, "Some Newspaper Men," p. 124-25.
60. The quotations are, respectively, from Blathwayt, "Literature in Journalism," p. 218, and C. E. Morland, "The Art of Interviewing," *Great Thoughts,* June 11, 1892, p. 373.

CHAPTER THREE

"Chinese Gordon for the Soudan"

‖◎‖

In the judgment of the London press, the *Pall Mall Gazette*'s first interview had fallen flat. It was with obvious satisfaction, therefore, that a little more than two months later, on January 10, 1884, Stead informed *PMG* readers: "Most of the leading papers in town and country reprint the report of our interview with Chinese Gordon, which is the subject of universal comment." The effect on the press and public of Stead's interview with Gordon vindicated his use of this form of reportage, but its importance went far beyond that. The campaign to send Gordon to the Sudan, which the interview triggered, was a demonstration of how newspapers could form public opinion and influence political decision making, and as such it is of no little significance in the history of journalism. Since a knowledge of the historical background is essential for an understanding of the *PMG*'s role in the Sudan crisis, it may be useful to begin by recalling the events that led up to this imperialist misadventure.

I

Gladstone had not been pleased when Disraeli purchased the Suez Canal shares in 1875, believing that financial control would entail political responsibility, and by April, 1880, when he formed his second ministry, his fears had in part been justified. The suspension of payment of debts to European creditors by the spendthrift khedive Ismail had led, in November, 1878, to the creation of an Anglo-French condominium, and in June, 1879, international pressure on the sultan forced him to depose Ismail in favor of his son Tewfik.[1] During that same year a mutiny of Egyptian army officers over arrears of pay had to be quelled, and in 1880, when Gladstone came into office, Egypt was on the brink of chaos, its army seething with discontent and its people resentful of supervision by foreigners, whether Moslem or Christian.

In 1881 an Egyptian nationalist movement got under way led by a military adventurer, Arabi Pasha; it aimed at abolishing European control and Turkish influence and establishing a constitutional government. In May, 1882, after Arabi had wrung a series of concessions from the hapless Tewfik, France and England dispatched a joint fleet to Alexandria to demonstrate for the khedive and to protect European interests. But Arabi's followers could not be contained. During an outbreak of rioting on June 11 some fifty Europeans were murdered, among them the British consul; and Arabi set about fortifying Alexandria. Although France, concerned by developments in Bismarck's Germany, ordered her ships home, on July 11 Admiral Sir Beauchamp Seymour, with permission from London, bombarded the forts of Alexandria into silence. Egypt no longer had a viable government, and England, with the Suez Canal to protect, could not allow another power to rush in and fill the political vacuum. Acting with unusual decisiveness, Gladstone's government on July 20 ordered an army to Egypt under Sir Garnet Wolseley. France was given another opportunity to make it a joint undertaking, but the crisis toppled her government and once again England was forced to act alone.

On September 13, 1882, after a spectacular march across the desert from Port Said, Wolseley scored a smashing triumph over Arabi at Tell el-Kebir; two days later Arabi surrendered in Cairo and was eventually exiled. However, this was only the beginning of England's involvement in Egypt. Common sense—and the canal —dictated that England must stay and help rebuild the Egyptian nation, although the Gladstone government was quick to declare that the British occupation would end as soon as order was restored and financial stability attained. In September, 1883, while Stead was settling into the editorial chair at Northumberland Street, Sir Evelyn Baring (later Lord Cromer) was sent to Egypt

1. As a tributary state of the Turkish empire, Egypt was ruled by a viceroy appointed by the sultan. The title of khedive was given to Ismail in 1867 by Sultan Abdul Hamid II.

as British agent and consul general, with plenipotentiary powers.[2] In October he informed the government that the situation was sufficiently under control to permit the reduction of British forces —a development which Gladstone was pleased to announce at the Lord Mayor's banquet. But almost on the heels of this announcement came disastrous news from the Sudan.

For sixty years this region had been inefficiently and often cruelly ruled by Egypt, although for a two-year period, from 1877 to 1879, an English governor, Colonel Charles Gordon, had brought about a semblance of order. Then in 1881 a former Egyptian official and slave trader, Mohammed Ahmed, declared himself to be a Mahdi, or Messiah, and launched a religious-nationalist uprising against Egyptian rule. During the next two years the Mahdi's followers gained control of much of the Sudan, leaving the Egyptian garrisons penned up in scattered strongholds, and in 1883 an Egyptian army of ten thousand men commanded by an Englishman, Colonel William Hicks, was charged by the Cairo government with the hopeless task of destroying the Mahdi in his own country. Instead, it was the Egyptian army which was destroyed —slaughtered almost to a man at the battle of El Obeid on November 5, 1883.

When news of the disaster reached London, Gladstone was under pressure from the Opposition and from the Queen to avenge this insult to England, reconquer the Sudan, and "liberate" the region from the Mahdists. Reluctant though he was to intervene, Gladstone did agree that the government had a moral obligation to help evacuate the beleaguered Egyptian garrisons. But there were some difficult tactical questions. The English-led garrison at Suakin, in the northwestern Sudan, could be evacuated by the Red Sea, but how could the withdrawal of the inland garrisons, centered at Khartoum, best be effected? And how much, if any, of the Sudan should be retained as a defense perimeter for Egypt itself? Gladstone lacked any real knowledge of the military situation in the Sudan, Baring was able to give him little guidance from Egypt, and the cabinet was divided over the action to be taken. While the government remained silent, the press clamored

2. Baring had been appointed British commissioner of the Egyptian public debt office in 1877, and he became the British controller general in 1879, when dual control was renewed by England and France. From 1880 to 1883 he had served as financial member of the Viceroy's Council in India, in charge of preparing annual budgets. He was created first Earl of Cromer in 1901.

for a declaration of policy at the very least. Admittedly the leader writers enjoyed the luxury of not being responsible for the consequences of the courses they advocated and of being able to speak in general terms; moreover, there was disagreement over whether Khartoum should be held or abandoned. But the leaders, the dispatches from correspondents, and the letters to the editors were unanimous in demanding that something be done.

II

The involvement of the *Pall Mall Gazette* in the Sudan controversy began on November 22, 1883, with a leading article, "The Catastrophe in the Soudan," on the fate of Hicks Pasha and his men. In the same issue was a signed article by Sir Samuel Baker, noted explorer and authority on the upper Nile region, which concluded: "Not an hour should be lost in deciding upon the plan of operations, which should be under the control of only one responsible individual, who should be unfettered in his action. That person should be an Englishman." On November 23 a leading article in the *Times* voiced the view shared by most of the London press that it was no time to talk of imminent withdrawal from Egypt, but Stead, during this first period of excitement, leaned toward a policy of evacuating the Sudan. Although he later berated Baring and the government for indecisiveness, the *PMG* leader on January 5, 1884, "Downing-Street and Cairo," defended the cabinet for not acting impulsively, observing that "statesmen responsible for the Government of the realm are properly less precipitate than their impatient advisers of the press." If matters did come to a head, the chief reliance should be on Baring—"for us as well as for the Khedive, his word in the crisis must be law." But two days later, on January 7, the *PMG* began to shift its ground: the leading article acknowledged that England might be forced to undertake the military defense of Egypt, which would also mean "taking in hand, for a time, the whole administration of the country."

On that same day, Charles Gordon, now a general, arrived in England to apply for military leave, intending to proceed to the Congo Free State on a mission for Leopold, king of the Belgians. The man who was to be the central figure in the Sudanese drama has been described as "perhaps the finest specimen of the heroic Victorian type—a Bible-taught Evangelical, fearless, tireless, incorruptible, following the call of duty through fields of desparate adventure." [3] At this time Gordon already was something of a popular hero. In 1863, after serving with distinction in the Crimean War and in the British reduction of Peking, he was given command of the small, motley Imperial Army of China, with orders to suppress the widespread and hitherto inextinguishable Taiping Rebellion. His accomplishment of this mission was a truly remarkable military feat, and he became Chinese Gordon to the British public. For a five-year period in the 1870s he served the khedive Ismail in Egypt, first in Equatoria, then as governor general of the Sudan, making an equally remarkable, if less spectacular, record. If he could not eradicate the slave trade, he at least curbed it, and he introduced reforms into the brutal, corruption-riddled government. In 1879 he met Baring at a conference on Ismail's financial difficulties. The meeting was not a propitious one; indeed, it was almost predictable that the cold, efficient civil servant and the impetuous, eccentric soldier of fortune would find it difficult to see eye to eye on anything. On this occasion Gordon sided with the khedive, who wanted a moratorium on Egypt's debts. When Ismail was deposed shortly after, Gordon resigned as governor general. Although he had no illusions about Ismail, he was loyal to him and had no use for Tewfik, the new khedive. At this time, too, he was in the throes of one of his periodic bouts of depression—the "doles," he called them—and he had come to despair of ever accomplishing anything in the Sudan.

Gordon's past experience and successes made him an obvious candidate to find a solution for the Sudanese dilemma. He knew the Sudan and its people well, and in China and the Sudan he had been able to triumph over armies that were numerically far superior. The suggestion that he should be sent to the Sudan seems to have been aired first in the *Times* on January 1, 1884, in a letter from Sir Samuel Baker. "A British High Commissioner, with full powers, should be dispatched to Congola and Berber without delay," Baker wrote. "Why should not General Gordon Pasha be invited to assist the government?" But there was no immediate response to this suggestion, from either Whitehall or Fleet Street, and the *Times* itself did not refer to it in its leader, which called for more positive action in Egypt. Then on January 5 Stead,

3. R. C. K. Ensor, *England, 1870-1914* (London: Oxford University Press, 1963), p. 81.

having learned that Gordon intended to serve King Leopold in the Congo, printed the following Occasional Note:

> "Chinese" Gordon is to undertake the administration of the business of the International Association on the Congo. Everyone will congratulate the International Association upon its good fortune in securing the services of such a man. But is it not a pity at a time when so much other work is urgently wanting to be done in Egypt and elsewhere, the ablest leader of irregular forces England has produced should be told off to the service of an International Association amid the swamps of the Congo.

Gordon's return to England on January 7 went almost unnoticed, but Stead, who had discovered he would be visiting his sister in Southhampton, sent a telegram asking for an interview on the Sudan question. Gordon replied that his opinions were not important enough to justify the trip from London, but to come ahead anyway. Stead lost no time in doing so. On January 8 the two men met for this first time, and—perhaps because of their remarkable similarity in character and temperament—seem to have quickly taken to each other. Both Stead and Gordon were men of action in their own worlds, impatient with the restrictions of orthodoxy, determined to remain unimpressed by pomp or authority. Both were physically small men, capable of an astonishing amount of work when caught up in a cause, and able to command deep loyalty from their close associates. Both were intensely emotional, given to moods which ranged from black despair to almost boyish exhilaration. Both sought solace, guidance, and justification in the Bible, though neither set much store by ritual and dogma. And both combined the selfless zeal of a crusader with a ham actor's love of the spotlight.[4]

The interview opened with a discussion of Gordon's new job in the Congo—Stead assured him that he was bound to quarrel with Sir Henry Stanley, his nominal superior—and then talk turned to

4. Unlike Stead, Gordon was a confirmed bachelor, but I could find no real proof of the suggestions of some biographers that he was a homosexual. Anthony Nutting says of this allegation, "So far as letters, diaries and the testimony of contemporaries go, there is little evidence one way or the other" (*Gordon, Martyr and Misfit* [London: Constable, 1966], p. 319). Another difference between the two men was that Stead was virtually a teetotaller and Gordon drank, although not as much as some writers have suggested.

the Sudan. Gordon conceded that the provinces of Darfur and Kardofan could not be held, but emphasized the dangers of abandoning the eastern Sudan: the threat was not an invasion of Egypt proper, but the influence that the Mahdi's success might have on the other Near East regions. Because of the lack of transportation Khartoum could not be evacuated; hence, said Gordon, "You must either surrender absolutely to the Mahdi or defend Khartoum at all hazards." The defense of the city would not be difficult, and if it were held, the Mahdi's forces would disintegrate. The great evil was not at Khartoum, but at Cairo; everything depended on "a firm hand placed at the helm of Egypt," and Gordon favored giving power to Nubar Pasha, "the one supremely able man among Egyptian ministers." A governor general with full powers also should be sent to Khartoum; Gordon's candidate was Sir Samuel Baker. The reason for the uprising in the Sudan, according to Gordon, was the same as for every popular revolt against Turkish rule: the people were oppressed, and Cairo paid no heed to their complaints. It was a mistake to see the Mahdi as a religious leader and the movement as a religious one. He had warned Khedive Ismail on three occasions that the Sudan could not be governed by the old ways; and while he was governor general he had taught the Sudanese something of liberty and justice. "I have laid the egg which the Mahdi has hatched," he told Stead. "I taught the people that they had rights." If reforms were instituted to help them and the people of Egypt, he saw "no reason why the last British soldier should not be withdrawn from Egypt in six months' time." He did not want to press his opinions on the public, Gordon said in conclusion, nor did he want to embarrass the government, but "if I can do anything for [the Sudanese] I shall be only too glad." [5]

On his return to London that night, Stead dictated the interview to his secretary, and the following morning it was checked by a Captain Brocklehurst, who had been present at the meeting between Stead and Gordon and had accompanied Stead back to London. ("A truly marvelous effort of memory," Brocklehurst wrote later to Stead's daughter Estelle, "for Gordon talked very fast and your father did not take a note.") [6] When it appeared in

5. *Pall Mall Gazette,* January 9, 1884.
6. Whyte, *Life,* 1:125. Many of Stead's contemporaries commented on his remarkable memory.

the *PMG* on January 9, the interview was spread all over page 11 and filled most of the first column of page 12; there was also a map on page 8 illustrating Gordon's ideas. Stead's leader, on page 1, trumpeted "Chinese Gordon for the Soudan" and began:

> It is a rare piece of good fortune that at a critical moment in the destinies of the Soudan and the Nile Valley the ablest Englishman who ever held command in Equatorial Africa should be once more within two hours of London. . . . It is, therefore, with peculiar satisfaction that we direct the attention of our readers to our eleventh page, where we are privileged to set forth in considerable detail the views of Chinese Gordon on the question of the Soudan.

Stead noted that Gordon's views were in conflict with those "in high quarters." Egypt's affairs were in the hands of the "able and experienced" Baring, "and, as we stated the other day, we have no option but reluctantly to acquiesce in his decision" that the Sudan should be evacuated. However, most authorities on Egypt disagreed, and Gordon maintained that the lack of transportation made such a move impossible. Khartoum should be relieved, Stead declared, and if Egypt's forces were not capable of doing so alone and no English troops were to be sent, the answer was to "send a man who on more than one occasion has proved himself more valuable in similar circumstances than an entire army." Referring to Gordon's "notorious" and "indisputable" qualities, Stead proposed that he be sent to the Sudan to assume absolute control, treat with the Mahdi, relieve the garrisons, and salvage what was possible from the situation. As a reminder of the need for prompt action, Stead ended with the warning that "before many days General GORDON will have left for the Congo, and the supreme opportunity may have passed away."

On January 10 Stead was able to report that the interview had been widely reprinted in the London and provincial press, and was "the subject of universal comment." The *Standard* commended Gordon on his knowledge of the situation, and the *Morning Advertiser* reached the same conclusion as Stead: it was a shame that a man with Gordon's experience in the Sudan was going off to the Congo. That evening the *Globe* took favorable notice of Gordon's remarks without mentioning the paper in which they appeared, and explained why he should know what he was talking about. On January 11, in an Occasional Note, Stead registered his dismay at the news, published that morning, that Gordon had been compelled to resign his commission in order to go to the Congo, and at the prospect of the government's leaving troops in the Sudan to be massacred without even asking Gordon's opinion. A number of the morning papers already had protested the policy of withdrawal on which the government now seemed set, with the *Times* printing that morning a second letter from Sir Samuel Baker strongly condemning it, and the *Daily News* approving Gordon's views on the matter. The *Times*'s leader praised Gordon's knowledge and experience and regretted that he could not help with the problem. Although the *Times* was adamant in opposing British withdrawal from Egypt, it saw no reason to hold on to the Sudan if the Khartoum garrison could be brought out safely. On January 12 the *Morning Advertiser* declared that all of England was looking for the employment of Gordon in the Sudan, while the *PMG* in its Occasional Notes painted a still blacker picture of the crisis and again lamented that without Gordon "it seems to be past praying for." The same evening the *Echo* sounded the only real note of skepticism in the London press by questioning what Gordon could do in the Sudan without an army.

On Monday, January 14, the *Times* reported that the War Office had not yet accepted Gordon's resignation, so there was still hope his experience "might be made available for the defense of Egypt, if not for the restoration of the Khedive's authority over a part of the Sudan." The *Times* also printed a letter, passed along by Sir Samuel Baker, in which Gordon stated that he supported intervention.[7] That evening Stead's leader, "Khartoum," noted that orders to evacuate the city had been given, and while granting the necessity to follow Baring's advice, expressed the fear, based on Gordon's views, that withdrawal was no longer possible. The *Evening News* for January 14 declared, "Chinese Gordon and a suitable contingent of Indian troops would ere this have . . . averted the evacuation and fall of Khartoum." The other morning papers all had commented on the grim prospects for evacuation of the Sudan, and on January 15 several, including the *Post* and the *Advertiser*,

---

7. A few days after his interview with Stead, Gordon talked with Baker, who urged him to forgo the Congo mission and return to the Sudan. Although Gordon did not want to commit himself, that same night he wrote to Baker supporting the plan of intervention. Baker promptly gave the letter to the Times. (Blunt, *Gordon at Khartoum* [London: Stephen Swift, 1911], pp. 172-73.)

picked up the theme that it still was not too late to call Gordon to the rescue. On January 16 the *PMG* came out with a follower, "How to Save the Khartoum Garrison," by Baker, which ran more than two full columns.[8] After analyzing the military, political, and diplomatic problems involved, which he made clear would be enormous, Baker concluded—expressing the same blind faith that seemed to have seized the press and public—"If General Gordon were in command in the Sudan he would solve the difficulty." The *Evening News* of the same date echoed this belief by insisting that "the Government must . . . send General Gordon to the scene of danger to make the best of the situation for us."

As newspapers all over England chorused their demand that the government make use of the services of Chinese Gordon, the cabinet, badly divided between advocates of a hands-off policy and those favoring a more positive approach, was trying to arrive at a plan of action. The imperialist group—Lord Granville, Lord Hartington, Sir Charles Dilke, and Lord Northbrook[9]—worked to overcome Gladstone's conviction that England already had taken on too many responsibilities in Egypt and to persuade him that a vigorous policy in the Sudan was essential. The very importance of the offices these men held gave them leverage, but their cause was unquestionably aided by the clamor in the press and by the widespread public reaction to it. On January 15 Gordon was summoned to a meeting with Lord Wolesley, adjutant general of the forces, and when questioned said that he would be willing to postpone his Congo mission and to serve under Baring if sent to Egypt. Some weeks earlier, in December, 1883, Granville had cabled Baring, sounding him out on the possibility of using Gordon in the Sudan. Baring had thrown cold water on the idea, which, he said, was favored by neither the khedive nor the Egyptian prime minister. After the *PMG* launched the "Chinese Gordon for the Sou-

8. The main news story on this date, occupying almost as much space as Baker's article, told of the arrival in Liverpool of P. T. Barnum's famous white elephant.

9. The Earl of Granville (1815-91) was twice Gladstone's foreign secretary (1870-74, 1880-85); the Marquess of Hartington (1833-1908), later the eighth Duke of Devonshire, had been the Liberal leader in the House of Commons, became Secretary for India in 1880, and had been transferred to the War Office in December, 1882; Sir Charles Dilke (1843-1911) was appointed Undersecretary of State for foreign affairs in 1880, and in 1882 became president of the Local Government Board, with a seat on the cabinet; the Earl of Northbrook (1826-1904) had been Viceroy of India (1872-76), and became First Lord of the Admiralty in 1882. He was a cousin of Sir Evelyn Baring.

dan" campaign, Granville again had queried Baring, and again his response had been negative. Now, on the day of his meeting with Gordon, Granville once more raised the question, and this time Baring gave in and assented to Gordon's coming to Egypt. On this day, too, the proposal was made to Gladstone that Gordon should go out to the Sudan, not in his military capacity, but simply to report on the situation. Presumably, he would be able to suggest the best way of effecting a withdrawal of the garrison, perhaps even how to come to terms with the Mahdi.

On January 16 Gordon went to Brussels to see King Leopold, who reluctantly granted a postponement of the Congo mission. Back in England two days later, he met with the war hawk members of the cabinet. Since Baring now had come around, the decision was made to send Gordon to Khartoum. His instructions were to report on the situation and to evacuate the Sudan. Gladstone, who had never met Gordon, was ill and resting at Hawarden when the decision was taken; in "an unhappy hour" he agreed to subscribe to it.[10] And on January 19 the morning papers printed a notice authorized by the War Office: "General C. G. Gordon, C.B., started yesterday evening for Egypt en route for Suakin or Khartoum on a special mission. He takes with him as his military secretary Lieutenant-Colonel Stewart, 11th Hussars, who was at Khartoum on duty last year."

Editorially, the London and provincial press expressed great satisfaction with the decision, and many were highly critical because it had not been made sooner. The Gordon mystique flavored the reaction, although some papers, among them the *Times*, cautioned against believing that the Egyptian-Sudan problem had been solved. That evening Stead's leading article began, "The whole Egyptian question has been revolutionized in an hour. At yesterday's informal meeting of the Ministers at the War Office there was taken one of those decisive steps that make or mar the destinies of empires." Stead opined that Gordon should have a free hand in the Sudan, just as Baring should have one in Egypt; the possible conflicts inherent in this dualism apparently did not bother him. Limited rule had been tried and had failed in Egypt, he said, so now England must be prepared to go all the way. The *PMG's* earlier recommendations for a policy of caution and nonaggression

10. Philip Magnus, *Gladstone: A Biography* (New York: E. P. Dutton, 1954), p. 310.

in Egypt did not deter him from declaring grandly that "the counsel which we have never ceased to press upon the Government has been tardily followed." Over the weekend other newspapers and magazines commented editorially on the cabinet's decision, and on Monday, January 21, Stead's leader reported: "No step taken by Her Majesty's ministers since the Egyptian troubles began has ever evoked such a universal outburst of approval as the despatch of General GORDON to Khartoum."

In retrospect it seems obvious that the decision to send Gordon to the Sudan was unwise. His powers to work miracles were overrated; indeed, he seriously misjudged the situation, for he underestimated the strength of the Mahdists and failed to appreciate the religious basis of the movement. And if these criticisms simply demonstrate the advantage of hindsight, it should at least have been apparent at the time that a man of Gordon's impetuosity and indifference to authority was not the ideal choice merely to send reports while deciding how to carry out the evacuation—a move which he was on record as firmly opposing. The story of what followed is well known. After conferring with Baring at Cairo and receiving an appointment as governor general of the Sudan, Gordon made a daring trip up the Nile to Khartoum. Once there he decided that the city could not be successfully evacuated but that it could easily be held and defended. By the middle of March Khartoum was surrounded and under siege by the Mahdists. Gladstone's delay in sending a relief expedition has been attributed to several factors: his preoccupation with Ireland and the Franchise Bill, his irritation at Gordon's defiance of the government's orders, and Gordon's own overly optimistic reports in the early stages of the siege. When, after numerous delays, the relief column finally reached Khartoum on January 28, 1885, they found the city had been overrun two days earlier and that during the ensuing massacre Gordon had been killed and decapitated.

Like the rest of the press, the *Pall Mall Gazette* had been carrying the running story of the relief expedition. When the news of the tragic climax to Gordon's mission reached London on February 5, it called forth from the *PMG* the boldest headline display it had yet ventured,[11] extending across two columns, with the top line set in twenty-four-point type:

11. Up to this time the *PMG*'s most daring use of large type had been a headline on January 28, 1885, which, ironically, told of "Another Victory in the Soudan." It was one column wide and the top head was in eighteen-point type.

TOO LATE!
KHARTOUM CAPTURED BY THE MAHDI
THE FATE OF GENERAL GORDON UNKNOWN
SIR CHARLES WILSON TWO DAYS LATE
THE STEAMERS WRECKED ON THE NILE

After February 5 the *PMG* headlines were reduced in size but for some days were more prominent than usual. Apart from this typographical departure, and despite Stead's personal involvement in the tragedy, the *Pall Mall* coverage of the story did not differ substantially from that of the other London papers; and on the confirmation of Gordon's death, it joined with the majority of the press in demanding that the Mahdist uprising be extinguished.

Most of the press and most of the public had wanted Gordon to be sent to the Sudan, but Gladstone had to bear the onus of delaying the decision to send the relief expedition and for weeks faced hostile, jeering crowds whenever he appeared in public. There were, however, a few voices which blamed Stead for the tragedy. On February 11 a particularly virulent denunciation of the *PMG* and its editor appeared in the pages of the *Echo*. A leader on Gordon's death, its implications, and the policy that the government should now pursue raged at the *PMG* and at the same time admitted that its influence on government policy was considerable.

> Well may Mr. John Morley warn his countrymen to disregard "the sanguinary ravings of delirious newspapers," more especially of the particular newspaper which arrogates to itself the right to order ministers about as though they were so many schoolboys. The *Pall Mall Gazette* addresses itself to "our bellowing brethren." Better the bellowing of the whole London Press than the incessant maniacal shriek of our contemporary. We do not suppose that ministers, weak as they have become, have been throughout the most humble, obedient servants of the *Pall Mall Gazette;* but they certainly on more than one occasion have taken the course, which it demanded they should adopt.

In succeeding days letters to the editor of the *Echo* spoke of "the War Office operating through that wild, hysterical, bloodthirsty paper, the *Pall Mall Gazette*" (February 12), and "that worst of Jingo prints, the reckless and blustering *Pall Mall Gazette*" (February 13). "It was an evil day," the writer of this letter observed, "when Mr. John Morley was shunted to give place to a man who sacrifices everything to his determination to produce a sensational sheet." [12]

III

As momentous and newsworthy as were the 1885 developments in the Sudan crisis, the events in January, 1884, leading up to Gordon's appointment were of far more significance in the history of journalism. There certainly had been earlier demonstrations of the influence of the press in political affairs, but, as R. H. Gretton has written, the campaign to send Gordon to the Sudan "was probably the first occasion on which a newspaper set itself, by acting as the organiser of opinion on a particular detail of policy, to change a Government's mind at high speed." [13] Gordon had been suggested to the public as a possible candidate to resolve the Sudan dilemma before Stead went into action, and nearly all the major dailies supported the campaign to some degree, but there is no question that Stead's interview with Gordon gave it the initial impetus. On the day after the announcement that Gordon had been ordered to the Sudan, Milner came into the *PMG* office and said to his editor as he unbuttoned his coat, "I think this is the biggest thing you have done yet" [14]—a judgment that was accepted by most of Stead's contemporaries and, needless to say, by Stead himself. The Gordon campaign was an example of what he meant when he used to say that he was busy "running the Empire from Northumberland Street." [15] Hugh Kingsmill, quoting the Stead leader of January 21, 1884, which warned the government not to interfere with Gordon after he reached the Sudan, hit the mark when he said, "There is a royal flavor about it." [16] And there was surely something royal in an article Stead wrote during a 1911 renewal of the debate about the Gordon mission. In one passage, which he headed "My Reason for Sending Gordon to Khartoum," he explained why he had "insisted" on the dispatch of Gordon, and declared, "I not only said so, but I was obeyed." [17]

12. The *Echo* leader and the letters to the editor were condemning not only the *PMG*'s part in the Gordon tragedy, but also its belligerent attitude toward France and Germany.
13. Gretton, *Modern History of the English People*, p. 124.
14. Stead, "Character Sketch: Milner," p. 21.
15. *Times*, April 18, 1912.
16. Kingsmill, *After Puritanism*, p. 181.
17. William T. Stead, "Books of the Month: More about General Gordon and the Men Who Sent Him Out," *Review of Reviews*, November 1911, p. 511.

Wemyss Reid, who saw in the episode a distressing example of
the dangers of newspaper influence and of Stead's arrogant manipu-
lation of it, depicted him in his *Memoirs* (1905) as reveling "in
his power with all the zest of a schoolboy" as he "calmly undertook
the direction of the foreign policy of Great Britain, and ordered
Ministers to do his bidding with an audacity which would have
been absurd but for the fact that Ministers seemed ready to take
him at his word. He it was who first advised them the evil course
of sending Gordon to Khartoum." The ministers "yielded to his
vehemence," Reid wrote, and Stead "was not in the least discon-
certed" when the course he had advised ended in tragedy. "Talking to me one day at that time, he said, 'John Morley told me
yesterday that I ought not to be able to sleep in my bed at nights
for thinking of all the men who have lost their lives over this business.'" If Reid had ever believed in government by newspapers,
he had been "cured of that delusion after seeing what a mess even
so brilliant a journalist as Stead made of the attempt to control
the policy of a nation from an editor's desk." [18]

The post-mortem of the Khartoum tragedy and the *PMG*'s role
in it was continued in 1908 when Baring, now Lord Cromer, published his *Modern Egypt*. Baring, who had endured considerable
vilification for his own part in the affair, still believed that sending
Gordon to the Sudan had been a mistake, but that once he got
there the best chance of success lay in following the *PMG*'s advice
to give him carte blanche. Baring himself had tried to act on this
advice, but Gordon had deluged him with contradictory opinions,
with the result that he never knew what to do from one minute to
the next. "During this stage of national excitement," Baring wrote,
"any one who had attempted to judge General Gordon's conduct
by the canons of criticism which ordinarily applied to human
action, would have failed to obtain a hearing." The English newspapers which carried feature articles glorifying Gordon and his
past exploits were largely responsible for his near-deification, but
what most disturbed Baring was that the press had helped to persuade the government to send Gordon on his ill-fated mission, and
he placed most of the blame on the *Pall Mall Gazette*. "'Anonymous authorship,'" he declared, "as one of the wisest political
thinkers of modern times has stated, 'places the public under the
direction of guides who have no sense of responsibility.'" [19]

18. Reid, *Memoirs,* pp. 345-46.
19. Earl Cromer, *Modern Egypt* (London: Macmillan, 1911), pp. 333,
336-37.

Stung by Baring's belittling of Gordon and by his views on the press, Stead replied in a *Contemporary Review* article, defending Gordon's actions, decrying Baring's inaction, and taking issue on the matter of newspaper influence. During the weeks after the massacre at El Obeid, he said, "it was the Press which possessed the prescience, initiative, resolution, and energy, and . . . it was [Baring] who was vacillating, procrastinating, and always too late." Stead pointed out, rightly, that the opinions expressed in the *PMG* were scarcely anonymous, and he steadfastly maintained that "the only redeeming feature in the whole dreary narrative of the ruin of the Soudan was supplied by the British Press in sending out General Gordon." [20]

The question of Stead's influence came up again in 1911 with the publication of Wilfred Scawen Blunt's *Gordon at Khartoum*. Blunt, who opposed British aggression in Africa and the Near East, said he did not think it could be "pretended that Stead's recommendation of Gordon for the post was so potent and instantaneous an influence at the Foreign Office, as to have forced Granville's hand unless Granville had been already willing." It was rather that Stead, by initiating the outcry for Gordon in the press, and, along with the other newspapers, whipping up the public demand for him, provided the support which enabled the war hawk ministers to carry out their policies. It was Blunt's theory that Stead actually had been the tool of the aggressively minded cabinet members and had acted on their advice; thus, "it was far more likely that those in the cabinet who wanted to send Gordon should have made use of Stead to popularize their plan than that Stead should have been able by his few words, however powerful, so suddenly to force it on them. Gordon's views . . . may possibly have quickened the pace, and this is all that can reasonably be affirmed about it." In support of his theory, Blunt alleged that throughout the crisis in January, 1884, Stead received "private information from within the Cabinet, probably from the War Office and communicated by Brett, who was Hartington's private secretary and his usual intermediary with the press, besides being an old member of the 'Pall Mall' staff." In regard to Stead's interview with Gordon, Blunt found it "impossible not to recognize in the sudden entrance of Gordon into the intrigue one of those who worked from time to time in the 'Pall Mall' columns through Lord Esher's agency."

20. William T. Stead, "Lord Cromer and Government by Journalism," *Contemporary Review*, April 1908, pp. 436-39.

After the publication of the Gordon interview, the *PMG*, as Blunt
saw it, became an organ of the cabinet faction that wanted to
intervene in the Sudan. Gladstone's objections to intervention could
be overcome only by the force of public opinion, and "the 'Pall
Mall Gazette' had more than once been used to coerce him. It was
the paper that he chiefly read." Thus, when Stead's campaign
caught on so spectacularly with the rest of the press and the nation
at large, Gladstone capitulated. Blunt rejected Morley's view that
"Granville and Hartington, Dilke and Northbrook, four level-
headed English politicians, at least as much rogues politically as
fools, went suddenly mad at Stead's persuading them that Gordon
was a miracle man. . . . It is cabinet ministers that inspire newspapers, not the newspapers them." [21]

Stead's refutation of Blunt's elaborate theory, published in his
Review of Reviews (November, 1911), was simple and unanswer-
able. He had never in his life met Hartington; he did not meet
Brett until after Gordon had left for Egypt; and Brett was never
a member of the *Pall Mall* staff. As for cabinet ministers inspiring
newspapers,

> The fact is that Mr. Blunt suffers from the Superstition of the
> of the Portfolio. If a man has a portfolio and a seat in the
> Cabinet he becomes at once a statesman who governs and
> directs. If a man has a newspaper and occupies an editorial
> chair he is of necessity of his position the puppet of the port-
> folio holder. That the statesman may be in the editorial sanc-
> tum and the puppet in Downing Street does not seem to have
> dawned on Mr. Blunt. But it was a tradition that Northumber-
> land Street had jealously preserved from the time when the
> Suez Canal shares were bought at Mr. Greenwood's sug-
> gestion.[22]

Stead's account has been confirmed by some of the others involved.
Lord Esher stated flatly that neither he nor Lord Hartington communicated in any way with Stead at this time and that "Mr. Blunt's
theory of a secret plot is all absurd nonsense, Stead started the
whole thing." Lord Milner was equally emphatic: "I remember
the circumstances perfectly; Stead's rush to Southampton was entirely his own idea. No one had suggested it, and he himself had

21. Blunt, *Gordon at Khartoum*, pp. 167-169.
22. Stead, "More about General Gordon," pp. 508-9.

not the least notion when he started, what would come of it." [23] Moreover, it would be just as unlikely that a man of Stead's temperament, holding his views on the mission of the press, would be directed by a cabinet minister as that a cabinet minister would be directed by him. But then Blunt saw Stead as playing the part of a puppet on more than one occasion. For example, in his diary entry for January 30, 1885, Blunt interpreted the appointment of the future Archbishop of Canterbury, Frederick Temple, as Bishop of London as the result of Hartington's intrigues with the press, particularly the *Pall Mall Gazette.* Since the *PMG* for weeks had been urging Temple's appointment, the "stupid public" believed that Stead was responsible for it; but the truth was, Blunt insisted, that "Hartington pulls all the strings and gives him the information" [24]—hardly the words of an astute and objective observer of the political scene.

IV

The splash made by the Gordon interview clearly confirmed Stead's belief in the value of this form of journalism, for during the first six months of 1884 the *PMG* ran no less than seventy-nine interviews with such diverse personalities as Edward Benson, the Archbishop of Canterbury; the American economic theorist Henry George; the head of the Pears Soap Company; the great Victorian preacher Rev. C. H. Spurgeon; Emile Zola; and a Mr. Stuart Cumberland, expert on the subject of thought reading. In addition, a number of people were interviewed on the Sudan matter, among them Wilfred Blunt. [25]

As well as employing the techniques of the New Journalism, Stead liked to call attention to their use, particularly when he could twit the more orthodox journalists for adopting the methods they had professed to scorn. In an Occasional Note for April 5, 1884, he wrote:

> One of the superstitions of the English press—superstitions which are fortunately on the wane—is that interviewing in England is a monstrous departure from the dignity and pro-

23. Whyte, *Life,* 1:131.
24. Blunt, *Gordon at Khartoum,* p. 369.
25. On December 22, 1884, Blunt granted Stead another interview, which was printed the next day. He stated in his diary that he had to rewrite it completely because it was so distorted (ibid., p. 355). Such complaints were rare; most of the persons Stead interviewed were impressed by his accuracy.

priety of journalism. None of our dignified contemporaries hesitates to interview anyone outside the British Isles, but interviewing . . . must not cross the channel. Thus the *Times* keeps an interviewer-general at Paris, in the person of M. de Blowitz,[26] and this morning it publishes much the most interesting report that has appeared on Bulgaria since our interview with Mr. Forster, in the shape of an interview with M. Jonin, the late Russian Resident at Sophia.

Another chance for a dig at the old journalism came three days later, on April 8, in an interview with Henry Labouchere, popularly known as Labby, a member of Parliament and proprietor and editor of a society weekly, *Truth*. Labby opened the conversation by asking Stead facetiously, "Are you aware how much you are degrading the dignity of the press by the introduction of the interviewer?" And he told of a conversation he had overheard between two clubmen who were lamenting the decadence of the *PMG*. "What are we coming to?" asked one. "Interviews in the *Pall Mall Gazette!*" "Yes," said the other, "and not only interviews, but pictures!" Labouchere recalled the consternation he had caused at the office of a London daily when he suggested a two-column advertisement, and then, in a Steadian vein, pronounced the dignity of the press "a superstition, a fetish, which is invoked when anything is proposed to be done that has not been done by our ancestors." The occasion for the interview was the sentencing of Edmund Yates, editor of the *World*, another society journal, to four months in jail for malicious libel, and Labouchere discussed aspects of the case, declaring his belief that good-natured gossip was harmless. In his concluding statements—he favored fewer and shorter leaders because Londoners did not like politics, and he averred that "one good bloody murder, from a newspaper point of view, is worth more than anything else that can happen"— Labouchere showed himself more attuned to the New Journalism of the future, the journalism of Sir George Newnes and Lord Northcliffe, than Stead himself.[27]

26. Henry Georges de Blowitz (1825-1903) was perhaps the best known of the Victorian foreign correspondents. He made a considerable reputation in Europe as an interviewer, based in part on a famous session with Bismarck at the time of the Berlin Conference of 1878.

27. According to Hamilton Fyfe, Labouchere "might, if he had gone in for daily journalism himself, have brought about the revolution which was due to Northcliffe holding exactly the same opinions as to how journalism should be run" (*Sixty Years of Fleet Street* [London: W. H. Allen, 1949], p. 35).

The Yates case had provoked a debate about gossip in news-papers, with the prevailing view of the more conservative press voiced by the *Morning Advertiser.* In an April 3 article, the *Adver-tiser* said that Yates and his contributors were by no means the only sinners in this connection. Further, it held that "details relat-ing to the private life of public men find their proper place else-where than in the columns of public journals, and whether founded or unfounded, true or false, ought equally to be excluded from a paper which professes to supply the public with news." Lining up with the *Advertiser,* the *Leeds Mercury* assailed the *World* for lowering the whole character of English journalism, and the *Man-chester Guardian* hoped that Yates's sentence would "administer a wholesome corrective to habitual abuses of the privileges of the press." Stead took the opposite side in an April 3 leading article, "A Plea for Tittle-Tattle." While he agreed that newspapers must be held to account for libels or false statements, he objected to the "wholesale anathema upon society journalism." The desire for this kind of news was a natural one, and shared by many people of all classes. "Everyone delights in a Boswell," he argued, "and what is the society journal but the Boswell to an innumerable num-ber of personages . . . known to the man in the street?"

Stead was using signed articles, as well as interviews and illus-trations, more frequently, and on April 15 he happily pointed out in an Occasional Note that the *Times* had printed a signed book review and that a signed article had appeared in the *Daily News.* "Universal anonymity has been a tedious superstition of English journalism," said Stead. "That there was no real reason for ad-hering to it so rigidly is shown by the fact that it has needed only a bold example to lead to the general infringement of the rule in six months."

During the summer Stead had an opportunity to deliver himself of some thoughts on the power of the press when Tory party leaders, concerned at the hostility of many papers, held a confer-ence in London for a number of editors of provincial Conservative newspapers. In a leading article on July 26, Stead made fun of the Tories for bringing the provincial journalists to London to make them feel important and then, in effect, telling them they didn't know their business. The leader of the Opposition, Sir Staff-ord Northcote (later Lord Iddesleigh), was quoted as saying that it was time to recognize the importance of the press in shaping public opinion, and Stead wrote that this was true in a wider sense than Northcote understood: "We began by governing England by Kings, we then governed her by nobles, after the Reform Act we tried government by the Commons, we are now well on our way to government by the Press." He described as "fatuous" the neglect of the press by statesmen of the old school—"they read it, they fear it, and they often obey it, but they never attempt to influence it." In promoting a policy, he said, ministers should seek newspaper support, and he complained that they failed to give even their trusted supporters among journalists "an inside view of the difficulties of Administration." Consequently, it often happened that a journalist who wanted to help was hampered by his lack of knowledge. "To put the truth frankly," he concluded, "it is time that statesmen recognize that if they are to carry out their policies they will have to pay court to the Press."

In August Stead returned to a favorite journalistic topic: the interview and its value. In a leader, "Interviewing versus Bookmaking," he expressed ironical astonishment that Lord Chief Justice Coleridge, who had spent ten weeks in America, was not going to write a book about it. Writing a book seemed to be the habit of returned travelers, and there was some demand for that sort of thing. However, it was "not really a demand for literature, but a demand for conversation. . . . It would be very absurd to hear Lord Coleridge philosophise about America. It is very natural to wish to hear him talk about it. But for a talk, a book is not the proper form." Perhaps the means to convey the talk of the "best men" to the public had been discovered, "with all humility, in the interview." The interview was maligned and occasionally it was absurd, but "it has a future before it" (August 16, 1884). When the *Saturday Review* poked fun at his thesis, Stead responded with another defense of the interview, which he termed "the most interesting method of extracting the ideas of the few for the instruction and entertainment of the many which has yet been devised by man. . . . Many notable men are more or less inarticulate, especially with the pen, and to them the intervention of the Interviewer is almost as indispensable as that of an interpreter is to an Englishman in China" (August 23, 1884). Three days later he chided the *Standard* for interviewing Ismail Pasha at Marienbad after ignoring him when he was in London. It seemed to him very odd, "but perhaps our contemporaries think that interviews become respectable by being telegraphed" (August 30, 1884). In that same issue

Stead reprinted in an Occasional Note a lighthearted comment by the *San Francisco Argonaut* on the *PMG*'s interviews, illustrations, and feature articles:

> If a barn be blown down there will appear in the *Pall Mall Gazette* next day a diagram of the premises; view of the barn while being blown down; view of the ruins; interview with the hired man who said he always knowed it was going to blow down; interview with the owner, and his and other theories on barns blowing down; interview with Professor Mugwump, the distinguished *savant*, with his views as to the reasons why barns blow down instead of up; comparative table of barn mortality for the last forty years, showing percentage of barns blowing down compared with the illiterate vote; and history of loss from the earliest times to the present.

"Alas! we must disclaim the compliment," said the *PMG*, "but we accept it as a sanguine prophecy of the pitch of perfection to which journalism may yet be carried."

Not only was Stead beginning to chip away at some of the most hallowed traditions of old-style journalism, but also his newspaper campaigns were gaining widespread recognition. Although the "Bitter Cry" and "Gordon for the Soudan" campaigns had been his most conspicuous efforts thus far, he had made a splash with such diverse projects as sending out a "circular," or questionnaire, soliciting the views of Liberal members of Parliament on certain political issues (it was denounced as an impertinence by some, but received a large response); conducting a forum on the virtues and defects of Henry George's philosophy; and agitating briefly in favor of cremation. Undeniably, Morley's erstwhile assistant had made his presence felt during the first year of his editorial tenure. Despite the *Pall Mall Gazette*'s rather small circulation, Stead was becoming one of the best-known journalists in England.

CHAPTER FOUR

Running the Country
from Northumberland Street

Stead's next two major campaigns, which ran from September, 1884, to June, 1885, at times overlapped and in some ways appeared contradictory. In one he seemed anxious to stir the country up and in the other to calm it down; in one he talked like a militarist (although he tried to dissociate himself from the jingoes), and in the other he assumed his more familiar roles of pacifist and Russophile; in one he spoke as an imperialist, in the other he apparently made common cause with the Little Englanders. Yet Stead saw no inconsistency in this, and in fact used one campaign to complement the other. Moreover, in both cases he showed that his support of the Liberal party would not override any violation of his personal philosophy, and that he believed an editor could— and should—exercise as much political power as a cabinet minister.

I

The most paradoxical of Stead's campaigns had its inception in August, 1884, when he received a visit at the Northumberland Street office from H. O. Arnold-Forster.[1] The nephew and adopted son of W. E. Forster, Arnold-Forster had been raised in his uncle's Yorkshire home and Stead had known him since childhood. The British navy was Arnold-Forster's concern; he believed that the expansion of the fleets of other European powers was posing a

1. Hubert Oakley Arnold-Forster (1855-1909) belonged to a famous and influential family; he was a grandson of Thomas Arnold of Rugby, and a cousin of Matthew Arnold. He served as a Unionist M.P. from 1892 to 1909 and secretary of state for war under Balfour (1903-1905).

serious threat to England's naval supremacy and that it was vital that she maintain her dominion of the seas in view of her vast and ever increasing trade and responsibilities overseas. Arnold-Forster had been greatly disturbed by a speech made in the House of Lords on July 10, 1884, by Lord Northbrook, the First Lord of the Admiralty. Northbrook had been defending the government's unwillingness to spend more money on the navy, and said that if granted an additional three or four million pounds, "the great difficulty the Admiralty would have to contend with . . . would be to decide how they should spend the money." [2] Arnold-Forster had taken issue with these statements, but few seemed to pay heed to the speeches he made in criticism of them. In his visit to Stead, however, he found a sympathetic listener who was impressed by his passionate conviction that England was in danger. It was a grim prospect he outlined for Stead: "Panic, disorder, suffering, starvation among our overcrowded population will bring home to us with painful clearness the error we make in neglecting to maintain a sufficiently powerful and, above all, a sufficiently numerous Navy." Realizing his country's complete dependence upon the navy, Stead saw it as a duty to remedy its weaknesses. He determined to make his own investigation of the matter, "and for a month or more I lived and moved and had my being in what may be called the world of the Navy." [3]

Stead's interviews with Sir Cooper Key, the First Sea Lord, and Admiral Seymour confirmed Arnold-Forster's pessimistic appraisal. Both believed that the naval estimates were too low and the Royal Navy was dangerously weak. Both had tried in vain to convince the prime minister of the navy's needs and doubted that anyone could change his mind. "Mr. Gladstone thinks of nothing but Ireland and home affairs," Sir Cooper said, "and we can get nothing

2. Great Britain, *Hansard's Parliamentary Debates,* 3rd ser., 290 (1884): 660. Northbrook's speech has been somewhat misinterpreted; he was making the point that since new guns had made it necessary to provide thicker, more costly armor, it would be foolish to spend much money on current types of ships. Also, with the increased efficiency of torpedos it was doubtful that any nation would want to spend huge sums on large ships. In his later account of the speech Stead mistakenly dated it May, 1884 (W. T. Stead, "The Rebuilding of the British Navy," *Review of Reviews,* July 1897, p. 78). See also Scott, *Life and Death,* p. 124 n.

3. Stead, "The Rebuilding of the British Navy," p. 77. The phrase "Panic, disorder, suffering . . ." was used by Arnold-Forster in an article he had written before Northbrook's speech ("Our Position as a Naval Power," *Nineteenth Century,* January 1883, 1-3).

for the Navy; not a penny." And when Stead asked Seymour what would happen in case of war with France, the admiral replied: "Within twenty-four hours of the declaration of war, Sir Cooper Key and I, and all the rest of us at the Admiralty, would be swinging by our necks from the lamp-posts in front of Whitehall." [4] Protests and threatened resignations had left the administration unmoved. The Liberal tradition of economy in government and of anti-imperialism did not jibe with a program of increased expenditures to discharge England's growing imperial commitments. The lower-ranking officers with whom Stead talked were equally pessimistic, but most of them were reluctant to put their careers in jeopardy by talking frankly to a journalist with Stead's reputation. Some did give him useful information, however, and one—young Captain Fisher—became an important though anonymous witness in the ensuing campaign. [5]

On August 12, the Secretary to the Admiralty, Sir Thomas Brassey,[6] speaking to the Portsmouth Liberal Association, echoed Northbrook's complacency. He gave the tonnage of major navies of the world, showing England comfortably in the lead, and asserted that despite general economies the Liberal administration had added one million pounds to the naval estimates. He also reported encouragingly on various elements of Britain's naval power: number of torpedo boats, merchant ships, shipyards, and so on (August 13, 1884). Exactly one month later a leading Conservative, Lord Henry Lennox, spoke to the Conservative Working Men's Club in Portsmouth, presenting a rebuttal to Brassey's conclusion. Brassey's tonnage figures were misleading, he claimed, and those for England must have included old and obsolete ships. Furthermore, said Lennox, even by counting ships in urgent need of repair, he arrived at a total of only 228,000 tons for the British navy as opposed to Brassey's figure of 329,000 tons. He then gave specific examples of areas in which England was deficient, including torpedo boats, ironclads, and shipyards. Commenting on the speech, Stead warned the Conservatives not to make partisan

4. Stead, "The Rebuilding of the British Navy," p. 78.
5. John Arbuthnot Fisher, first Baron Fisher of Kilverstane (1841-1920), served as Lord of the Admiralty and First Sea Lord (1904-10, 1914-15). It was only after Fisher's high rank gave him immunity that Stead revealed the identity of his informant (Whyte, *Life,* p. 150).
6. Thomas Brassey, first Earl Brassey (1836-1918), was the author of *The British Navy* (1882-83) and founder of *The Naval Annual* (1886).

capital out of the issue, for it was originally the policies of their leader, Lord Beaconsfield, which triggered the French naval expansion that—as Stead saw it—now threatened England (September 13).

The *Pall Mall Gazette* campaign for a bigger and better navy was officially launched on Monday, September 15, with a two-column leading article, "What Is the Truth about the Navy?" In it Stead took cognizance of the struggle for empire which was beginning to absorb many European nations.

> The scramble for the world has begun in earnest. In the face of that phenomenon how far are we able to prevent our own possessions being scrambled for by our neighbours? The answer to that question depends upon the condition of our navy. If it is as strong as it ought to be we have nothing to fear. If, on the other hand, it is no longer in a position of incontestable superiority to the navies of the world, we are in a position of peril too grave to be capable of exaggeration. Not only our Imperial position, but the daily bread of twenty millions out of thirty millions of our population depends entirely upon our dominion of the sea. If that is lost, or even endangered, our existence is at stake.

He said again that the issue must not become enmeshed in party politics, but opined that the Liberals were in a better position to build up the navy than the Conservatives, who were suspect in matters relating to military expenditures. Moreover, the Liberals were the free-trade party, which needed the navy to survive; hence, the antimilitary Cobden was willing to spend money on the fleet, and even Gladstone, in his Midlothian campaign of 1880,[7] had expressed his determination to maintain English naval supremacy. The great question, as Stead saw it, was not whether the navy was as good as ever, but what its strength was relative to that of other powers. He asked a dozen questions which could be answered by yes or no—they related to overall superiority, the future of ironclads, the defense of outposts, the number of torpedo boats, etc. If the Admiralty's answer to any of them was negative, it should

7. During his Midlothian campaign Gladstone gave a series of impassioned speeches, designed to appeal to the masses, which many Conservatives, including Queen Victoria, thought were demagogic and degrading to a man in his position. The theme of his major speech, given in Edinburgh on March 17, was opposition to Beaconsfield's jingoistic imperialism.

ask for as much money as was needed to correct the deficiency, and "no party in this country will refuse them as many millions as is necessary to put things right."

For two days after the opening salvo the matter rested and the *PMG* was content to tell its readers of the situation in the Sudan, of the anti-Lords agitation over the Franchise Bill to extend male suffrage, and of a debate on the question of whether school children were being overworked since the passage of the Education Act of 1870. Then, on September 18, came the full barrage. The first six pages of the sixteen-page issue were devoted to the naval question: twelve of twenty-four columns of news were given over to Stead's leader, "A Startling Revelation," and an article, "The Truth about the Navy," signed "By One Who Knows the Facts." Since most of the future declarations and debates over particular aspects of England's naval strength reiterated or elaborated the points made in this issue of the *PMG*, they will be considered in some detail.

Stead's leader, which occupied most of page 1, noted that the *PMG* was publishing "at a length which though fully warranted by the importance of the subject is entirely without precedent in the history of this journal, a detailed statement of what purports to be the truth about the navy made by one who is in a position to know the facts, although for obvious reasons we withhold his name." The information was so alarming that it had been given to competent naval authorities, who "agreed with the general accuracy of the writer's presentation of the facts." Although using the most optimistic estimates, "he sets forth one of the most gloomy pictures of the condition of our navy that has probably ever been published in an English newspaper, and one which, unless its substantial accuracy can be promptly disproved, must arouse the nation to energetic and immediate action." The report showed that England no longer enjoyed the unquestioned naval supremacy which she had held in 1868, when she was spending as much on her navy as France, Italy, Germany, and Russia combined. Now she was spending eleven million pounds, compared to fifteen million by these four powers. Yet during the intervening years her territorial and commercial responsibilities had increased, and with two-thirds of her food supplies imported, naval supremacy had become a life-and-death matter. An immediate increase in naval expenditures was necessary for survival, even though "no words are too strong to express the repugnance which we feel to any such demand. . . . But what is the alternative?" England "leads the progress of the world in civilization"; England "alone among the Great Powers of the older world . . . stands for liberty"; England could not be jeopardized "for the sake of a penny on the income tax. . . . If France is rich enough to pay for her glory, is England not rich enough to pay for her insurance?"

The rest of page 1 and the following pages carried the report for which Captain Fisher apparently supplied much of the material. It opened with a survey of the past fifteen years, pointing out that there had been a great increase in prosperity and population, in overseas possession and trade, which imposed a heavier burden on the navy. Yet, the naval estimates for 1883 were lower than those for 1868, despite increased construction costs. Breaking down naval power into categories, the report conceded that England had a superiority in first-class ironclads, but not in relation to a coalition of powers, and England's advantage disappeared when second- and third-class vessels were taken into account. Throughout the campaign it was clear by direct statement or inference that France was the power which the advocates of a larger navy most feared, and the report referred to France when discussing ironclads in the process of construction. England was building more of these vessels than before, but France was building them at an even faster rate and in two years would lead England in ironclads of the second and third class. Moreover, French ships were better armed and had more modern guns.

So far as foreign stations were concerned, if war suddenly broke out with France "the whole of our Chinese squadron would be at her mercy." The Pacific and Australian squadrons were safe from France, but "we could not face Chilian ironclads without reinforcements." England's position was tenuous with regard to the stations at the Cape, West Africa, East India, and southeastern America (where the menace of Brazil was invoked), and "only on the Australian and the North American stations have we an incontestable superiority over any enemy that we could encounter." Even most home harbors were inadequately protected, and outside of the United Kingdom there were only four docks equipped to refit ironclads. England's commerce was insecure because there were not enough ships for the protection of all trade routes and most coaling and telegraph stations could be destroyed with impunity—"perhaps the most fatal flaw in England's armour." Since the number of seamen had been reduced by 16 percent during the past fifteen years, in case of war England would have to call on the reserve, which was less than half the size of France's. French gunners were better trained, and the men of England's trained reserve "would hardly keep us going two months." But "the most incredible" aspect of England's naval weakness was that there was not one first-class torpedo boat ready for action, and the current building program was inadequate. Thus, "'the truth about the Navy' is that our naval supremacy has almost ceased to exist."

In succeeding issues over a period of three months Stead kept the question of England's naval strength to the fore in leading articles, signed articles by naval officers, statesmen, and interested citizens, and summaries of letters to the editor. Some articles dealt with specific weaknesses, others with general proposals for future action; most managed to steer clear of party antagonisms. From time to time the French menace was invoked, as, for example, when Fleet Admiral Sir Thomas Symonds wrote, "If a war broke out tomorrow with France I do not see how we could possibly avoid the most awful disasters" (September 25, 1884). On a number of occasions the articles were accompanied by maps and illustrations, including the first full-page illustration run by the *PMG*—a map of the world showing British naval stations and coaling ports (October 17). The bulk of the articles and letters supported naval expansion, and Stead, as was his wont, also printed some opposing views. The longest expression of the other side, a one-and-one-third-column article by Henry Richard, M.P., written from the point of view of the "Friends of Peace," opposed an increase in naval expenditures. The voices of dissent were few and thin, however, as once again a Stead campaign caught on with the public.

Although other newspapers and magazines joined Stead in the campaign, the British press was neither as unanimous in its support, nor as quick to climb on the bandwagon, as during the Gordon campaign. The first to join up was the Conservative *Morning Post*, which on September 18 mentioned the *PMG* article and welcomed its exposé of unpreparedness. Other London papers did not move with such alacrity, though the weekly magazines were more attentive than the metropolitan press. On September 20 the *Spectator* reacted sympathetically to the *PMG* analysis of the problem, but it changed its tune the following week. While the *Saturday Review* was usually a political foe of the *PMG*, it had itself carried articles on the need for naval expansion, and it hoped that "The Truth about the Navy" might be thought worth reading by "advanced Radicals" who had sneered at the *SR*'s own campaign. The *Tablet* injected a partisan note, predicting that if the concern over the navy made the nation forget its anger at the House of Lords for rejecting the Franchise Bill, "the Tory party might be saved from the blundering of its leaders by the *Pall Mall Gazette*" (September 20).

Two days after its big spread, the *PMG* published a page 3 article, "'The Truth about the Navy' Confirmed," which averred that the exposure of England's naval weakness had "placed this journal in a position of responsibility more serious, perhaps, than that in which any newspaper has been placed since Dr. Russell's letters to the *Times* from the Crimea."[8] The report had brought "confirmation and assent from every quarter, including the highest," and offered as proof were letters sent by high naval officials whose names could not be made public and by two officers whose names were given. But Stead was annoyed by the indifference of some of his fellow journalists, and he referred indignantly to the "conspiracy of silence" being observed by most London papers, although "the provincial papers are speaking out freely" (September 20, 1884).

On Monday, September 22, an Occasional Note referred to the many letters from naval men and politicians (both Liberals and Conservatives) praising the exposé. About half believed that the "Truth" article had understated the case; however, several provincial papers, while agreeing on the necessity of maintaining naval supremacy, had questioned whether the facts had been proved. In response, the *PMG* said it was willing to submit the question of the accuracy of the account to the lords of the Admiralty "from Lord Northbrook downwards." Over the weekend the Sunday *Observer* joined the fray and by September 22 the

8. Sir William Howard Russell (1820-1907), was the famous British war correspondent who covered the Crimean War for the *Times*, as well as the Sepoy Mutiny, the American Civil War, the Austro-Prussian War, and the Zulu War. He coined the phrase "the thin red line" in reporting the action of the British infantry at Balaklava. His grim and candid accounts from the Crimea revealed the suffering of the British troops as well as the inefficiency of the British military authorities.

PMG printed excerpts from twenty-two provincial, three Scottish, and three Irish newspapers which had expressed themselves on the issue. As might be expected, the strongest support came from the Conservative papers, and a number of them mentioned that the attack on the naval estimates had first appeared in a Liberal outlet. Many Liberal papers supported the campaign, but some felt that the *PMG* conclusions were unwarranted and expressed their confidence in the administration. The Liberal *Bradford Observer*, for example, spoke of the "very energetic and effective fashion" in which the *PMG* had "called public attention last winter . . . to the condition of the 'outcast poor,' [and] is this winter in the mind to perform the same service for the British navy. But the general public must trust the Experts in this matter." The *South Wales Daily News*, which was opposed to the arms race, wrote that the *PMG* "has often rendered great service to the Liberal party and to the country generally, but it has just taken a leap in a direction in which we must emphatically refuse to follow." Stead's old paper, the *Northern Echo*, took the Little Englander line: "The figures quoted do not strike us as particularly alarming. . . . That we cannot properly defend our empire is no new story. Mr. Gladstone has preached it for many a year." Better to risk losing part of the empire, said the *Northern Echo*, than to crush the whole of it under the burden of arms expenditure. Such reactions, the natural expression of a traditional Liberal, were in the minority in the provincial press. More typical were the views of the *Liverpool Courier*, which thought that "our evening contemporary has placed the country under very real obligations by not only publishing this document, but by practically vouching for its accuracy," and of the *Western Daily Mercury*, which declared that the *PMG* had earned the country's gratitude "by bringing before it in terms that can scarcely be challenged the truth about the British navy" (September 22).

On September 23, Stead again took the London press to task for its refusal to give the *PMG* its due. He was particularly nettled by the Conservative *Telegraph*, which had printed a letter from W. H. Smith, First Lord of the Admiralty under Disraeli, asking for a parliamentary inquiry into the state of the navy, but had deleted the part of it in which Smith referred to the *PMG*; and, on top of that, had praised Smith—excluding the *PMG*—"for giving an articulate voice to the cry of patriotic anxiety which is filling the land." Stead's Occasional Note reads:

The Rip Van Winkles of the London Press are awakening at last, and the readers of the *Daily Telegraph* learn with astonishment this morning that "a cry of patriotic anxiety is rising in the country to which no ministry dare close its ears." This is no doubt quite true; but is it not a little odd that no echo of that ever reached its ears until six days after the publication of "The Truth About the Navy," on which our contemporary's article is based? So curious a thing is journalistic jealousy that the leading organ of the Opposition refused to publish without mutilation the letter of the Conservative First Lord, because it contained reference to the *Pall Mall Gazette*. This, indeed, is worthy of Eatanswill.[9]

Smith sent his letters to other London papers, and it induced them to take public notice of the controversy. The *Times*, which supported Smith's request, said that Northbrook could be sure the nation would agree to expenditures necessary to support the navy (September 23). The *Morning Post* commented on the growing public feeling about the issue, and the *Daily Chronicle* was more interested in the political aspects, criticizing Smith for turning the navy over to Northbrook in such bad shape. Labouchere, the Radical editor of *Truth*, claimed that the Radical press had always believed in the need for a strong navy, but warned Smith and "his Jingo friends that taxation has its limits," citing the waste of money on the Afghan, Zulu, and Egyptian expeditions (September 24). On September 25, Stead declared in an Occasional Note that "there can no longer be any doubt that the public is thoroughly aroused." All branches of the service concurred, and with two or three exceptions the press also saw the need for England's naval forces to be "irresistably superior" to those of France and any of her potential allies. The newspaper excerpts printed for that date were generally in accord with this statement, but the *Northern Echo* was unconvinced and insisted that the *PMG* had merely awakened alarmists who wished to impose an impossible burden on England (September 26).

During the second week of the "Truth" campaign, letters of support continued to flood into the *PMG* offices, and other newspapers and periodicals joined the movement, although some came in halfheartedly. An unlikely supporter was the new Socialist periodical, *Justice*, which fumed: "The miserable faction-fighters of

9. The name of the pocket borough in the election episode in *Pickwick Papers*, Eatanswill became the synonym for a corrupt constituency.

our capitalist House of Commons have not even been able to look
after the safety of their own precious commerce" (September 27).
Occasionally a voice of caution was raised in the face of the growing excitement. The *Spectator* substantially altered its earlier position, pointing out that the *PMG* housing campaign had not resulted in any practical accomplishments and that sending Gordon
to Khartoum had not cleared up that problem. "Nor will the
British Navy be strengthened by demands which, if they were
granted, would compel us to vie with combined Europe in a race
of expenditure, only to discover in the end we could not keep our
overgrown fleet afloat or in decent repair for want of men and
money." The statements in the *PMG* articles were "exaggerations
used to create public emotion, which they only exhaust prematurely." The *Spectator* also belittled the threat of starvation, the
prospect of a combination of powers allied against England, and
the idea of "sea-wolves" preying on British commerce. "We do
not mean in any way to deprecate a demand for further extension
of the Navy," the *Spectator* said; it did not believe in false economy,
but it should be made clear just how much expansion was necessary
for security. It agreed that the navy was important for maintaining the empire, and conceded that war against two major powers
must be reckoned as a possibility—but not against "the whole
civilized world." [10]

Some journals took an even more skeptical view of the uproar,
but by and large Stead was correct in saying that the impact of
the "Truth" campaign was immense because the press "with few
exceptions" took up the cause.[11] One of the exceptions was the
Standard, whose refusal to take note of the controversy moved the
St. Stephen's Review to remark, "The *Pall Mall* published the
most remarkable article of modern times, which is quoted far
and wide, and creates a sensation without parallel; but the
Standard quotes it not, and it is probably the only news sheet in
the three kingdoms which didn't" (October 10).

Throughout October the parade of leaders, signed articles, press
summaries, Occasional Note paragraphs, and news stories con-

10. "The Condition of the Navy," pp. 1260-61. In his summary of press
comments on the campaign for this day Stead quoted, "We do not mean in any
way to deprecate a demand for further extension of the Navy," but not the
more skeptical passages, thus distorting the degree of approval expressed in the
article.
11. Stead, "The Rebuilding of the Navy," p. 78.

tinued to bear witness to the weakness of England's navy. On October 2 Stead wrote that, among the reviews, only the *Fortnightly* gave the navy question "its proper place among the events of the month," but by October 31 he could say that " 'The Truth About the Navy' has left a definite impress on the monthly miscellanies." In addition to articles in the *National Review* and *North American Review*, there were articles by Arnold-Forster in the *Nineteenth Century* and Sir Edward Reed in *Contemporary Review*, both praising the *PMG*. Arnold-Forster declared that highly paid men in the Admiralty were "about to be galvanized into activity solely and simply by the action of a penny newspaper." [12] A mild dispute broke out during the month over the meaning of a speech by Sir Thomas Brassey at Hastings on October 21. It was intended as a defense of the Admiralty, but Stead's interpretation of it is indicated by the heads for his leading article, "The Official Admission at Last," and for the news story on the speech, "An Official Defence and Confession." The *Daily News* had hoped that the speech would "assuage alarm," but Stead maintained that Brassey had confounded the *PMG*'s critics, for his speech had verified the statistics in the "Truth" series and it left many of the charges unanswered (October 23). He chided "that unfortunate *Daily News*" for saying that the speech proved that things were not as bad as had been represented. [13] That such divergent conclusions resulted from Brassey's remarks was simply a matter of different interpretations of the statistics. Brassey was concerned with the immediate position and did not consider the possibility of an alliance of powers against England, while the *PMG* throughout had emphasized potential dangers.

Lord Northbrook had been in Egypt, and when he returned in November he found that the pressure of public demand had drastically altered the situation with respect to the naval estimates. They were, as the *Morning Post* said, "the question of the hour" (December 1). The proponents of a naval buildup now had convincing national support, and according to the *Liverpool Post* the agitation was "the work of a single journal, the *Pall Mall*

---

12. H. C. Arnold-Forster, "The People of England *versus* Their Naval Officials," *Nineteenth Century*, November 1884, p. 702.

13. On October 18 Stead condemned the *Daily News* as a mouthpiece of the administration: "No one expects the *Daily News* to admit that two and two make four until it has a certificate from Downing-street to that effect."

Gazette" (December 3). "The net result of it all," Stead later
wrote,

> was that within three months of the publication of "The Truth
> About the Navy" I had the supreme satisfaction of going
> down to hear Lord Northbrook stand up in his place in the
> Senate, and from the very bench where, in the month of
> May [*sic*], he had declared that the Navy was so perfect he
> would not know what to do with £2,000,000 if he got it as a
> gift, he declared that the state of the Navy was such that he
> must have at least three and a half million over and above
> the ordinary estimate of the year.[14]

At the time, however, Stead felt that Northbrook's request, although
a good start, was still inadequate, as he said in a leader on
December 3. A summary of the statements by Northbrook in the
Lords and Brassey in the Commons showed a request for total
defense expenditures of nine million pounds, of which some five
million would go for new ships. This figure was later pared down,
and Stead believed that the reduction was due to the influence
of Joseph Chamberlain, who "was then in a state of the blindest
ignorance concerning all naval matters." [15]

The press reaction to Northbrook's appropriations request was
mostly favorable. A number of papers, notably those associated
with the Conservative party, pointed out the inconsistency of the
Admiralty's first claiming that the naval defense was strong enough
and then asking for increased estimates to strengthen it; and some
papers, including the *Times*, agreed with Stead that the new
estimates were still insufficient. While the London papers, as usual,
tended to ignore the *PMG's* contribution, many provincial newspapers gave it full marks. However, the *Cork Examiner,* admitting
that "no single newspaper probably could ever before distinctly
claim to have by its own action put the country to a cost admittedly
exceeding five millions," wondered if this was a good thing for the
nation. Good or bad, there can be no question that the new naval
estimates were the result of Stead's enterprise, employing the
techniques of the New Journalism. On a visit to the Portsmouth
dockyard after the "Truth" series appeared, Captain Fisher
introduced Stead to the commander-in-chief with the words

14. Stead, "The Rebuilding of the Navy," p. 79.
15. Ibid., p. 79.

"Admiral Hornby, I wish to present to you a man who has done more for the British Navy than any Englishman since the days of Lord Nelson." Stead himself said of the "Truth" series and the pamphlet reprinting it, "I have never written anything in my life which produced so immediate and so overwhelming an effect on public opinion." [16]

Stead could accept criticism cheerfully and he was known for his willingness to print adverse points of view in the *PMG*, but lack of recognition infuriated him. When John Morley said that it was "undoubtedly the professional heads of the Departments" in the Admiralty who decided that "the cry [for increased naval estimates] must be raised in the press," Stead replied, "We have only to say as courteously as the circumstances permit that there is not a word of truth in the whole of this story," and that the agitation was "purely journalistic." Although Morley admitted that newspaper pressure had caused the increase in the estimates, he had ignored the "Truth" series, and in the same Occasional Note Stead observed acidly that "Mr. Morley used to know something about newspapers in general, and about one newspaper in particular, but he comments upon the recent naval agitation in a fashion which seems to show that he has hardly kept in touch with the journalism of the day" (December 23).

After mid-December there was a lull in the naval agitation, although from time to time the *PMG* published articles and features on various aspects of naval power. The campaign went into a new phase in March, 1885, when debates on appropriations resumed with the new session of Parliament and Stead was enraged to learn that the navy estimates were going to be less than promised in December. With the threat of war with Russia looming over the Afghan dispute,[17] Stead seized upon this as further proof that the English navy was dangerously weak. His leader for March 13, "The Truth about the Navy Once More," opened with an attack on a government policy which could mean European war against Russia in alliance with "the unspeakable Turk." "One by one," he wrote, "all the cherished principles of Midlothian have been given up," and nothing was left to differentiate Gladstone's policy from Disraeli's. He then considered England's fitness to fight, after noting that an evening paper had claimed the military forces in

16. Ibid., pp. 80, 78.
17. See pp. 111 ff.

India were utterly inadequate, and said that he was more immediately concerned with the state of the navy. He admitted that a war with Russia would not be a naval war—a fact that had been glossed over in the earlier phases of the campaign—but insisted that the inadequacy of England's fleets and ports was "notorious to every Government in Europe" and that a more general war might ensue. The follower, "Is Our Navy Ready for War?," was another by "One Who Knows," and ran almost three pages. It dealt again with specific weaknesses in England's naval position, and its general tone was summed up in the assertion that "there is an unpreparedness for war on the part of our navy almost inconceivable by man." Once again the menace across the Channel was dragged in, with the observations that France might well use an Anglo-Russian conflict as an opportunity to dictate terms in Egypt and that a Franco-Russian alliance was a real possibility. "I am making no extravagant claims," said the anonymous writer, "when I ask that our navy should be strong enough to protect our shores from fear of invasion by France."

Stead's March 17 leader, "Breaking Faith with the Nation," was a column-and-a-half attack on Brassey for trying to lull the nation into a false sense of security. Promises made in December had not been kept, declared Stead, and Brassey was completely wrong in asserting that the Admiralty request had not been cut down. A full-page account of the previous night's debates on the naval estimates appeared on page 11 under a two-column head: "THE NAVY OF OLD ENGLAND—IS IT READY FOR WAR?" Although purporting to be a straight news story, it was obviously slanted; even the crossheads indicated the editorial bias. Brassey's reply was labeled "A Quibble, A Misrepresentation, Or, A Misstatement"; and other sections were headed "We've Got the Ships—i.e. Some of Them—in 1887" [18] and "Are We Doing Enough, Hardly." Such a treatment of parliamentary debates on serious matters might seem unexceptional today, but it was unusual for the respectable press of 1885. According to this report, it was remarkable that although admirals and other experts had been complaining about appropriations for years, no one paid any attention until the *PMG* also complained.

18. An allusion to the music hall song, popular during the 1878 crisis, from which the word *jingoism* derived: "We don't want to fight, but, by jingo, if we do, / we've got the ships, we've got the men, we've got the money too. / We've fought the Bear before, and while we're Britons true, / The Russians shall not have Constantinople."

Thus it was mainly due to the *PMG* that the government proposed an expenditure of £5,525,000 on the navy, which, however, was cut from the Admiralty recommendation of £11,000,000.

The rest of the press at this time was supporting the demand for increased estimates, but not so vociferously and dogmatically. Some of the Liberal papers blamed the Admiralty or the government for any naval deficiencies rather than singling out Brassey. As usual the *Pall Mall's* part was ignored except by the Liberal *Leeds Mercury*, which stated that the *PMG* "may fairly claim a leading voice in the discussion of naval affairs" (March 18, 1885).

Stead's last leader on this phase of the naval campaign appeared on April 8 during the height of the Russian war scare, and again he made a connection between unpreparedness and the threat of war. He wrote that it was "with a certain grim satisfaction that we note the flurry at Whitehall," referring to the frantic stopgap measures adopted by the Admiralty in preparation for a fight with a second-rate naval power. While he did not think "either Russia or England will be so criminal as to go to war about the claim to survey a patch of wilderness," he saw some good coming from the "periodical Russian scare . . . as inevitable as the measles," since it was opening the public's eyes to "the inadequacy of our navy and the inefficiency of its administration." Nimbly leapfrogging over the question of prospective opponents, Stead concluded that unless the navy was "ready to meet and vanquish the fleets both of France and any of her allies," England was secure neither in her commerce nor from invasion.

In assessing the results of the *PMG* "Truth" campaign, the first question to be considered is whether or not the agitation was justified. Had England's most vital arm of defense really been weakened to a dangerous degree? The point of view of those who believed that naval weakness had been vastly exaggerated was most comprehensively expressed by F. W. Hirst in his 1913 study, *The Six Panics*.[19] The reason for the book, Hirst explained in the preface, was not to prevent false alarms in the sensational press, since nothing could do that, but to point out to "the governing classes and the leading statesmen" how they had been tricked in the past and to warn them against "panic-mongers" in the future.

In his account of the 1884 panic, Stead was described as "a

19. F. W. Hirst, *The Six Panics and Other Essays* (London: Methuen, 1913).

clever journalist who indulged in an unfortunate talent for
sensations" and who "resorted to the old business of Naval Panic-
Monger in the Pall Mall Gazette." There was no trace of popular
panic, "but Mr. Stead and his fellow conspirators managed to
produce a feeling of nervous disquietude in high society." Tracing
the development of the campaign from its initiation in September,
Hirst called the original "Truth" article "five pages bristling with
bloodcurdling figures and technical horrors of all sizes and shapes."
He assailed Stead for "selecting a particular year when Italy and
Germany were spending practically nothing" on which to base
some of his figures, and for comparing English naval expenditures
with those of France, Italy, Germany, and Russia, "four strangely
chosen bedfellows who could not on any conceivable hypothesis
have united in war against us." With obvious skepticism Hirst cited
the catalog of perils publicized by the *PMG*—the visions of Chile
defeating England in the Pacific and Brazil sweeping the British
South American squadron from the seas, of unprotected merchant-
men, of coaling stations at the mercy of a single hostile cruiser, of
crippling shortages of men and torpedo boats: "In a word we were,
as usual during panics, hopelessly inferior." In Hirst's view, the
panic was fostered by a combination of Admiralty officials
"ingeniously maintaining a thesis for the sole purpose of extracting
more money from the pockets of the people, and of enlarging the
patronage of a great spending department," of business interests,
especially the shipyards in the "armour-plate ring," and of the
jingoists. Stead himself was "actuated probably by no worse motive
than an irresistable desire to be the centre of a journalistic sensation." [20] Like most polemicists, Hirst was guilty of oversimplifi-
cation, and he utterly failed to appreciate Stead's motives. Stead
sincerely believed that the navy needed to be strengthened, and as
usual, his sensationalism was a means, not an end. Nor is there
any tangible evidence of a politico-military-industrial cabal
organizing a panic to promote profits.[21] Nonetheless, Hirst's basic
assumption that the situation was not as alarming as Stead and
others presented it can not easily be dismissed.

20. Ibid., pp. 41-58. Referring to the leading article with which Stead
opened the campaign (see above, pp. 91-92), Hirst said that it was "in the too
familiar style which now palls on the public palate. But then perhaps it
seemed strong; for the mixture of Burke, Penny-a-Liner, and the Penny Dreadful was comparatively new" (p. 47).
21. The *Pall Mall* did upon occasion call attention to the empty shipyards
in England in its leaders and articles on the naval situation.

Among Stead's defenders was Sir John Briggs, formerly Chief Clerk of the Admiralty, who, in a survey of naval administrations published in 1897, praised the "Truth" articles for the results they obtained. But Briggs admittedly had an ax to grind: his purpose was "to set before the public the extent to which the defences of the Empire and the requirements of the navy have been neglected by successive administrations." [22] Another defender, Frederic Whyte, stressed the touchy international situation in 1884: Russia's drive toward India and the growing Anglo-French tensions, particularly in respect to Africa. Yet, Russia's fleet was a tragic joke, and in perspective it is clear that France, with her almost pathological concern over Germany, was not about to challenge England to the point of war; further, a Franco-Russian alliance against England was not in the realm of the possible. Whyte also brought forward in Stead's defense Archibald Hurd, author of a number of works on the navy and manpower, whom he quoted as saying, "We have been saved by our panic-built Navy from the worst consequences of war—the invasion of these islands, the disintegration of the Empire, the destruction of our vast mercantile marine, and the strangulation of our ocean-borne commerce, which is the very lifeblood of the British people." [23] But the ships built as the result of the 1884 campaign had already become obsolete when World War I broke out, and Hurd, writing in 1915, was referring more immediately to the "Two Keels for One" campaign which had preceded the war. Indeed, many of those who justify Stead's naval campaign by its result have confused, or blurred together, these two periods of concern over foreign threats; and there is little reason to believe that the increases of 1884-85 contributed directly to the British navy of 1914. Perhaps the best analysis of the situation is that England's navy did need some refurbishing, but was not in the alarming state that Stead and the proponents of the navy buildup led the public to believe.

It is because Stead is remembered today as a pacifist and promoter of international arbitration that "The Truth about the Navy" has been called one of his more paradoxical agitations. But the paradox is more apparent than real. The best explanation was provided by Stead himself at the request of the Nobel Committee

22. Sir John Henry Briggs, *Naval Administrations, 1827-1892*, ed. Lady Briggs (London: Sampson, Low, Marston, 1897), pp. 214 ff.
23. Archibald Hurd, "Our Panic-Built Navy: Before and after the War," *Fortnightly Review*, October 1, 1915, p. 644, quoted in Whyte, *Life*, 1:145.

in 1901 and published in the *Review of Reviews* (June, 1912). He was a lifelong advocate of arbitration, he said, not as an ultimate solution to international problems, but as a step toward the creation of a United States of Europe. However, "it was not by the abandonment of force on the part of the advocates of law and of peace that anything could be done, but by the use of force in the defence of law and for the suppression of anarchy." He was as earnest as any propagandist of peace "to cast out militarism and dethrone the soldier, but my observations and reflections crystallized in one phrase—you can only exorcise the soldier by the aid of the policeman." He was, he said, "for several years one of the foremost, if not the foremost, advocate of what I may call the Imperialism of Responsibility, as opposed to the Jingoism, which is the Imperialism of pride and avarice, on the one hand, and to Little Englandism, which seemed to me almost as selfish and unworthy a policy, on the other." He saw British imperial power as "the instrument for maintaining peace among races which would otherwise have been cursed by internecine warfare, and of putting down the horrors of slavery and of other barbarous works in vast regions. . . . I became an impassioned Imperialist, but my Imperialism was always an Imperialism of Responsibility, or, as I phrased it nearly thirty years ago, an Imperialism plus common sense and the Ten Commandments. . . . Empire was to me not a source of pride, excepting so far as it was the emblem of duty done, of burdens borne for the benefit of humanity."[24] To Stead, as this document makes clear, a strong navy was but an instrument for preserving international peace and for spreading the glories of European civilization (particularly English civilization) throughout the world.

II

The emphasis on Stead's campaign did not mean that the *PMG* was unconcerned with other issues and news of the day. During the autumn of 1884, while the drumbeating for the navy went on, some of the leading stories concerned Gordon and the Sudan and the agitation resulting from the rejection of the Franchise Bill by the House of Lords. Occasionally Stead's crusades seemed to limp along beyond their time, and articles connected with slum housing

24. W. T. Stead, "The Great Pacifist," *Review of Reviews,* June 1912, pp. 609-20. The last article Stead ever wrote, it was finished only a few days before the sailing of the *Titanic.*

still continued to appear now and then. On October 1, in an Occasional Note, Stead recalled, "It is just a year since the bitter cry of outcast London found articulate expression, and one can see 'how loud and clear' it has sounded in the fact that its consideration was the first business submitted to the Church Congress yesterday"—surely an anticlimax.

He resumed his running attack on the London press for its persistent refusal to acknowledge the existence of its "contemporaries." On October 10 when the *Standard* published an advance outline of a proposal for the redistribution of parliamentary seats prepared by a ministerial committee, every London paper except the *PMG* ignored the story. In an Occasional Note Stead branded as absurd the policy of silence because of journalistic jealousy, although he could not resist adding that the *Standard* itself was one of the worst offenders. Suppression of news of the day, he said, "merely because it does not first appear in 'our columns' is little better than a fraud upon the public." He returned to the matter the next day, Saturday, October 11, observing sarcastically that "every newspaper in the country is discussing the Redistribution scheme except the *Times, Daily News, Morning Post* and *Daily Chronicle,* which are still pretending to know nothing about the most important political news of the day." The farce would end on Monday, he predicted, for it was "too silly to be kept up a day after a reference has been made to the scheme by a single statesman of the first class." The prediction was fulfilled, and on October 13 the *PMG* crowed, "The conspiracy of silence has ludicrously collapsed, and this morning all the dailies condescend to recognize the existence of the *Standard* and its draft Redistribution scheme."

As he had done earlier, Stead continued to encourage by example and by comment the use of the interview, and on December 17 welcomed the most recent "convert to the more reasonable faith," the *Daily News.* He noted that "the curious superstition of the morning 'dailies' that 'interviews' are only consonant with their dignity when telegraphed from abroad is fast fading away." On the last day of 1884 he viewed with even more complacency the progress of this *PMG*-sponsored contribution to contemporary journalism.

Among the permanent gains of the year the acclimatization of the "interview" in English journalism certainly should be reckoned. That this form of influencing public opinion supplied, as the phrase goes, a real want, is proved by the fact that it only needed a single example to make most of the newspapers follow suit. . . . Before this time next year we confidently expect to see the interview acclimatized in the columns of the "leading" journal.

The new year began placidly enough with Stead espousing another of his longtime dreams—imperial federation. The Imperial Federation League had been founded in November, 1884, with the blessing of important statesmen from both parties—among them were Lord Carnarvon, W. H. Smith, W. E. Forster, and Lord Rosebery [25]—and the *PMG* already had carried articles endorsing the idea. In Stead's leading article on January 1, 1885, "Programme 1885," the first item called for "The Unity of the English Realm" through imperial federation. The term meant all things to all men, but Stead, whose conception of it was primarily political, proposed as "the first practical step toward the establishment of some system of Imperial Federation" the creation of a Colonial Council, with representatives from the self-governing colonies. His program—which also included a Royal Commission with colonial representation to deliberate on the problem of maintaining British naval supremacy—did not go as far as the proposals of some who foresaw colonial representatives sitting at Westminster. The second plank of "Programme 1885" called for British expansion in various overseas areas and recognition of responsibilities in Egypt and South Africa. Also on his program were some form of home rule for Ireland, the establishment of a Royal Commission on local government, and a number of domestic reforms, including "prudent progress in the direction of Socialism . . . rigidly restrained by securities against intolerable interference with individual liberty."

On January 9, Stead's leader, "A Practical Suggestion," clearly indicated that he was launching another campaign. "For some time

25. Lord Carnarvon (1831-90), as Colonial Secretary in the Derby and Disraeli ministry of 1866-67, had brought in the North American Confederation Bill. He was also Colonial Secretary in Disraeli's second ministry (1874-78), and resigned over his disagreement with the administration's policy in the Russo-Turkish dispute. Lord Rosebery developed his ideas on a "commonwealth of nations" as the basis for imperial relations during an 1883-84 tour of Australia and New Zealand. He became one of the leading spokesmen for what was called "Liberal Imperialism" and succeeded Gladstone as Liberal party leader and prime minister (1894-95).

past," it began, "Imperial federation has been in the air. Every one has been talking about it, and writing about it, for some months. It is now time that the general desire both at home and in the colonies should assume a practical shape. Otherwise there is some danger the movement may end in smoke." And he called attention to the concluding installment of an interview with Earl Grey, "the Nestor of English Colonial Ministers," in which Grey talked of a plan essentially the same as Stead's own.[26] During the next weeks articles and leaders, interviews and letters, kept the idea of imperial federation—or at any rate, closer imperial ties—before the public. Opposing views were presented, too, although they usually were answered in the same issue. Thus, on January 19, in a front-page follower, Lord Blachford gave his objections to a colonial advisory board.[27] He expressed his preference for department heads and picked professionals because advisory groups were conducive to "friction, delay and indecision," but he admitted that he was "one of that apparently small minority who looked upon Federation as an unattainable phantom." Stead replied in the Occasional Notes that Blachford's views were "vitiated by two fatal flaws": his lack of faith in the unity of "Greater Britain"—a favorite Steadian phrase—and his "assumption that bureaucratic is preferable to representative government." Stead also rather unfairly called Blachford's article "an argument for autocracy."

In fact, however, Blachford was not in a minority in believing federation unattainable. One of the reasons for the failure of the movement to draw the empire closer together was simply that the league members were often at odds over specific political and economic proposals. Stead, for example, in an Occasional Note written during a conference on imperial federation, took issue with "the economic heresies of the chairman of the Conference. The dream of a British Zollverein is nothing within the range of practical politics" (January 15, 1885). He maintained that insistence on imperial free trade would destroy the dream of federation

26. Earl Grey was the third Earl and uncle of the fourth Earl. Now in his eighties, he had been Undersecretary for Colonies in his father's administration when the great Reform Bill of 1832 was passed, and had been interested in colonial matters throughout his career. The first installment of the interview had appeared on January 7.

27. Lord Blachford (1811-89) had been Permanent Undersecretary of State for Colonies (1860-71); he was described as presenting the "Bureaucratic Point of View."

without bringing free trade, and he assured colonials that England would not ask them to abandon their tariffs. Yet imperial preference, if not imperial free trade, was the basis of federation to many in the league. At any rate, although Stead returned to the subject of imperial federation many times during the first half of 1885, he had too many other irons in the fire to indulge in a long-range, sustained campaign.

An example of the imagination which set the *PMG* apart from the rest of the press was its coverage of an attack on Westminster Hall and Tower by Fenian dynamiters on January 24. Since the explosions occurred on a Saturday, there was more time to prepare for Monday's editions, and on January 26 the paper carried a series of sketches, large and small, illustrating the incident and the damage done. Although the sketches were crude in detail, particularly in their depiction of figures, they were the most ambitious attempt yet of a daily paper to illustrate a story. Curiously, when the *PMG* carried a follow-up two days later with a full page of sketches, they were of even poorer quality.

In May Stead poked gentle fun at one of the morning papers for the glacial slowness which it had exhibited in adopting some of his typographical innovations. "We really must congratulate the *Standard*," he wrote. "It has at last, about two years after we introduced the practice, contrived to produce a little map in its own office by typography. It is a very little one, quite infantile in fact, with only three names in it, and one of these on the wrong side, but it does our enterprising contemporary much credit, and we hope it will be encouraged to persevere in the upward road" (May 2). During May also there appeared the first leading article in many months on the housing issue. The occasion was the publication of the report of the Royal Commission upon the Housing of the Working Classes. Stead found points to criticize in the report, but felt that it would do good. He asserted that there was "nothing which the most advanced school of State Socialists have ever dreamed of which is not advocated in principle," and that there was no longer a conflict between laissez faire and state interference, but rather between different schools of Radicals (May 8). But by all odds the major issue of the first half of 1885 was an international crisis which for a time threatened to involve England in a major war.

III

The 1885 Afghanistan crisis between England and Russia was the latest chapter of a long story of conflicting expansionist pressures. After the Crimean War Russia accelerated her drive through Central Asia and it appeared to many that one of the objectives was India, where Britain's own policy of aggrandizement had pushed the frontier northward. Afghanistan's position between Russia's southern empire and the Northwest frontier of India; its inherent weakness, which was exacerbated by frequent dynastic struggles; and its lack of well-defined boundaries made it a natural stage for playing out the climax of this imperialist struggle. From the end of the war until the 1870s, in part because of the influence of the Little Englanders, the British attitude toward Russian expansion and Afghan internal difficulties was a passive one of watchful waiting. In 1874, however, the election of a Conservative government brought a marked change of policy as Disraeli, the new prime minister, and Lord Lytton,[28] the new governor general of India, favored a more aggressive policy to restore England's prestige and strategic position in Central Asia.

In 1878, in order to check what seemed to be growing Russian influence with the Afghan emir, Shere Ali, Lytton demanded that a permanent British representative be established at Kabul. Afghanistan's refusal to accept Lytton's envoy led to an armed invasion by the British on November 20, 1878. There followed a series of military actions, known as the Afghan War, which resulted in the acquisition of some Afghan territory bordering India, the deposition of Shere Ali, and, when his son proved to be a frail reed, negotiations with Abdu-r-Rahman, his nephew. Abdu-r-Rahman had been living under Russian protection since 1868, but he seemed to be willing to come to terms with the British, and was the only candidate for emir with the strength to reestablish order in the country. At this point a general election in England once again altered the situation in Afghanistan. Disraeli's imperialist aggression, as the Liberals portrayed it, was a major issue in the 1880 election campaign, and the victorious Gladstone government was pledged

28. Lord Lytton (1831-91) was the son of Edward Bulwer-Lytton, the first Baron Lytton, and a poet as well as a statesman. He held a number of minor diplomatic posts before being appointed British minister at Lisbon in 1872. He introduced a number of reforms in India, and ended his days as a popular ambassador in Paris (1887-91).

to withdraw from England's recently acquired territory and to return to a policy of noninvolvement in Afghanistan affairs. However, Lord Ripon,[29] who succeeded Lytton as governor general, soon came to the conclusion that the Liberal policy of withdrawal would be disastrous and ultimately lead to further Russian expansion or war. Thus he continued the negotiations along the same lines initiated by his predecessor, and in an accord reached in August, 1881, Abdu-r-Rahman agreed to put the management of Afghan foreign relations in British hands in return for an annual subsidy and a guarantee against aggression. The British also relinquished only part of the territory they had seized, and the Gladstone government allowed its election pledges "to fall into a convenient if dishonest oblivion." [30]

In 1882 there were Anglo-Russian conversations in London about formally defining Afghanistan's northern boundary, but nothing was resolved. In February, 1884, Russia took advantage of Gladstone's embarrassments in the Sudan and occupied the Merv region, only two hundred miles north of Afghanistan's principal western city, Herat. The two great empires were now another step closer to the direct confrontation which neither really wanted, and it was agreed in the spring of 1884 that Russia, England, and Afghanistan would set up a joint commission to establish the northern Afghan frontier. The English mission under Sir Peter Lumsden was sent to the disputed area in the autumn of 1884, but Russia delayed until the following February, apparently in order to gain control over as much territory as possible before the commission's work began. The next obvious Russian target was the area of Panjdeh, south of Merv, over which Afghanistan's claims were, at best, shadowy. In November Russian forces moved to within twelve miles of Afghan outposts there, and as the tension built up between local commanders of the czar's and the emir's forces, the stage was set for the crisis of the early months of 1885.

The English people became aware that some sort of Anglo-

29. Lord Ripon (1827-1909) was born at 10 Downing Street while his father, first Viscount Goderich, was prime minister. An active member of the Christian Socialist movement in his twenties, he held several positions in the War and India offices after succeeding his father as Earl of Ripon in 1859. (He was made first Marquess of Ripon in 1871).

30. H. H. Dodwell, "Central Asia, 1858-1918," *The Indian Empire*, vol. 5 of *Cambridge History of the British Empire* (Cambridge: Cambridge University Press, 1932), ch. 23, p. 422.

Russian clash was brewing in Afghanistan in February, 1885, although in its earliest stages the crisis had to compete for public attention with a censure motion against the government over Egypt. On February 21 a story on the *PMG*'s main news page carried the headline:

ALARMING NEWS FROM CENTRAL ASIA

ALLEGED RUSSIAN ADVANCE ON PENJDEH

SIR PETER LUMSDEN FALLS BACK ON HERAT

The article was based on a report in the *Times* that the Russians had advanced into an area held by troops of the emir, causing the English boundary commission to withdraw. The *PMG*'s own comment was "On making inquiry in well informed quarters we are told that the statement of the *Times* is believed to be correct, and that unless the Russian advance is checked, hostilities are almost certain to break out between the Afghans and the Russians, from which the gravest consequences may ensue."

On Monday, February 23, the only mention of the incident was in a paragraph under the paper's "City Notes." Remarking that Russian stocks were down, the story spoke of "reassuring statements from St. Petersburg" on Russia's peaceful intentions, and attributed the current difficulty to Russophobes on the staff of Sir Peter Lumsden. On the next day in a follower datelined "St. Petersburg, Feb. 19(7), 1885," Mme Novikoff wrote on "The Truth about the Russian Advance." Her article began, "I have just had a most interesting conversation with one who is of the highest authority on all matters relating to the foreign policy of our empire." Predictably, this anonymous authoritative source denied any Russian interest in Herat. He claimed that the advance was a reaction to certain members of Lumsden's party having incited the Afghans to occupy areas beyond the frontier, including Panjdeh, which had never been under Afghan rule. The "authority" admitted that the Russian military response went further than necessary and mistakes had been made on both sides, but hoped that an understanding between the rival nations could be reached. In an Occasional Note on February 24, Stead, also predictably, accepted Mme Novikoff's version on the affair and hoped that Lumsden would "keep his youngsters well in hand." It was Stead's tendency to accept the Russian rather than the English version of the incidents which followed, making him anathema to many of his countrymen during his campaign to avoid a war over Afghanistan.

At the beginning of the dispute, Stead seemed to take a more balanced approach than later on. A follower on February 27 "By a Russian" tried to document the assertion that Panjdeh was not really in Afghanistan and that the emir was at fault for moving first. It was answered in a follower on March 2, "By an English-man" who claimed that Panjdeh was Afghan territory by the terms of the 1872-73 agreement, and that England was committed to aiding the emir in the case of "foreign unprovoked aggression." An Occasional Note on the same day pointed out that the followers were both written by qualified men and served only to show that the two nations were far from agreement on the issue to be de-cided by the boundary commission. A leader for March 4 declared that Russia's proposed frontier was better and more realistic than England's, but at the same time thought that Russia had advanced too far, and spoke of "serious blundering on both sides." Even this rather neutral stance set Stead apart from most of his journal-istic contemporaries. As the crisis deepened, only the *Echo* among London papers took a nonbelligerent position and opposed the war-like utterances of the rest of the press, although the *Daily News* did show less Russophobia than most. Much of the provincial press also found Russia to be hopelessly in the wrong, and more than a few sabers were rattled in proclamations about England's sacred obligation to defend the emir.

On March 5, in a leader, "Russia and the Afghan Frontier," Stead began to climb down on the Russian side of the fence, depicting the tension as a result of Russian responses to Afghan aggressive-ness. Russia claimed to have notified England of her intention to counter Afghan advances, but Foreign Secretary Granville denied it. Stead implied his concurrence with the Russian view, asking Granville to publish the dispatches between the two nations on the subject. At the same time, the editor remained optimistic. If the Tories were in office, he declared, war would be all but inevitable, but under the Liberals "it is still possible for Russia and England to work together as allies not foes." The lines were thus being drawn more sharply between Stead and his fellow journalists. That morning the *Times*, in effect, gave Russia three options: to show her honesty by withdrawing; to stay, which would mean any accident could trigger a war; and to advance still further, which would mean "war at once, both with Afghanistan and with England." The *Standard* took even more of a no-nonsense line: although the ministry had blundered badly, "this country has not yet sunk to the depth of degradation imagined by these hysterical and wormish journalists." There was also difference of opinion over whether or not England was ready for a fight with Russia. On March 6 Stead introduced that anomalous feature in his campaign for peace, the warning that England's navy was inadequate and should be better prepared for war. But the next day's *Spectator* stated that if Russia did not withdraw it would mean war, and "we were never more ready for war than now." [31]

In the week that followed, Stead continued to promote the Russian interpretation of the crisis and to point out how inadequately England was prepared for war. He made clear what he thought the next step should be in his leader for March 12: both powers must "turn round and go back," and England must take the first step by recalling the Afghans. However, on the same day many of the other London papers were displaying their belligerence. The *Telegraph* proclaimed, "Better war than weakness in a crisis so dishonestly forced upon us," and the *Morning Post* railed at "scuttle-at-any-price advocates of submission and surrender." Even the *Daily News,* more pacific than most of its colleagues, described war as probable, having been forced upon England by "the recklessness of the Russians." Some of the major provincial papers were taking much the same approach. To the *Liverpool Post,* the whole matter was "in the hands of Russia. If she withdraws, well and good; if she does not, we shall make her." The *Leeds Mercury* felt that the proposal of those "friendly to Russia" to get the Russian troops out by promising the Czar the frontier he was after "cannot be seriously discussed" (March 12). On the weekend the Conservative *Saturday Review,* naturally a critic of Gladstone throughout, took Stead more specifically to task, declaring that the government must not "listen for a moment to any such unblushingly worthless pleas as those put forward by the *Pall Mall Gazette*." [32]

On March 13, Gladstone announced in the House of Commons that Russia and England had agreed to make further inquiry into

31. "England and Russia," *Spectator,* March 7, 1885, p. 302.
32. "The Afghan Situation," *Saturday Review,* March 14, 1885, p. 340.

the exact frontier. The *PMG* welcomed the relaxation of tension, while noting that danger still existed and that the warmongering of the press would poison Anglo-Russian relations for a long time. On the other hand, the London morning papers had been angered at what they considered to be a surrender to the foe. As the *Morning Advertiser* put it, Gladstone had "caved in" (March 14). In the provinces, the Liberal press tended generally to support Gladstone at this point, while the Conservative papers were more in agreement with the *Liverpool Courier*, which spoke of the prime minister's "humiliating surrender" (March 14).

On the following Monday (March 16), Stead began his call for arbitration. In a leader headed "Why Not Call in 'The Honest Broker'?" he asked, "Why not refer the dispute about twenty miles of steppe to the arbitration of our very good friend, the honest broker at Berlin?" On Friday the *PMG* printed a follower in which Henry Richard, M.P., joined Stead's call for arbitration. Other journals, however, continued to see surrender in the government's actions. The *Saturday Review* for March 21 renewed its assault on both Gladstone and the *PMG*, in an article which said that the prime minister "has once more struck the *English flag* to a foreign power." It also castigated "Mr. Gladstone's apologists in the English press, or rather his apologist—for we are not aware that he has more than one, and one only at his service when he is cordially co-operating with Russia." [33]

The coverage of Afghanistan slackened early in the following week, but Stead fanned the sparks of controversy again in his leader for Thursday, March 26. In it he offered "A Direct Challenge" to ministers and opposition leaders, editors of key newspapers and periodicals,[34] and "eminent authorities" on Central Asia to reply to what "we believe to be the absolute Truth about the Afghan Frontier." The leader repeated the various points raised by Stead during the past weeks, with the major theme being that the Afghans, not the Russians, were the real aggressors and that "England is distinctly in the wrong." Even while this issue was being sold in the streets, the government was challenging the Russians by calling up the reserves. The next morning the only London

33. "The Surrender in Afghanistan," *Saturday Review,* March 21, 1885, p. 372.
34. Specifically, the *Times, Daily News, Standard, Morning Post, Daily Telegraph, Saturday Review,* and *Spectator.*

paper to pick up Stead's gauntlet was the *Chronicle*, in a first leader which ran for more than a column. It began by denying that calling up the reserves was jingoism. "The only persons, indeed," it said, "who just now rant and rave and play the bully are the Anglo-Russians—a small and, we wish to believe, somewhat crazy clique of political charlatans." Speaking of "the cool-headed determination of England to insist on justice being done," the leader warned Russia that the government was not going to surrender as, it claimed, Beaconsfield had done at the time of the Congress of Berlin. "The Rhetorical delirium" served up by the *PMG* was being used by Russian jingos, who pretended that it truly reflected English public opinion, but it no more did than "the erratic periodicals which the inmates of some of our more respectable madhouses now and again amuse themselves by printing." It further insisted that the danger of war would be great if Russia deluded itself into thinking that England would evade her responsibility under the pretext suggested by "the most violent and most demented of the Muscovite organs in London"—that Russia only pushed close to Herat as a response to threatened expansion by Afghanistan. Panjdeh had always been part of the administrative district of Herat, according to the *Chronicle*, and the crisis was simply a matter of Russian evil opposed to Afghan innocence. The leader concluded with the warning that Russia had occupied places which enabled her to menace India and she must either withdraw peacefully or be dislodged. The rest of the morning press generally joined the *Chronicle* in applauding the calling up of the reserves, although some of the Liberal provincial papers deplored the government's actions as jingoism.

Irritated when his challenge brought some evasive correspondence but no direct reply, that evening (March 27) Stead wrote a middle entitled "Waiting for an Answer." He gave a lengthy extract from the *Chronicle* leader, after observing that it "alone essays to deal with the challenge, and by way of fortifying a worthless case it abuses those who differ from it in the following good set style." He also reprinted a letter he had received from the editor of the *Morning Advertiser*, who had declined his "trap," knowing the way the Russian government conducted its controversies. To Stead the other newspapers were begging the real question, namely, "Was Penj-deh, or was it not, debatable territory within the scope of the reference to the Joint Commission?" In the leader for this issue Stead objected to calling out seventy thousand reservists on the ground that as preparation for war it was inadequate, and as a political move it was dangerous. Perhaps concerned with the increasing bitterness of the attack against supposed pro-Russians, he argued, "We are by no means defending the whole course of Russian diplomacy in relation to this boundary question." But he also maintained that in all of the Afghan frontier negotiations "Russia has been most reasonable." The outlook for peace was bleak, he believed, and the only hope was "the intervention of some impartial third party."

On the following Sunday (March 29) the Liberal *Sunday Observer* stated that an Anglo-Russian war over India was inevitable anyway, and that it was "obviously a gain for us to fight while the odds are still in our favour." The *PMG* "challenge" was dismissed out of hand: "Since the days when the fable of the wolf and lamb was first framed, no more audacious attempt has even been made to represent the assailant as the assailed."

During the weeks of controversy the *Echo*, although not a Russophile, had been the only other London paper to voice restraint in the atmosphere of nationalistic belligerence. On Monday, March 30—a day on which, unknown in London, the Russians launched a full-scale attack and drove the Afghans from Panjdeh —the *Chronicle* emphasized just how unrepresentative the position of the two evening papers was. It expressed its regret that the Russian newspaper *Nord* did not take England's "warlike demonstrations" seriously: "The *Nord* is a much more intelligent and trustworthy organ of the Russian government than the only two so-called Liberal evening newspapers in London, whose emotional pleadings for the Muscovite are becoming so notorious that they might without any disadvantage to their readers be stereotyped." The *Nord*, the article continued, was misleading when it claimed that only some English papers were opposed to Russian aggression, for "it is not 'some' but 'all' English newspapers, with the exception of the two it quotes, that take sides against Russia in this controversy. . . . There never was a point about which Englishmen were less divided in opinion." Almost all Englishmen were ready to make any sacrifice to stop the Russian advance on India, the *Chronicle* claimed, and surely Russia must be aware of it. Otherwise the Russian "advocates in the English press [would not] make such frantic efforts to assure the Russians not only that England is in the wrong, but that Englishmen have neither ships nor guns fit to enable her to go to war." The "hysterical reiteration" by the "Muscovite agents" that the vital question was whether or not Panjdeh was debatable territory did not justify the Russian advance in the area. The article concluded that "nothing is more curious than the ease with which [Russia] has inoculated her chief champion in our metropolitan press with her own semi-Asiatic moral obliquity" in its supposition that occupation by force gives title to an area. Most of the other morning papers also dealt at length with the crisis, and many reflected the attitude of the *Chronicle*, although their attacks on Stead and the *PMG* were less specific and direct. The *Post*, for example, merely spoke of "one or two influential voices which raise the craven cry of surrender and arbitration."

In his leader that evening (March 30), "An Appeal to Reason," Stead agreed that he had stood virtually alone on the issue, but now detected a change in climate. Despite the fact that "nearly every newspaper in the country" had been "bellowing . . . morning and evening for war," he was convinced that the people of England really wanted arbitration, and claimed that seventy or eighty M.P.'s had already signed a memorial to that end. The chief object of Stead's scorn was not the *Chronicle*, but the more moderate *Daily News*, which had said that the question could not be referred to arbitration. "The *Daily News*," he wrote "is almost always wrong —and never so utterly wrong as when it masquerades as a demented Jingo." Stead also denied the contention of those who saw as the real issue the long-developing duel between British and Russian expansion. By his interpretation, the two nations were "linked together by destiny for better or for worse."

During the next few days, as Anglo-Russian discussions continued, prospects for peace did improve, and the rest of the press seemed to become a little more sanguine about the state of negotiations. However, there were frequent warnings that England must keep her guard up and some outbursts of bellicosity and denunciations of arbitration. On April 9 the news of Russia's major attack on Panjdeh reached London, and with it the crisis became more critical than ever. The *PMG* used four heads, the first in large bold-face type, for the page 8 story:

GREAT BATTLE ON THE
AGHAN FRONTIER

THE AFGHANS TOTALLY ROUTED BEFORE
PENJ-DEH
FIVE HUNDRED AFGHANS KILLED
BRITISH OFFICERS PRESENT AS
SPECTATORS

There followed over a column of news and a sketch of the Russian general, Komaroff, who had led the attack. On a later page there was a reasonably objective chronological table of the dispute between February, 1884, and April, 1885. Stead's leader for the day obviously anticipated the furor which was about to break when the morning papers had time to react to the news "Keep Cool, and Be Sure of Your Facts." Pointing out—needlessly—that a false step could mean war, he modulated for the time the pro-Russian tenor of some of his previous writings, saying that although always opposed to the advocates of a Russian war, "we have never denied that war may be rendered inevitable by acts of bad faith and unprovoked aggression." If Russia should be guilty of such conduct, "we shall be second to none" in demanding vindication of national honor. If the Russian actions were as flagrantly aggressive as others seemed to believe, Stead would agree with the war party. "All that we ask is that the Russians should not be condemned unheard." [35]

The next morning the London press was in full cry. To the *Times*, Komaroff's action established "a state of belligerency between Russia and Afghanistan." The *Standard* proclaimed even more shrilly, "The Muscovite Menace must be disposed of, once and for all." Although some of the dailies were more dogmatic than others, the general demand, as the minimum act by which Russia could atone for her crime and secure peace, was to recall Komaroff and evacuate all occupied positions. Most of the provincial papers went along with this demand, although, as usual, there were more voices of dissent outside of London. The Liberal *Manchester Examiner*, for example, reminded its readers how insignificant the incident would seem in a few months, and suggested that the best course of action would be "to repress all feelings of indignation" and continue to seek the facts. Stead's old

35. The same issue of the *PMG* carried two Occasional Note paragraphs which praised a ringing defense of British expansion given by Professor Seeley at Toynbee Hall—but Stead was always selective in his imperialism.

journal, the *Northern Echo,* also called for moderation and maintained that the czar really wanted peace. As for Stead, he echoed his urging of the previous day in his leader, "Keep Cool and Be Sure of Your Dates." He now claimed that dispatches from Sir Peter Lumsden himself indicated that "the Russian attack was occasioned by a movement of Afghan forces," and that the latter, under the British Captain Yates, had actually been the ones who destroyed the uneasy equilibrium in Panjdeh. Stead also suggested that the cabinet look closely at the information which would tell them whose troops were where on what dates. Once more the implication was clear that such data would support the Russian contentions on the matter.

On the inside pages, the *PMG's* news stories on the crisis ran to almost two full pages. One of them had a second head, "The Russian Explanations," which promised more than it gave, for all that could be said at this time was "It is probable that the Russian Government will reply to the demands of the English Government for explanations of 'the unhappy incident.'"

That night in the House of Commons Gladstone gave a reasonable speech which toned down some of the growing hysteria, stating among other things that the czar had already called on Komaroff to explain his actions. Stead eagerly seized at this straw, and his leader for Saturday, April 11, began with the assertion that there was "a perceptible abatement in the excitement." His new analysis of the situation was interesting: the main obstacle to a peaceful settlement had been the presence of the Afghans "in the very heart of the debatable land," but since they no longer held this territory, the Russian troops could withdraw. Conceding that he was "proceeding on the assumption that General KOMAROFF did not wantonly attack an inoffensive Afghan force," Stead nevertheless disclaimed the charges that he would support Russia no matter what she did. "If General KOMAROFF be as guilty as most of our contemporaries assume . . . further negotiations are impossible while he remains in command." If his government had sent Komaroff orders to attack, "it would be as impossible to continue on good terms with Russia as with a declared enemy of the human race." The difference between the *PMG's* attitude and that of the rest of the press was that "we refuse absolutely to believe that the Russian Government can have been guilty" of such an offense. To Stead the "greatest securities for peace" at the moment were the good sense of the czar and Gladstone, the German emperor's determination to prevent war, European financial interests which were exerting pressure for peace, and his own belief that the emir did not want British troops to pass through Afghanistan even in order to fight the Russians. In a news story entitled "The Russian Explanations" in the same issue, Stead made his personal convictions even clearer with the statement "The fact that the Afghans moved first is incontestable."

In his leader for Monday, April 13, Stead spoke as though the issue were settled. He completely accepted General Komaroff's explantion that Russia had only attacked the Afghans in self-defense (since the latter were taking up positions to launch an attack themselves), and expressed the hope that Captain Yates could explain his actions as well as had Komaroff. On the next day he berated the other newspapers for "demanding reparation while the whole question of who is to blame is *sub judice*." He also observed that the lack of telegraphic communication at the site, and the consequent delay in the sending of messages, might actually help to prevent war by giving people time to think. Later in the week Stead introduced a note which he was to repeat in later campaigns—his inability to understand how clergymen could fail to respond to what he saw as their Christian duty by not supporting his stand on the issue. In the leader on Wednesday he berated the clergy for their silence, and the *PMG* followers for both Friday and Saturday maintained the same theme.

During this week, as dispatches trickled in and messages crackled between Saint Petersburg and London, there was another brief period of somewhat lessened tensions. The general ignorance of the geography of Afghanistan, the difficulty in ascertaining the timing of various moves on that remote frontier, and the contradictory nature of the reports made the crisis—not all the details of which are clear to this day—difficult to understand. Although the press remained belligerent in tone, some of the newspapers—particularly in the provinces—began to suggest that perhaps there was a Russian side to the story. By Friday, April 17, Stead felt that matters had calmed down enough to permit him to deal with another continuing problem on the fringes of the empire. "Now that there seems to be a fair prospect of a speedy and pacific issue of our troubles on the Afghan frontier," he began his leader, "it is high time to turn our attention once more to our trouble in the

Soudan." (Now it was Stead the imperialist talking, as he called for a firm stand and the British subjugation of the area.) The possibility of a peaceful settlement of the Afghan problem did not bring joy to all of the press. "It may appear ungracious," mused the *Standard* on Saturday, "to regret that the nation is saved from the great calamity of war. But no one who has the honour of England at heart can help feeling that we are paying a disastrous price for the respite. Russia has once more triumphed, and triumphed at our expense." The feeling that England was abdicating her interests in order to prevent war was shared by some other journals, and the *Spectator* strongly implied that Gladstone lacked courage in his handling of the crisis. Still, whether with regret or not, most of the press now seemed to be convinced that war was not going to come over the latest incident, but that the outcome of the boundary settlement would determine future Anglo-Russian relations.

Early in the next week, when further information had been received, including a strongly anti-Russian dispatch from Lumsden, the winds of press opinion shifted once more. In his leader for Monday, April 20, Stead insisted that the dispute was virtually settled, but the following morning the *Times* opined that the prospects for peace had declined and the *Standard* that it was now clear that the "Russian onslaught" was "deliberate, unprovoked aggression," while even the more moderate *Daily News* found the Russian claims unacceptable. Undaunted, Stead headed his leader that night "Why Peace Is Certain" and gave his reasons, stressing the emir's reluctance to admit British troops into his territory. It would be unprofitable to recapitulate the details of the dispute over just what the reports of Komaroff and Lumsden had proved, but the confusing and contradictory character of the various dispatches is indicated by the different conclusions men of reasonable intelligence, if not of good will, could derive from them. Thus, while Stead could assert in a leader, "Komaroff Confirmed by Lumsden," the *Times,* on the same day and using the same information, could say, "We have learned nothing new about the essence of the matter," and the *Standard* could maintain that Lumsden's report stamped Komaroff's as "simple fiction" (April 22).

The *Standard*'s conclusions were pretty much supported by the other morning dailies, including the *Daily News.* Among the evening papers the *PMG*'s position, at least to the extent that it supported a peaceful settlement, was more or less followed by the *Echo*. In an Occasional Note, Stead, who professed to believe that he was also supported by the *St. James's Gazette,* voiced his surprise that its editor, Frederick Greenwood, was advocating peace (April 23). (In fact, except for an occasional warning that England was ill-prepared for war, there was little in the *Gazette* to justify Stead's assumption that it supported him.) By Saturday, April 25, when the *PMG* leader was headed "Deadlock, but No War," the *Times* was expressing the belief that Russia wanted war, the *Standard* could see no escape from the impasse, and the *Spectator* was calmly speaking of "the struggle upon which we are about to enter."

A decided turning point in the Anglo-Russian conflict over Afghanistan came on Monday, April 27, when Gladstone appeared before the House of Commons to ask for a vote of credit of eleven million pounds for military preparations. This unwonted display of belligerence was at least in part dictated by domestic political considerations: the government could not afford the appearance of another international humiliation so soon after Khartoum. Whatever the reasons, the new stance brought the desired results, for Russia certainly did not want a war with England at that time. The response to Gladstone's speech and his proposals for arbitration was conciliatory, although the czar refused to consider an inquiry into Komaroff's actions. It was agreed, however, that the question of whether the Anglo-Russian understanding in the area had been violated might be referred to a third party for arbitration. Here again England deferred to Russia's wishes, agreeing to accept the king of Denmark as arbiter. Most of the London press praised Gladstone's speech the next day, seeing the request for eleven million pounds as a demonstration of England's determination to stand firm, although the *Standard* did not think it was definite enough. That evening the *PMG* gave a full page, with a two-column head and seven crossheads, to a report of the speech, which an introductory paragraph termed "one of the greatest oratorical triumphs on record." The leader also praised it, although somewhat less effusively.

For the rest of the week most of the discussion of the crisis in the press centered on Gladstone's offer of arbitration and such questions as whether or not the prime minister had actually delivered an ultimatum, just what points were to be arbitrated, and whether there should be a third party involved in the arbitration. By Saturday, May 2, Stead was back to his optimistic posture, in a leader entitled "A Settlement in Sight." To him, the conciliatory way in which the czar had received the English proposals—he did not like to call them an ultimatum—showed that the *PMG*'s confidence in peace had been justified. Representing the opposing camp, the *Standard* on the same day reiterated its call for firmness and denounced arbitration as a plan for dragging the matter out. That night Lord Granville announced Russia's conciliatory response to the English proposals, and in the leader for Monday, May 4, Stead gloated that the "alarmist writers" who had been calling the *PMG* traitorous were "now beginning to perceive what fools they have been making of themselves," and were busy inventing excuses for Russia doing what they said she would never do. Stead also reminded the public that the *PMG* was "the only journal whose forecasts have been entirely justified by the events." The rest of the press did not entirely share Stead's bland assumption that the crisis was over. The *Daily News* did find peace prospects "still clearer," but the *Times,* for example, insisted that it would be rash to conclude from Russia's conciliatory reply that the issue was settled. Many of the other papers were also skeptical, and the *Post* maintained that negotiations with Russia must be regarded with "suspicion and mistrust."

In Parliament on May 4, the announcement of the agreement to arbitrate was answered with a bitter denunciation by the Conservatives, led by Randolph Churchill, of the ministry's handling of the matter. On the next day the press was somewhat divided in its reactions to Gladstone's policy. On the negative side, the *Morning Advertiser* saw the agreement to arbitrate as a diplomatic defeat and the *Standard* spoke of the "wholesale slaughter" of Afghans, insisting that arbitration was not what Parliament had in mind when it voted the eleven-million-pound credit. The *Times* was also dubious, believing that there was "little to be thankful for beyond the fact that war has been avoided," for everything depended upon Russia's good faith. The *Daily Chronicle* was better satisfied and did not think the terms of the settlement justified the "violent language" of Churchill, while the *Daily News,* sure that the prospects for peace were brighter than for a long time, accused the Conservatives of acting like a war party. The provincial press, particularly of Liberal persuasion, was more enthusiastic about the agreement and in general denied that it was a surrender to the Russians, while decrying what the *Sheffield Independent* described as the "bitter Tory partisans and Jingo journalists."

On May 6, for the first time in many days, the Afghan crisis did not make the first page of the *PMG*, and only brief coverage was given to it on the inside pages—mostly concerning relief in Europe that war had been averted. From this point on, the controversy tended to slip gradually out of public and press consciousness. Further negotiations were, of course, reported; editorial comment appeared from time to time; and the *Standard* kept referring to England's "humiliation." However, for all practical purposes the crisis had passed.[36]

During the final months of the crisis, the coverage of it by the *PMG*—and the rest of the press—became more sporadic and gradually dwindled to an occasional article. With the story growing cold, there was no need for the other papers to continue baiting Stead, particularly since they were always averse to giving journalistic rivals any publicity. Stead's transgressions were not forgotten, however, and the assessment of the *Pall Mall Gazette* in *Deacon's Newspaper Handbook* for 1886 included the statement that it had recently caused "much amazement and speculation in regard to the strangely unpatriotic position it assumed during the Anglo-Russian crisis."[37] Stead had given a summation of his own in a follower for June 1, 1885, entitled "Reflections on the Late Crisis." He felt that the incident showed that when the Liberal party was in office, the Opposition would apply no brake to the development of warlike policies. War, indeed, had been averted on this occasion only because of the emir's refusal to accept British military aid and Russia's forbearance. In England itself, "all the usual forces which operate for peace were silenced." Returning to some old themes, Stead decried the lack of any real effort to avert war on the part of the Peace Society and most Nonconformist ministers, but declared that the position of the Radicals—except for Morley and

36. Although the matter quieted down, Granville was to discover that the Russian Foreign Office was still troublesome when it came to working out the details of the negotiations, and no settlement had been reached when the Gladstone ministry fell in June. Lord Salisbury took over the problem for the Conservatives and, after continued difficult discussions, on September 10 the two nations signed a protocol delineating a frontier which gave Panjdeh to Russia.

37. "The Pall Mall Gazette," *Deacon's Newspaper Handbook, 1886* (London: Samuel Deacon, 1886), p. 76.

Labouchere—was the "worst of all." He also repeated his lament over English "insanity" when confronted by Russia, and said of the press—somewhat unfairly—that "provincial editors were as mad as their London brethren." If Stead had been in a more objective mood he would have had to admit that many of the provincial papers, particularly those with Liberal convictions, had been quite restrained and had often backed the *PMG's* position. Still, Stead might be forgiven for his testiness. In the same article he quoted from two letters he had received which accused the *PMG* of literally selling out the country. Years later there were still critics who described his position during this period in similar terms.

CHAPTER FIVE

"The Maiden Tribute"

Not long after the Afghan controversy subsided into relative quiescence, Stead undertook the crusade for which, more than any other, he is remembered. From first to last, his campaign to raise the legal age of consent for girls from thirteen to sixteen mirrored many of the paradoxical elements which make the character of the man so complex and controversial. Here we see Stead the Puritan calling on the techniques and talents of Stead the New Journalist; the stern moralist defying conventional Victorian morality; the experienced professional guilty of astonishing reportorial carelessness; the sincere, selfless reformer flaunting his egocentrism; the protector of the virtue of womanhood objecting to proposals to raise the age of consent still further because many young prostitutes would thus be deprived of their livelihood. Even the name that he bestowed on the series launching the crusade, grandly—jumbling allusions to Greek myth and the Old Testament, stamped "The Maiden Tribute of Modern Babylon" as a quintessentially Steadian venture.

I

William Stead's receptiveness to appeals for help in behalf of seemingly lost causes was by now well known, and it drew to his office Benjamin Scott, chamberlain of the City of London and a reformer who had campaigned against vice for many years. He told Stead that the Criminal Law Amendment Bill, which offered protection to young women through such measures as raising the age of consent, was in danger of being dropped by the govern-

128

ment. If Stead could rouse public opinion once more, Parliament might be pressured into reconsidering and passing the bill.

Scott had helped to set in motion the train of events which led to the first introduction of the Criminal Law Amendment Bill in 1883. In 1880, as chairman of a group determined to expose and suppress the transportation to the Continent of young English girls for the purpose of prostitution, he had written to Lord Granville asking Parliament to enact preventive legislation. Partly through his efforts, in 1881 a Select Committee was established by the House of Lords to investigate the situation. The committee, which concluded its sittings in July, 1882, confirmed the extent of the white-slave traffic and the increase in juvenile prostitution. Its report called for vigorous measures and made nine recommendations which were the basis for the Criminal Law Amendment Bill. This bill, which raised the age of consent from thirteen to sixteen and contained penalties against indecent assault, soliciting a woman to enter a brothel overseas, and admitting into any premises a girl under sixteen for the purpose of sexual intercourse, passed the House of Lords in 1883 but was dropped by the House of Commons. In 1884 it again passed the Lords but was sacrificed in the Commons to the struggle over that year's Parliamentary Reform Bill. Stead had been cognizant of the problems which the Criminal Law Amendment Bill was supposed to solve, and he later spoke of the *PMG* as protesting when the bill was dropped in 1884, but the protest was mild enough. An Occasional Note which listed eight different bills about to be dropped in the Commons concluded, "It is a pity that the Criminal Law Amendment Bill was not plucked like a brand from the burning. The poor children might at least have been spared" (July 11, 1884). In April, 1885, the bill, now somewhat watered down by the lowering of the age of consent from sixteen to fifteen, again passed the House of Lords, but once more seemed doomed in the House of Commons. On May 22, as Parliament was preparing to rise for its Whitsuntide recess, Sir William Harcourt, the Home Secretary, moved the second reading of the bill in the Commons. Only about forty members were present, and in an atmosphere of apathy mixed with hostility the measure was debated until adjournment and no vote was taken. On the next day Stead wrote in an Occasional Note, "Once more we regret to see that the protection of our young girls has been sacrificed to the loquacity of our legislators. Mr. Bentinck talked out the Criminal Law Amendment Bill yesterday afternoon, and we fear that the chance of proceeding with this measure before the general election are of the slightest."

At this point Benjamin Scott decided that Stead's talents for journalistic agitation must be more fully committed to the cause. He came to the editor on May 23 with grim tales of juvenile prostitution, of the abduction of young girls by brothel keepers, of the sale by their own parents of innocent young virgins to those who would induct them into a life of vice. Stead was shocked and dismayed by the recital, yet at first he was uncharacteristically reluctant to get involved. According to his own account,

> I naturally wanted to try [to force the Commons to take up the bill] but every instinct of prudence and self-preservation restrained me. The subject was tabooed by the Press. The very horror of the crime was the chief secret of its persistence. The task was almost hopeless. No ordinary means could overcome the obstacles which were presented by the political situation.

Stead paid a call on Howard Vincent, whose experiences as the director of criminal investigation at Scotland Yard from 1878 to 1884 gave him a great deal of first-hand information about the problem. When Vincent confirmed Scott's sordid descriptions, Stead determined to act. "Be the results what they may," he wrote, "no nobler work could a man ever be privileged to take. Even a humble part in it is enough to make one grateful for the privilege of life." [1]

A "Special Commission," consisting of Stead and two or three assistants, proceeded to investigate the nether world of London prostitution. Their activities were conducted with the foreknowledge, and at least partial approval, of such irreproachable figures as the Archbishop of Canterbury, Cardinal Manning, Mrs. Josephine Butler, and high officials of the Salvation Army. Scores of interviews were held—mostly by Stead himself—with active and retired brothel keepers; with procurers, pimps, and prostitutes; with rescue workers, jail chaplains, and former police officials. At the outset of the investigation, on June 3, Stead showed his keen sense of the dramatic, as well as his disregard for legal niceties, when he purchased a young girl named Eliza Armstrong from her mother,

1. Scott, *Life and Death*, pp. 125-26.

to prove that it could be done. The actual transaction was conducted by Rebecca Jarrett, a reformed prostitute now working for the Salvation Army, whom he met through Mrs. Butler. Mrs. Jarrett assured Stead that Mrs. Armstrong not only took money for turning over her daughter to a stranger, but also believed that she was being purchased for the purpose of sexual intercourse. Young Eliza, who was thirteen and completely unaware of the implications of what was going on, was taken to a midwife and known abortionist, who examined her, attested to her virginity, and sold Stead a bottle of chloroform to make the supposed seduction easier. She was next taken to a room in a brothel, which she believed was a hotel, and given a whiff of chloroform. A half hour later Stead entered the room, and when Eliza, who was still awake, cried out in alarm, he immediately left her alone. The next morning she was turned over to Bramwell Booth, son of the founder of the Salvation Army, who arranged for the girl to be taken to France and given a position there.

Sickened and horrified, Stead continued with his investigations and interviews throughout June and most of July. The chances of the Criminal Law Amendment Bill's passing seemed even bleaker after June 8, when Gladstone's government resigned after a defeat on an amendment to the budget. The new government, formed under Lord Salisbury, intended to dissolve as soon as the new registration lists, required by the Parliamentary Reform Act of 1884, were completed; and because of its tenuous position it did not intend to take up any major or controversial legislation for the remainder of the session.[2]

Stead launched his great crusade while his investigations were still going on, beginning with what might be called a teaser in the *Pall Mall Gazette* of Saturday, July 4, 1885. There was nothing unusual about the appearance of this issue; in fact, throughout the entire series no effort was made at a more eye-catching format. It was the content of the articles, leaders, and crossheads which made them offensive to many, and indeed some might be considered objectionable even today. The July 4 follower was headed "Notice to Our Readers" in modest, eight-point italics, with the underlining

2. In Stead's manuscript account of these events, written at a later date, there is again a confusion in dates. He indicates that Benjamin Scott, on his May 23 visit, was afraid that Gladstone's regination would lessen the chances for the passage of the bill; but Gladstone did not step down until June 8. See Scott, *Life and Death*, p. 125.

the only concession to attention getting. The second head, "A Frank Warning," showed that Stead understood the technique of intriguing the curious reader. The follower explained that the Criminal Law Amendment Bill was about to be dropped and announced in an underlined sentence: "We have, therefore, determined, with a full sense of the responsibility attaching to such a decision, to publish the report of a Special and Secret Commission of Inquiry which we appointed to examine the whole subject." The report would deal with "those phases of sexual criminality which the bill . . . was found to repress" in order to prevent yet another suppression of the legislation. Since the editor did not want to inflict a sordid story of vice on "unwilling eyes," he warned

> that all those who are squeamish, and all those who are prudish, and all those who prefer to live in a fool's paradise of imaginary innocence and purity, selfishly oblivious of the horrible realities which torment those whose lives are passed in the London Inferno, will do well not to read the Pall Mall Gazette of Monday and the following days.

The humor magazine *Punch* responded in its next issue with a satirical warning to its readers that it intended to publish a "diabolically sensational story," with "scarifying" illustrations of love, crimes, and "unparalleled atrocities." Thus *Punch* advised the public not to look into the next two numbers. "By the time this appears," it observed, "the *Pall Mall Gazette* will have made our flesh creep, and of course the rush for the paper will have been enormous." But *Punch* did concede the possibility that "the end, which the *PMG* keeps steadily in view, may justify the means."[3]

Having whetted the appetite of his readers, on Monday, July 6, Stead began his leader, "The report of our Secret Commission will be read to-day with a shuddering horror that will thrill throughout the world." He asserted that since the evidence compiled showed both the reality of the crimes and the efficacy of raising the age of consent, the House of Commons would undoubtedly find time to pass the bill. This result, however, would be only a small part of the justification of the report, which would reach the conscience of the English people, and lead them to put a stop to this "veritable slave trade." Nothing had yet been done because of a "conspiracy

3. "Steady, Sir, Steady," *Punch*, July 11, 1885, p. 17.

of silence maintained by the Press, the Home, the School and the Church. The Press, which reports verbatim all the scabrous details of the divorce courts, recoils in pious horror from the duty of shedding a flood of light upon these dark places." After noting that the failure of the Church was, perhaps, the most complete, Stead introduced a theme that was woven through the entire fabric of the crusade but is generally overlooked by biographers and press historians. In the "Maiden Tribute" campaign the *Pall Mall Gazette* made common cause with the "New Democracy" by frequently presenting the scandal of juvenile prostitution and white slavery in terms of class outrage. Thus Stead avowed that although the Church had failed, there was another force to which the crusaders could appeal. "The future belongs to the combined forces of Democracy and Socialism, which when united are irresistible," and those movements would unite to protest this "sacrifice to the vices of the rich." Socialism in particular would be stimulated by the revelations of the abuse of wealth in the English social system, and, in an immoderately sweeping indictment, Stead condemned "princes and dukes, and ministers and judges, and the rich of all classes" for the evils about to be exposed. He acknowledged that abolition of prostitution was too idealistic and unattainable a goal, but the revelations could at least save "innocent victims."

The first installment of the report appeared as a follower under the title "The Maiden Tribute of Modern Babylon," and continued through page 6. The crossheads sprinkled throughout, while not large, were provocative enough to help explain the excitement with which the issue was greeted: "The Violation of Virgins," "The Confessions of a London Brothel-Keeper," "How Girls Are Bought and Ruined," and "A Child of Thirteen Bought for £5." Drawing an analogy with the plight of the maidens sent from ancient Athens to perish in the Labyrinth at Crete, the report pointed out that the Athenian tribute was paid only once in seven years, while in London every night many times seven "will be offered up as the Maiden Tribute of Modern Babylon. Maidens they were when this morning dawned, but tonight their ruin will be accomplished, and tomorrow they will find themselves within the portals of the maze of London brotheldom."

It was hoped that this tribute could be ended altogether, but "if the daughters of the people must be served up as dainty morsels to minister to the passions of the rich, let them at least attain an

age when they can understand the nature of the sacrifice which
they are asked to make." Stead proclaimed "the hour of Democracy has struck," and warned that if there was no reform, there
would be revolution against those of the upper class who "purchased the wives and daughters of the poor to satisfy their lust."
He did not ask the police to interfere with sexual immorality, which
could only be cured by education, but to act for the prevention of
crime; and he listed the criminal acts which by his "personal knowledge" were freely committed in London, including:

I. The sale and purchase and violation of children.
II. The procuration of virgins.
III. The entrapping and ruin of women.
IV. The international slave trade in girls.
V. Atrocities, brutalities, and unnatural crimes.

The report recounted how the facts had been verified by the
"Chief Commissioner" and his assistants, with their nightly explora-
tions of "the London Inferno." Stead was struck by the overlapping
of the respectable worlds of business and politics with the world
of vice.

> I heard of much the same people in the house of ill-fame as
> those of whom you hear in caucuses, in law courts, and on the
> 'Change. But all were judged by a different standard. . . . To
> hear statesmen reckoned up from the standpoint of the brothel
> is at first almost as novel and perplexing an experience as it
> is to hear judges and Queen's Counsel praised or blamed . . .
> for their addiction to unnatural crimes or their familiarity with
> obscene literature.

He offered to authenticate his charges, providing there would be
no criminal action against his informants, by turning over "names,
dates, localities referred to together with full and detailed explanations of the way in which I secured the information" to a committee consisting of the Archbishop of Canterbury, Cardinal Manning, Samuel Morley, M.P., the Earl of Shaftesbury, the Earl of
Dalhousie, and Howard Vincent.[4]

4. Cardinal Manning (1808-92), left the Anglican clergy to become a
Roman Catholic in 1851, and was made Cardinal in 1875. In religious affairs
he was an autocratic, conservative ultramontane, but from his days as an
Anglican parish priest he had a deep interest in the education and the general

Stead next described how young girls were lured into brothels and not allowed to leave "until they have lost what woman ought to value more than life." At certain houses virgins could be purchased at relatively high prices—young girls who were rarely willing and often did not know why they were in the house. One informant (Vincent) had told him that although the very thought of these rapes "ought to raise hell, it does not even raise the neighbors." The victims were in an almost hopeless position legally because they did not know their assailants by name, and because their seduction took place in a brothel. "A woman who has lost her chastity is always a discredited witness," Stead observed. The "Chief Commissioner" admitted that there were those who questioned the reluctance of the girls involved, and he told of a well-known member of Parliament who declared, "I myself am quite ready to supply you with 100 maids at £25 each, but they will all know very well what they are about." The M.P. allegedly added that, while some of the virgins might be unwilling, most of them "take a very businesslike view of the saleable value of their maidenhead." In rebuttal, Stead quoted at length a number of active and retired brothel keepers who described the techniques of procuring unwilling virgins, the practice of sadism and flogging, and the sale of young girls by their mothers. One tale concerned a man who could be satisfied only by very young maidens; they were strapped down so that their resistance to him was limited to their screams. And yet, Stead wrote, there was virtually no protection for a girl as young as thirteen even when her permission had been gained by fraud or when she did not understand the nature of the act. This first installment of the revelation ended with a story of the purchase for five pounds of a child of thirteen named Lily. Stead later claimed that he had only heard the story and that it had inspired him to follow the same pattern of abduction with another girl, but his statement at the beginning that he could "personally

---

welfare of the poor. In 1889 he warmly championed the cause of the workers in the famous London dock strike. Samuel Morley (1809-86) amassed a fortune as a businessman, and was very active in religious, philanthropic and temperance movements. He became a proprietor of the *Daily News* in 1868, and, sitting as M.P. for Bristol (1868-85) was a strong supporter of Gladstone. The Earl of Dalhousie (1847-87) had given up a career in the navy (1861-79) to devote his time to studies and politics. He was elected M.P. for Liverpool in 1880, but succeeded as the thirteenth earl the same year. In 1884 he introduced the Criminal Law Amendment Bill in the House of Lords.

vouch for the absolute accuracy of every part of the narrative" and
the dates and details make it clear that he was telling in essence
the story of Eliza Armstrong.

The impact of the report on the public was immediate, and despite the fact that W. H. Smith and Son, which had a monopoly
on England's railway news stands, refused to handle the *Pall Mall
Gazette* while it carried the "Maiden Tribute" revelations, its sales
rose spectacularly. By Tuesday, July 7, letters had begun to pour
into the *PMG* office and that afternoon the crowd gathered at
Northumberland Street awaiting the next issue was so large that
vendors and cart drivers had difficulty in picking up their papers.
The *PMG* leader for Tuesday dealt with the more prosaic subject
of the new cabinet, but it was followed by the second installment
of the "Maiden Tribute" revelations, which again continued for the
next five pages. Among the crossheads, which to some *PMG*
critics were as damning as the text, were "The Forcing of Unwilling Maids," "I Order Five Virgins," and "Delivered for Seduction."
The second report stated that the victims described in the preceding installment were "almost always very young children between
thirteen and fifteen," for the reason that "the law at present almost
specially marks out such children as the fair game of dissolute men.
The moment a child is thirteen she is a woman in the eyes of the
law." Repeating the Victorian maxim that her virtue was "the most
precious thing a woman ever has," Stead pointed out that whereas
she could not legally dispose of other valuable possessions until
the age of sixteen, she could sell her person at thirteen.

The report also had some observations on the incredible ignorance of physiology and sex of many of the girls entrapped in the
"labyrinth." In an interesting example of the way in which he
sometimes rejected aspects of the chapel training which shaped
so much of his career, Stead opined that "Catholic children are
much better trained; and . . . the chastity of Catholic girls is much
greater than that of Protestants of the same social strata." He
blamed "the soul and body destroying taciturnity of Protestant
mothers," which left their daughters in total ignorance of sexual
realities.

Much of Tuesday's account was filled with more details of the
strenuous recruiting needed to keep the brothels filled, and told
more of the wiles used to entrap girls and young women. Under
the crosshead "Procuration in the West End," Stead made the

rather obvious point that young virgins brought more money there than in the East End of London, and cited prices, fees for maidens, and procuresses' commissions. He also provided a number of case histories of victims of the "systemized business" of procuring, which indicated that in their innocence and ignorance many of the girls thought that the seduction for which they had been purchased was accomplished once the midwife had examined them to certify their virginity. Finally, Stead described the process by which, over a period of a few days, he was able to arrange for the purchase of seven girls between the ages of fourteen and eighteen, four of whom had doctors' certificates attesting to their virginal state, and all of whom had signed agreements to allow their purchaser to have them for a stipulated fee. The actual purchases, which were not completed, would have cost between thirty-four and forty-four pounds.

The Tuesday issue was sold out almost as soon as it hit the streets, and that evening in the House of Commons George Cavendish-Bentinck, who was to become one of the most determined opponents of Stead's crusade, rose to call the Home Secretary's attention to "publications relating to objectionable subjects" by the *Pall Mall Gazette*. When he asked if the authors and publishers could not be subjected to criminal proceedings, there were cheers and laughter. He pointed out that sale of the paper had been suspended in the railway stations and many private bookstalls, and that it was now being sold in the streets by under-age children displaying "indecent placards." Another member asked if it were true that the trade price of the paper had been boosted by 25 percent. Secretary Cross replied that publishers of obscene material could be prosecuted, but that a jury would have to decide what constituted an obscene publication and that he had no information on the sale and price of the paper.[5]

On the following day, July 8, the crusade returned to the *PMG* leader column, which began on a typically Steadian note of self-congratulation: "The report of our Secret Commission, as is now evident, has produced an effect unparalleled in the history of journalism. The excitement yesterday in London was intense. The ministerial statements were comparatively overlooked in the fierce dispute that went on everywhere over the revelations of our Com-

5. *Hansard's Parliamentary Debates*, 3d ser., vol. 298 (1885): pp. 1827-28.

mission." The editor accepted the challenge of W. H. Smith and
Son, whose head sat in the Salisbury cabinet, by noting ironically,
"The great monopoly of railway bookstalls that bears the name of
one of the members of our administration which has just declared
in favour of amending the law to deal with the criminals we have
exposed, forbade the sale of the most convincing demonstration of
the necessity for such legislation." More provocative was his statement that the crusade was fortunate in its critics. "When we
learned by whom the attempt to hide these crimes from the eye
of the public was headed in Parliament and in the Press we took
courage," he wrote, and went on to exult in the honor of leading
a cause which was attacked by the "worst men." Drawing the lines
for the coming battle, Stead scoffed at threats of criminal prosecution which had been made in the House of Commons by Cavendish-
Bentinck, particularly since "we might subpoena almost half the
Legislature in order to prove the accuracy of our revelations." He
vowed that he would not follow the example of Mrs. Jeffries—a
well-placed brothel keeper, whose trial had recently been a cause
célèbre in London—and plead guilty in order to save "noble and
Royal patrons from exposure." The leader claimed overwhelming
support for the crusade from people all over England, including
churchmen, and blamed the "men of the world" for the relatively
small opposition. Against a dozen or so anonymous letters of abuse,
Stead said he had received assurances of support from moral and
religious leaders all over England. He commented on the objections raised to the class implications of the campaign with the
assertion that the whole sordid story was evidence "of the extent
to which wealth was used to corrupt, to demoralize, and to destroy
the daughters of the poor." To Stead the "supreme criminal" was
not the pimp or brothel keeper; it was the "wealthy and dissolute
men." Such talk might be considered dangerous and revolutionary,
but "it is not so dangerous as allowing this havoc to continue un-
checked, nor so revolutionary as the attempt to gag the single voice
that is raised to impeach the rich for their crimes against the poor."
With what must have seemed to many dangerous radicalism, Stead
again warned that if "such rottenness" were not reformed, revolution might well be the result, and "in view of that contingency, possibly even those gentlemen who cheered Mr. Cavendish-Bentinck
yesterday may see fit to do what they can to expedite the passing
of the vital clauses of the Criminal Law Amendment Bill, with

which the Government, in more or less half-hearted fashion, intends to persevere."

In the third chapter of the "Maiden Tribute" revelations which followed were two items that probably disturbed some of Stead's supporters and gave comfort to those who felt that Stead was dealing in sensationalism for its own sake. One was the story of a five-year-old girl who had been raped, accompanied by a small illustration depicting the victim with an officer of the Society for the Protection of Children. This story and another about two girls who had been victims of incest were indeed tragic, but not really relevant to the crusade, since raising the age of consent would obviously not help such unfortunates. The other questionable part of the report was less a reflection of sensationalism than a bad lapse in taste. Under the crosshead "A Close Time for Girls" Stead drew a clumsy analogy between the legal age of consent and game laws. Citing the existence of closed seasons for the protection of birds, he suggested, "Why not let us have a close time for bipeds in petticoats as well as for bipeds with feathers?" Then, in a vein which must have made even some of his dedicated supporters wince, he continued, "Fish out of season are not fit to be eaten. Girls who have not reached the age of puberty are unfit even to be seduced." He concluded with the questionable assertion, "It is also a scientific fact that such children are far more likely to transmit disease than full grown women. Scientifically, therefore, the close time should be extended until the woman has at least completed sixteen years of life." The third report also concerned itself with deficiencies in the existing law which, it claimed, virtually prevented parents from recovering a child from a brothel without the expenditure of at least thirty to fifty pounds in legal fees.

Other topics were dealt with under such self-explanatory crossheads as "Entrapping Irish Girls" and "Imprisoned in Brothels," and the installment ended with the stories of two of the villains in the melodrama, one of whom, if Stead's account was accurate, surely demonstrated remarkable virility. A certain wealthy retired doctor required three virgins every night, "but his devastating passion sinks into insignificance compared to that of Mr. ———, another wealthy man whose whole life is dedicated to the gratification of lust." Stead told of running across the man's name constantly during the course of his investigations, and "the fact that he exists ought to be put on record, if only as a striking illustration of the extent to which it is possible for a wealthy man to ruin not merely hundreds, but thousands of poor women. It is actually Mr. ———'s boast that he has ruined 2,000 women in his time. . . . Exercise, recreation, everything is subordinated to the supreme end of his life."

By now "The Maiden Tribute" had spread well beyond the leader and follower columns of the *PMG*, and Wednesday's issue included articles on the enormous demand for the paper, the attacks by Cavendish-Bentinck in the Commons, and the railway bookstall boycott imposed by W. H. Smith. Added to the crush of vendors and would-be purchasers outside the *PMG*'s offices were spectators who came to goggle at the brawling, surging crowd, and finally the police had to be called to Northumberland Street. At first only four were sent and they were unable to cope with what was becoming a riotous mob. The pressure was so great that men were pushed through windows, and eventually it took forty policemen to restore order. Meanwhile the little Marinoni press continued to hum and the press run halted only when the paper supply gave out. On top of the W. H. Smith boycott at railway news stands, the City Solicitor banned the sale of the *PMG* within the limits of the City, but nonetheless, as on the previous two days, the issue sold out completely.

Although Stead complained repeatedly about the "conspiracy of silence" on the part of the London press, that afternoon Frank Harris's *Evening News* took ample notice of the "Maiden Tribute" crusade, with a scathing denunciation of its revelations. The entire right-hand column of page 1 for July 8 was devoted to the attack, which was couched in the vituperative terms characterizing all of this paper's accounts of the campaign:

> The evening organ of advanced Radicalism has this week succeeded in earning for itself a notoriety of infamy never approached, certainly in English journalism, and which, so far as our experience goes, has never been gained by the most sensational journalism either of Europe or America. We have long been accustomed, unfortunately, to see from time to time some filthy sheet appear in the gutter of London streets, and maintain just a brief existence as a vile insect reared on the putrid garbage of the dunghill. Public decency has been outraged by its presence, and the police have winked at the evil. But that a journal that addresses itself to the most educated

classes of the country, which has maintained a brilliant reputation for twenty years, which has been conducted by such
journalists as Frederick Greenwood, and John Morley, and to
whose columns some of the foremost pens of the kingdom have
contributed, should descend to the same level, is a new departure which must inspire every decent man with disgust.

There are at least two passages in Harris's later autobiography
which make this diatribe curious: his boasts about his own use
of sensationalism—with its emphasis on "kissing and fighting"—to
boost the sales of the *Evening News,* and his sneers at John Morley's
abilities: "His work remains fruitless, academic, jejune, divorced
from life, unillumined by genius, unconsecrated by art. A bleak
face and a bleak mind!"[6] With reference to the Panjdeh campaign,
Harris noted, "The management of the *Pall Mall Gazette* has already won an unenviable notoriety by its unpatriotic attitude in
the face of English embarrassments in the East." However, he
said, this notoriety was short-lived, and it was necessary to discover
a new sensation. Thus, the true motive of the revelations was
profit, not morality. The result of broadcasting "matter which we
should have thought no man would willingly risk being read by
his wife or daughter, or even his son rising to manhood" was not
the ending of an evil, but simply an enormous increase in sales.
Why, Harris asked, if the *PMG* actually knew names, dates, and
other details of these horrible crimes, had it not turned the information over to the proper authorities? He agreed with Cavendish-
Bentinck that criminal action should be taken against Stead's paper.

The *PMG*'s leader for the following day, Thursday, July 9, was
headed "To Our Friends the Enemy," and thanked the City Solicitor for suppressing the sale of the paper in the City of London.
"After Mr. Cavendish-Bentinck," Stead wrote, "he has probably
contributed the most to break down the conspiracy of silence which
our contemporaries are maintaining." Amazed at the violation of
the freedom of the press, he again threw down the gauntlet to the
authorities in a passage that tells much of both the techniques and
motives of his crusading journalism: "We challenge prosecution,
we court inquiry. We have reluctantly been driven to the only
mode—that of publicity—for arousing men to a sense of the horrors

6. F. Harris, *My Life and Loves* (New York: Grove Press, 1963), pp. 628-
31, 694-96.

which are going on at this very moment." Convinced that his revelations could be proved without betraying confidences given during the investigation, Stead said that so far he had avoided exposing individuals, but if put in the witness box he would "confront in the courts of justice brothel-keepers with Princes of Blood, and prominent public men with the unfortunate victims of their lawless vice." Since Stead did get his day in the witness box and failed to expose any "Princes of Blood" or "prominent public men," it might be assumed that he was not above using a calculated bluff to bolster his offensive. On the other hand, he and his supporters could counter this charge with the observation that his trial did not involve an attempt to suppress the paper nor, technically, the validity of the whole of the "Secret Commission's" report.

There was no installment of the revelations in Thursday's paper, but in the follower, "The Truth about Our Secret Commission," which ran for over three columns, Stead answered charges of inaccuracy and reiterated his eagerness to submit to a judicial investigation which would expose "the men in high places whose misdeeds our commission is exposing." He described "the origin and the constitution of the Commission," and explained that the fourth report had been postponed for a day in order to complete certain evidence which "will astound the world." He welcomed the support, encouragement, and assistance given by various secular and religious leaders, social and welfare organizations, and the *PMG* staff, and also sardonically thanked Sir William Harcourt, the erstwhile Home Secretary. Harcourt had refused to offer police cooperation in his investigation, but Stead was now convinced that this was all to the good, since the brothel keepers would have been more reticent if the commission had also interviewed the police. He described the chief method of the investigation as "the sound journalistic principle of the universal interview," and in another of those asides which pained some of his supporters, he praised the aid given him by the "much maligned" Mrs. Jeffries. Compared to many houses of ill repute, he declared, hers "were well conducted" and "on as respectable a footing as that ghastly calling permits." As appalling as were the facts brought to light, Stead continued, they only skimmed the surface, and the three hundred pounds which the investigation cost was "less than a rich man will spend in procuring the corruption of a single shop girl of the better class." The one thought which sustained him throughout the terrible ordeal was that he was about to shatter the "conspiracy of silence."

William T. Stead in 1881

FOURTH EDITION.

TERRIBLE EXPLOSION AT WESTMINSTER.

ATTEMPT TO DESTROY THE LOCAL GOVERNMENT BOARD OFFICE.

LATEST PARTICULARS.

A terrific explosion occurred last night at the offices of the Local Government Board, Parliament-street, Westminster. The sound of the explosion was succeeded by the shrieks of women and the sound of falling windows, and the whole of the thoroughfares in the immediate neighbourhood were covered with a thick coating of the broken glass. The inhabitants turned out of their houses in intense alarm, and thousands rushed to the spot, followed quickly by the police. At first it was thought that a serious gas explosion had occurred, but very soon a more serious view was taken of the case. The explosion, it was found, had occurred in the ground floor of the Local Government Board Offices, smashing the stonework into splinters and breaking into fragments the windows, portions of which lay strewn in all the surrounding streets. The massive stonework and stone balustrade in front were thrown forward into the street, and the interior of the room was completely wrecked, and the stonework torn up into splinters. The porter who has charge of the Local Government Offices was on the premises at the time, and he stated that the explosion sounded quite close to him, "like the report of an 80-ton gun," and the crash of the front portion of the building was accompanied by the flash of a large body of flame. After the explosion there was a smell of gas in the premises, even in the occupied rooms ; but this is to be explained by the fact that the force of the explosion was such as to extinguish all the lights in the premises, and thus caused an escape of gas until it could be turned off at the meter. This sudden darkness intensified the alarm which the terrific force of the explosion naturally excited on the part of the wife and servant of the office-keeper, who were at the time sitting in their private room. For the moment they were powerless. Upon recovering their presence of mind they went out into the passage, and were nearly blinded by the dense choking clouds of lime-dust with which the place was filled. Their first endeavour was to grope about in search of candles, and when these were lighted it became possible to form some idea of the actual damage.

The men left in charge of the other public offices were also much alarmed, each being apprehensive that the premises under his own care had suffered or were in danger, and much alarm was also created at the Premier's residence. Police-sergeant Rose, who was in King-street at the time, was within fifty yards of the spot, and his first impression was that an earthquake had occurred. The ground trembled beneath him. He involuntarily put his hands to his helmet to keep it from falling, and, a shower of glass raining on him, his hands were cut. Sergeant Rose and a constable hearing screams proceed from a house at the corner of King-street, ran upstairs and brought out a woman and her two children. The apartment was completely wrecked. The children had been asleep, but their bed was overturned and their faces were cut and bleeding. The little ones were wrapped up and taken to the adjoining police-station. Mr. Fisher, principal clerk to Lord R. Grosvenor, the Government whip, was in the Parliamentary offices in King-street when the explosion occurred, and was forced off his feet at the same moment that the plate-glass windows were blown in, from the fragments of which, however, he was happily protected by a screen. An official of the House of Lords who was passing states that he was startled by a sudden burst of blue flame darting upward like a rocket, followed by a sharp, detonating explosion, and a heavy shower of broken glass. A person who witnessed the explosion from the end of the street, and who declared himself to have some experience of explosions, said that the report had the hard metallic sound which is characteristic of gun-cotton, dynamite, or such other explosives as contain nitro-glycerine.

The report was heard about half a minute after nine o'clock in the House of Commons, while Mr. Gourley was speaking. So great was the force of the explosion, that the floor of the House and the galleries shook.

The scene of the explosion this morning was visited by immense numbers of persons on their way to business, but all access to Charles-street was barred early in the morning by a posse of policemen, and subsequently by the erection of a strong barricade at each end. Colonel Majendie, C.B., Inspector of Explosives, was early on the spot conducting a close personal examination of the wrecked room. Orders were despatched before nine o'clock in the morning for photographic apparatus to photograph the scene of the explosion, in order that permanent record might be preserved of the evidence afforded by the broken stone of the nature of the explosive employed. The scene was a striking one. Most of the windows in the lofty pile of buildings in which the Local Government Board is installed are broken. The high wooden hoarding which fenced off the vacant piece of land adjoining the police-station is blown down. The actual spot where the explosion occurred is the window immediately adjoining the entrance to the Local Government Board Office, and the sixth from Parliament-street.

The explosion took place almost immediately opposite the end of King-street. The wall of the police-station, which is fortunately unpierced by windows, stopped the stones which were blown through the wooden fencing, and prevented any serious damage. A heavy stone, said to weigh two hundredweight, struck the brick wall with such force as to knock a hole through it, but its force being spent it fell back without penetrating to the other side. At the bottom of the wall several fragments of the balustrade are lying with other fragments of broken stones. Being round, they somewhat resemble stone cannon-balls. Ten of the stone pillars supporting the balustrade in front of the window of the room wrecked by the explosion were blown to pieces, and the pediment upon which they stood was hurled across the street.

In Delahay-street the force of the explosion is very apparent. The offices of Sir Francis Reilly, K.C.M.G., have their windows blown in, and the sashes of some of the upper rooms are destroyed. The windows in the offices of Mr. Brunel Mr. Barry and Mr. Brereton, though of plate glass, have been destroyed, but at the adjoining offices of the Society for the Propagation of the Gospel in Foreign Parts there is little damage done.

In King-street there are over ninety windows more or less smashed, the great majority being completely blown out. Of the windows in that part of Parliament-street which adjoins the Post-office all the glass has shared the same fate ; while in the main portion of the street, the greatest destruction has occurred at the premises of Messrs. Waterlow and Sons and the Messrs. Mitchell. These establishments present a very wrecked appearance. At the Whitehall Club almost every window is gone, both in Derby-street and Parliament-street. The next two houses have escaped, but beyond them there are several windows smashed here and there. Inside this enclosure men have been busy for some time in sweeping up the shattered glass which strews the whole of the roadway. Members of Parliament and a great many ladies have been allowed to pass into this enclosure to view the havoc made by the explosion.

The chief force of the explosion seems to have spent itself upon the stone balustrade in front of the window in the basement room No. 8, which has been completely wrecked. It has been blown to pieces. The window-sill has disappeared, but the left jamb of the window has been blown away, leaving a jagged edge of broken stone. The effect of the explosion on the building will be best understood by a glance at the accompanying rough sketch of the window as it now is and the companion window adjoining, which it resembled before the explosion occurred.

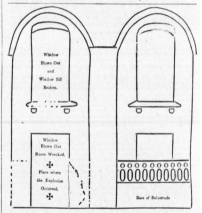

The broken lines show the rough outline of the jamb of the window and other places which bore the brunt of the explosion. The whole balustrade is blown clean away. The explosive—which could not have been gunpowder, for there are none of the traces left by that explosive, nor gas, which is equally out of the question—seems to have been dropped within the balustrade and the window. The theory that it was placed in the sub-basement or cellar under room No. 8 is untenable. No damage has been done to the brick wall supporting the floor, and the floor itself has suffered only in one place, a broad strip being torn up in the centre of the room, stretching from the fireplace to the opposite wall. Any explosive powerful enough to smash and pulverize the solid blocks of Portland stone, some of which twenty inches thick form the base of the balustrade, would have done much more damage to the brick supports of the floor itself if it had been fired from the sub-basement. The brunt of the explosion seems to have been borne by the balustrade, its base, and the jamb of the window, and this points to the infernal machine having been dropped over the balustrade by a passer-by. No one was seen to do it, but the street is dark and unfrequented, and a package of dynamite or of panclastite might easily have been placed there without attracting any attention.

The room that has suffered most from the explosion is a small room usually occupied by clerks, known as No. 8 in the basement story. It is about 18 or 20 feet square, and is entered by two doors lighted by one window, and heated by an ordinary fireplace. When the writers left it last night, one press containing packets of envelopes addressed to urban and rural sanitary authorities, ran the whole length of the right wall, and a desk ran down the middle. There were several chairs, stools, and the usual furniture of an office. The floor was of ordinary flooring deals covered with oilcloth, the roof was vaulted, crossed with iron girders, and cemented. All the contents of the room have been blown into a chaotic mass of wreck and rubbish. A great gulf yawns in the centre of the room, while on the floor that yet remains intact lies heaped a mass of broken furniture, mixed with fragment of oil-cloth, and half buried beneath a great heap of envelopes. A stray book was lying open here and there, and a pair of slippers lay near the fireplace. The roof and the sides of the room were indented as if they had been made the target for innumerable pistol-shots. The plaster cornice was crushed. A piece of timber, hanging loosely by one end, stretched downward from the roof into the room, and everything—timber, envelopes,

An early attempt at pictorial representation of the news in the
Pall Mall Gazette. (See page 26)

THE
PALL MALL GAZETTE
An Evening Newspaper and Review.

No. 5808.—Vol. XXXVIII.　　　*TUESDAY, OCTOBER 16, 1883.*　　　*Price One Penny.*

IS IT NOT TIME?

"THE Bitter Cry of Outcast London" is the striking title of a small pamphlet the contents of which we condense in another page. If this were the first time that this wail of hopeless misery had sounded on our ears the matter would have been less serious. It is because we have heard it so often that the case is so desperate. The exceeding bitter cry of the disinherited has come to be as familiar in the ears of men as the dull roar of the streets or as the moaning of the wind through the trees. And so it rises unceasing, year in and year out, and we are too busy or too idle, too indifferent or too selfish, to spare it a thought. Only now and then, on rare occasions such as the present, when some clear voice is heard giving more articulate utterance to the miseries of miserable men, do we pause in the regular routine of our daily duties and shudder as we realize for one brief moment what life means to the inmates of the slums. But one of the grimmest social problems of our time should be sternly faced, not with a view to the generation of profitless emotion, but with a view to its solution.

Is it not time? There is, it is true, an audacity in the mere suggestion that the problem is not insoluble that is enough to take away the breath. But can nothing be done to abate the horrors of the slums? If, after full and exhaustive consideration, we come to the deliberate conclusion that nothing can be done, and that it is the inevitable and inexorable destiny of thousands of Englishmen to be brutalized into worse than beasts by the conditions of their environment: so be it. But if, on the contrary, we are unable to believe that this "awful slough" which engulfs the manhood and womanhood of generation after generation is incapable of removal; and if the heart and intellect of mankind alike revolt against the fatalism of despair, then indeed it is time and high time that the question of the homes of the poor is faced in no mere dilettante spirit, but with a resolute determination to make an end of the crying scandal of our age. It is true that that is much easier said than done. But at present who can even be got to say it, much less to set about the doing of it? Yet it is the one great domestic problem which the religion, the humanity, and the statesmanship of England are imperatively summoned to solve.

What the evil is every one knows. It is the excessive over-crowding of enormous multitudes of the very poor in pestilential rookeries where it is a matter of physical impossibility to live a human life. Men, women, and children are herded together in filthy styes ; there is a family in every room ; morality is impossible, and indeed has ceased to exist ; and in these reeking tenements are bred the stunted, squalid savages of civilization. The tentative attempts hitherto made to deal with this foul ulcer of London have only intensified the evil. Some rookeries have been pulled down, but those that are left are more crowded than ever. The new dwellings are filled with a better class, and, as the author of the pamphlet remarks, "The outcasts are driven " to huddle more closely together in the few loathsome places " still left to them." These fever dens are said to be the best-paying property in London, and owners who, if justice were done, would be on the treadmill, are drawing from 50 to 60 per cent. on investments in tenement property in the slums. " Entire courts are filled with thieves, prostitutes, and liberated " convicts. In one street are thirty-five houses, thirty-two of which " are known to be houses of ill-fame. In another district are forty- " three of these houses and 428 fallen women and girls, many of " them not more than twelve years of age." The grim Florentine might have added to the horrors of his vision of hell by a sojourn in a London slum. For in his Inferno the damned at least did not feed. With us they do. Every year sees an addition to the long roll of the new born lost. Born in the fetid atmosphere of a crowded cellar, suckled on gin, and cradled in the gutter, they never have a chance. When they are five or six they are driven into the public school to infect it with the moral miasma of their lairs. Many are lucky enough to die, others live on, in turn to propagate their kind, and to hand down to another gene-ration the curse which never leaves them from the cradle to the grave. All this seething mass of misery and vice exists at our doors. It is getting no better, it is rather getting worse. Is anything to be done?

What a satire it is upon our Christianity and our civilization, that the existence of these colonies of heathens and savages in the heart of our capital should attract so little attention. It is no better than a ghastly mockery—theologians might use a stronger word—to call by the name of One who came to seek and to save that which was lost those churches which in the midst of lost multitudes either slumber in apathy or display a fitful interest in a chasuble. Why all this apparatus of temples and meeting-houses to save men from perdition in the world which is to come, while never a helping hand is stretched out to save them from the Inferno of their present life. Is it not time that the churches, forgetting for a moment their wranglings about the infinitely little or the infinitely obscure, should concentrate all their energies on a united effort to break this terrible perpetuity of perdition, and to rescue some at least of those for whom they profess to believe their Founder came to die?

It is unfair to lay all the blame on the churches. They have failed, it is true. No one goes to church or chapel in the slums. Whole streets full of people live and die without ever having entered a place of worship. But it is unjust to ignore the fact that ⸢ most of those who have flung themselves bravely into this Malebolgic pool of London's misery are inspired by the sacred compassion which has ever been one of the most potent influences of the Christian Church. And outside the Churches there are sufficient men, and more than sufficient means, to solve this problem. Here, if anywhere, is a question demanding the most anxious consideration—a huge cancer eating into the very heart of the realm—and yet, with a few notable exceptions, who spares it a thought? Those who have no concern about another life have all their energies at command for the amelioration of this —but what is being done? What rich man except the American PEABODY leaves his fortune to rehouse the poor? How many thinkers dedicate themselves to an exhaustive study of the method of ameliorating the condition of the homeless? Where is the leader of men who will preach a new crusade against the crying evil of our times? As for the politicians, they make no sign. We do not suggest that the housing of the poor should be made a party question, but is it not time that all those who are really concerned about the welfare of their fellows should attempt at least to bring the subject to the front? If the few—and there are several—who have bestowed long and anxious thought upon this question were to lay their matured convictions before the public, who knows but that at last some clear, practical agreement might be reached which, when once plainly set before the nation, might result in united and energetic action for the abatement of this great evil? Even if it should not be successful, is it not high time to make the attempt?

ALPINE PHENOMENA.

THE threat of winter came early to the Alps this year. On the morning of the 6th of September snow, not deep, but uniformly spread, covered everything. It was soon, however, disposed of by a powerful sun. We had afterwards, oft repeated, the calm glory of the sky and mountain, in the early morning, followed by serenity at night. During the day the firmament was usually chequered with clouds, lifted by the sun's heat from the humid earth. At this season of the year they frequently form like hoods around the mountain heads. At times they detach themselves, and, retaining the shape of the "block" on which they were formed, sail away through the azure. The clouds thus produced are usually very lustrous and fine-grained. Sometimes they hang motionless for hours over the mountains. Their feathery edges resembling plumage, a trifling supplementary act of the imagination gives them the form of "angels sleeping on the wing." One rare and beautiful cloud effect claims a passing notice here. Shake common housemaid's dust over a plate of glass, and look through the glass at a candle ; you see n' colour. But shake over the glass a dust composed of the spores o lycopodium, which are all of the same size ; on looking at the candle through such dust rich rings of colour are seen to surround the flame. When, instead of a candle, the electric light is looked at

The leader which launched Stead's first major crusade, the "Bitter Cry" campaign. (See page 50)

TOO LATE!

KHARTOUM CAPTURED BY THE MAHDI.

THE FATE OF GENERAL GORDON UNKNOWN.

SIR CHARLES WILSON TWO DAYS TOO LATE.

THE STEAMERS WRECKED IN THE NILE.

FOURTH EDITION.

We regret to have to announce that the worst has happened in the Soudan. Khartoum has fallen into the hands of the Mahdi ; and of the fate of its brave commander nothing is at present known.

Sir Charles Wilson, with a picked party, left Metammeh for Khartoum in Gordon's three steamers on January 24th, and arrived before the city only to discover that it had fallen into the hands of the Mahdi two days before their arrival.

As Sir Charles Wilson left Metammeh on the 24th and Khartoum can be reached in thirty-six hours by water, it would appear that Khartoum must have fallen into the hands of the enemy—whether by treachery or by open assault we have not yet been able to ascertain—about the day after General Gordon's steamers were making the reconnaissance at Shendy.

Sir Charles Wilson found Khartoum held by an enormous number of the Arabs, whose heavy fire rendered it impossible for the steamers to approach the city.

He was thus unable to obtain any news concerning the fate of General Gordon.

On his return down the river bearing this melancholy intelligence, two of his steamers were stranded on an island, where Sir Charles Wilson, with his crew and their small escort were left entrenched but exposed to the attacks of the enemy on either side.

Colonel Stuart Wortley brought the intelligence to Meta mmeh, when a steamer was at once detached to bring away Sir Charles Wilson and his gallant comrades.

No official confirmation of this intelligence has been received, but from the reticence of the departments to whom we have communicated the information we have received we have no reason to doubt that it is substantially correct.

No Ministers are at present in town except Sir Charles Dilke and Mr. Chamberlain, but a Cabinet meeting will probably be held to-night to decide upon the course to be adopted.

The position of General Stewart at Goubat is said to be very strong, and the two steamers still remaining will enable his force to supply their camels with forage from the river banks.

LORD WOLSELEY'S TELEGRAM.

We have received the following from the War Office :—

Telegrams have been received at the War Office from Lord Wolseley announcing the fall of Khartoum on the 26th of January :—

Sir C. Wilson arrived there on the 28th, to find the place in the hands of the enemy. He returned under a heavy fire from the river banks.

The steamers in which he returned were wrecked some miles below the Shabluka Cataract The whole party were saved and landed on an island, where they are in safety. A steamer had gone to fetch them.

The fate of Gordon is uncertain.

Lord Wolseley reports that Sir H. Stewart is doing well, and that nearly all the wounded were being brought to Gakdul.

The Central News says :—The Government has received a long despatch from Lord Wolseley which it is believed contains the official confirmation from Sir Charles Wilson of the fall of Khartoum. There is no longer any doubt that the Mahdi holds the town of Khartoum, but hopes are entertained that General Gordon may still be safe in the citadel, and able there to hold his own against the rebel attacks. It is believed he has his provisions stored there as well as ammunition, and it is known that he has small pieces of artillery there.

DIARY OF GORDON'S MISSION AND THE RELIEF EXPEDITION.

General Gordon left London for Khartoum on the 18th of January, 1884. On the 9th of January Colonel Coetlgon telegraphed from Khartoum to the Khedive strongly urging an immediate withdrawal from Khartoum to the Khedive. He said that one-third of the garrison was unreliable, and "even if were twice as strong as it is it would not hold Khartoum against the whole country." On the 5th of January, 1884, General Gordon had accepted a commission from the King of the Belgians to proceed to the Congo. On the 8th of January, our representative had an interview with Gordon at Southampton. On the following day the account of that interview appeared in the *Pall Mall Gazette*. It was strongly urged that Gordon should be sent out with *carte blanche* to do the best tha

he could. This view was strongly supported by the press, irrespective of party, and the Government finally determined to accept the suggestion. On the 13th he arrived in town rom Southampton and had an interview with Lord Wolseley at the War Office, and expressed his confidence that the Soudanese difficulties could be settled. The following is a diary of the mission :—

1884.

Jan. 18.—Gordon left Charing-cross, at 8 P.M.
Jan. 24.—Arrived at Port Said.
Jan. 25.—Arrived at Cairo.
Jan. 27.—Gordon and Stewart left for Khartoum.
Feb. 2.—Gordon arrived at Korosko and entered Desert.
Feb. 4.—Massacre of Baker Pasha's force at El Teb, near Tokar.
Feb. 9.—Gordon arrived at Berber.
Feb. 13.—Gordon left Berber.
Feb. 18.—Arrived at Khartoum. Issued proclamation to inhabitants remitting taxation and sanctioning slave trade.
Feb. 29.—Battle of El Teb.
March 7.—Gordon proposed that Zebehr should be sent to Khartoum to succeed him.
March 13.—Defeat of Osman Digna at Tamai.
March 16.—Defeat of Gordon at Halfiheh.
March 21.—Fighting reported at Khartoum ; relief of the garrison of Halfiheh by Gordon.
March 24.—Whole country south of Berber in a state of revolution ; Khartoum invested.
April 9.—News received from Gordon dated March 30. From 24th to end of month Gordon had frequent successful engagements with the enemy.
April 16.—Zebehr at Cairo received Gordon's appointment as Assistant-Governor of the Soudan, which Zebehr declines.
April 23.—Berber invested.
May 5.—Blue-book issued showing that on April 16 Gordon telegraphed to Sir E. Baring as follows :—" As far as I understand the situation is this: You state your intention of not sending any relief up here or to Berber, and you refuse me Zebehr. I consider myself free to act according to circumstances. I shall hold on here as long as I can, and if I can suppress the rebellion I shall do so. If I cannot I shall return to the Equator, and leave you the indelible disgrace of abandoning the garrisons of Senaar, Kassala, Berber, and Dongola, with the certainty that you will eventually be compelled to smash up the Mahdi under great difficulties if you would retain peace in Egypt.
May 9.—News received that Gordon had defeated rebels on White Nile.
May 10.—British military authorities in Cairo ordered to prepare for the despatch in October of an expeditionary force for the relief of Gordon. Twelve thousand camels to be purchased. Active war preparations in England.
June 10.—News received of fall of Berber and massacre of garrison ; 3,500 persons killed.
July 20.—General Gordon had written to Mudir of Dongola dated June 22. Gordon said he had 8,000 men with him at Khartoum, and asked if reinforcements were coming.
July 23.—Mudir of Dongola defeats 5,000 rebels near Debbah.
August 5.—Credit vote for expedition for £300,000 passed in Commons.
Aug. 7.—News received that Gordon, Stewart, and Mr. Power were all well, and on 29th that he had provisions for four months.
Aug. 10.—Gordon gains victory, in which 1,800 rebels were killed.
Aug. 14.—Nile route adopted.
Aug. 28.—Lord Wolseley appointed.
Sept. 10.—Lord Wolseley arrives at Cairo.
Sept. 12.—News that Gordon had attacked Berber ; also report that he had been actively engaged on the river south of Khartoum, and that he had captured two islands from the rebels.
Sept. 17.—Despatch received from Gordon at Khartoum, dated August 26, in which he says :—" I am awaiting arrival of British troops in order to evacuate garrison. Send me Zebehr. I shall surrender the Soudan to the Sultan as soon as 200,000 Turkish troops have arrived. If the rebels kill the Egyptians you will be answerable for their blood.
Sept. 19.—Telegrams arrive from Gordon complaining of slackness of expedition, rebels increasing.
Oct. 4.—Lord Wolseley arrives at Wady Halfa.
Oct. 6.—Wreck and massacre of Colonel Stewart and party near Berber.
Oct. 17.—Bombardment of Metammeh by Gordon, with three steamers and eighteen nuggars.
Nov. 2.—At Dongola.—1st battalion South Staffordshire embark on 5th. Practically commencement of advance.
Nov. 8.—Letter received from General Gordon, confirming report of Colonel Stewart's death, and saying he has sufficient provisions to hold out till expedition arrives.
Nov. 25.—Guards camel corps arrive at Handak.
Nov. 28.—Naval brigade formed under Lord Charles Beresford.
Dec. 12.—Headquarters transferred to Ambukol. Sir Herbert Stewart proceeds to Korti with mounted infantry and Guards camel corps.
Dec. 15.—Sir Herbert Stewart arrives at Korti.
Dec. 16.—Lord Wolseley arrives at Korti.
Dec. 29.—General Stewart ordered to take the desert route to Metammeh. General Earle to go up the Nile.
Dec. 30.—Departure of General Stewart for Metammeh.

1885.

Jan. 1.—Message from Gordon—" Khartoum all right, December 14. C. G. Gordon."
Jan. 2.—First portion of Stewart's force arrived at Gakdul.
Jan. 14.—Advance from Gakdul for Metammeh.
Jan. 17.—Attacks the Mahdi's forces at Abu Klea Wells, gaining a victory.
Jan. 18.—Reported capture of Omdurman by the Mahdi.
Jan. 19.—General Stewart again attacked by the Mahdi's forces at Gubat, when enemy were once more defeated. General Stewart wounded.
Jan. 20.—Established on the banks of the Nile at Gubat.
Jan. 21.—Reconnaissance in force of Metammeh, assisted by four steamers sent down by General Gordon, with message dated December 29, " Khartoum all right, could hold out for years."
Jan. 22.—Reconnaissance on Shendy.
Jan. 24.—Sir C. Wilson left for Khartoum with two steamers and a detachment of the Sussex Regiment.

The headline display announcing the fall of Khartoum.
(See pages 77–78)

THE
PALL MALL GAZETTE
An Evening Newspaper and Review.

No. 6336.—Vol. XLII.   MONDAY, JULY 6, 1885.   Price One Penny.

"WE BID YOU BE OF HOPE."

THE Report of our Secret Commission will be read to-day with a shuddering horror that will thrill throughout the world. After this awful picture of the crimes at present committed as it were under the very ægis of the law has been fully unfolded before the eyes of the public, we need not doubt that the House of Commons will find time to raise the age during which English girls are protected from inexpiable wrong. The evidence which we shall publish this week leaves no room for doubt—first, as to the reality of the crimes against which the Amendment Bill is directed, and, secondly, as to the efficacy of the protection extended by raising the age of consent. When the report is published, the case for the bill will be complete, and we do not believe that members on the eve of a general election will refuse to consider the bill protecting the daughters of the poor, which even the House of Lords has in three consecutive years declared to be imperatively necessary.

This, however, is but one, and that one of the smallest, of the considerations which justify the publication of the Report. The good it will do is manifest. These revelations, which we begin to publish to-day, cannot fail to touch the heart and rouse the conscience of the English people. Terrible as is the exposure, the very horror of it is an inspiration. It speaks not of leaden despair, but with a joyful promise of better things to come. *Wir heissen euch hoffen!* "We bid you be of hope," CARLYLE'S last message to his country, the rhythmic word with which GOETHE closes his modern psalm—that is what we have to repeat to-day, for assuredly these horrors, like others against which the conscience of mankind has revolted, are not eternal. "Am I my sister's keeper?" that paraphrase of the excuse of CAIN, will not dull the fierce smart of pain which will be felt by every decent man who learns the kind of atrocities which are being perpetrated in cool blood in the very shadow of our churches and within a stone's throw of our courts. It is a veritable slave trade that is going on around us; but, as it takes place in the heart of London, it is a scandal—an outrage on public morality—even to allude to it. We have kept silence far too long. There are a few devoted workers who have been labouring for years endeavouring to save those who might well address GORDON'S homely reproach to the "majority of us: "While you are eating and drinking and "resting on good beds, we, and those with me, are watching by night and by day"—working against this great wrong—happy, indeed, if they escaped obloquy and abuse for endeavouring to remind us of our duty. No longer will good men be able with easy conscience to join in that indignant "Hush!" by which the evil-doers have hitherto silenced every attempt to make articulate the smothered wail that rises unceasing from the woeful under-world. There is now an end to that conspiracy of silence by which, after every inquiry, "the door was each time quickly closed upon "the question, as the stone lid used to be shut down, in the "Campo Santo of Naples, upon the mass of human corpses that "lay festering beneath." That "stone lid" is raised now, never again, we may hope, to be closed until something has been done. Under the ruthless compulsion of publicity even those but indifferent honest will do more good than many of the most virtuous when the evil could be hidden out of sight.

That much may be done, we have good ground for hoping, if only because so little has hitherto been attempted. A dull despair has unnerved the hearts of those who face this monstrous evil, and good men have sorrowfully turned to other fields where their exertions might expect a better return. But the magnitude of this misery ought to lead to the redoubling, not to the benumbing of our exertions. No one can say how much suffering and wrong is irremediable until the whole of the moral and religious forces of the country are brought to bear upon it. Yet, in dealing with this subject, the forces upon which we rely in dealing with other evils are almost all paralysed. The Home, the School, the Church, the Press are silent. The law is actually accessory to crime. Parents culpably neglect even to warn their children of the existence of dangers of which many learn the first time when they have become their prey. The Press, which reports verbatim all the scabrous details of the divorce courts, recoils in pious horror from the duty of shedding a flood of light upon these dark places, which indeed are full of the habitations of cruelty. But the failure of the Churches is, perhaps, the most conspicuous and the most complete. CHRIST'S mission was to restore man to a semblance of the Divine. The Child-Prostitute of our day is the image into which, with the tacit acquiescence of those who call themselves by His name, men have moulded the form once fashioned in the likeness of GOD.

If Chivalry is extinct and Christianity is effete, there is still another great enthusiasm to which we may with confidence appeal. The future belongs to the combined forces of Democracy and Socialism, which when united are irresistible. Divided on many points they will combine in protesting against the continued immolation of the daughters of the people as a sacrifice to the vices of the rich. Of the two, it is Socialism which will find the most powerful stimulus in this revelation of the extent to which under our present social system the wealthy are able to exercise all the worst abuses of power which disgraced the feudalism of the Middle Ages. Wealth is power, Poverty is weakness. The abuse of power leads directly to its destruction, and in all the annals of crime can there be found 'a more shameful abuse of the power of wealth than that by which in this nineteenth century of Christian civilization princes and dukes, and ministers and judges, and the rich of all classes, are purchasing for damnation, temporal if not eternal, the as yet uncorrupted daughters of the poor? It will be said they assent to their corruption. So did the female serfs from whom the seigneur exacted the *jus prima noctis*. And do our wealthy think that the assent wrung by wealth from poverty to its own undoing will avert the vengeance and the doom?

If people can only be got to think seriously about this matter progress will be made in the right direction. Evils once as universal and apparently inevitable as prostitution have disappeared. Vices almost universal are now regarded with shuddering horror by the least moral of men. Slavery has gone. A slave trader is treated as *hostis humani generis*. Piracy has disappeared. Intestine war is now almost unknown. Torture has been abolished. May we not hope, therefore, that if we try to do our duty to our sisters and to ourselves, we may greatly reduce, even although we never entirely extirpate, the plague of prostitution? For let us remember that—

> Every hope which rises and grows broad
> In the world's heart, by ordered impulse streams
> From the great heart of GOD.

And if that ideal seems too blinding bright for human eyes, we can at least do much to save the innocent victims who unwillingly are swept into the maelstrom of vice. And who is there among us bearing the name of man who will dare to sit down any longer with folded hands in the presence of so great a wrong?

THE MAIDEN TRIBUTE OF MODERN BABYLON.—I.

THE REPORT OF OUR SECRET COMMISSION.

IN ancient times, if we may believe the myths of Hellas, Athens, after a disastrous campaign, was compelled by her conqueror to send once every nine years a tribute to Crete of seven youths and seven maidens. The doomed fourteen, who were selected by lot amid the lamentations of the citizens, returned no more. The vessel that bore them to Crete unfurled black sails as the symbol of despair, and on arrival her passengers were flung into the famous Labyrinth of Dædalus, there to wander about blindly until such time as they were devoured by the Minotaur, a frightful monster, half man, half bull, the foul product of an unnatural lust. "The "Those who entered it could never find their way out again. If they "hurried from one to another of the numberless rooms looking for "the entrance door, it was all in vain. They only became more hopelessly "lost in the bewildering labyrinth, until at last they were devoured by "the Minotaur." Twice at each ninth year the Athenians paid the maiden tribute to King Minos, lamenting sorely the dire necessity of bowing to his iron law. When the third tribute came to be exacted, the distress of the city of the Violet Crown was insupportable. From the King's palace to the peasant's hamlet, everywhere were heard cries and groans and the choking sob of despair, until the whole air seemed to vibrate with the sorrow of an unutterable anguish. Then it was that the hero Theseus volunteered to be offered up among those who drew the black balls from the brazen urn of destiny, and the story of his self-sacrifice, his victory, and his triumphant return, is among the most familiar of the tales which since the childhood of the world have kindled

The opening salvo in Stead's most sensational crusade, "The Maiden Tribute of Modern Babylon." (See page 132)

The mob outside the *Pall Mall Gazette* office on July 8, 1885—the third day of the "Maiden Tribute" crusade. (See page 140)

Stead in his convict uniform, which he donned annually on the
anniversary of his imprisonment. (See page 183)

THE
PALL MALL GAZETTE

An Evening Newspaper and Review.

No. 7255.—Vol. XLVII.   *MONDAY, JUNE* 18, 1888.   *Price One Penny.*

NOTICE.

The special articles on "WAR OR PEACE" which we begin to publish to-day will be read at the present crisis in European history with universal interest. It has for some time been patent to close observers that the centre of power in Europe has been shifting to St. Petersburg. The accession to the German throne of a young and untried ruler accentuates the change, and it is more than ever upon St. Petersburg that the issue of "War or Peace" in July depends. In his investigations directed to solving that issue, our Special Commissioner has had altogether unique opportunities of learning "the best that is known and thought" by the best authorities. The series of articles in which he embodies his conclusions will, therefore, be read with all the living interest that is always excited by stories of real life, and with more than all the anxiety, in proportion as the stage is more wide and the issue more important.

BLOWN INTO AIR.

LIBERAL Unionism in Scotland is dead—blown into air. West Edinburgh scotched the animal. Ayr has killed it. This moral of the Ayr election is writ so large in the stubborn facts and figures of the case that the Unionist apologists are driven either to turn the facts inside out or to add up the figures wrong. Thus, the *Times* actually confuses the Mr. SINCLAIR who has won now with the Mr. SINCLAIR who lost in 1886. "Mr. SINCLAIR," it says," has assiduously nursed the constituency for some time past, and, *although he had no chance against* Mr. CAMPBELL, he had no doubt made himself too strong to be beaten by any but a good local candidate, at all events at a by election" Mr. SINCLAIR is not a local man at all; he is a Free Kirk minister from Grangemouth, and no connection whatever with the Mr.—or rather Captain—SINCLAIR who stood last time. Then there is the *Standard*, which says that the Unionists lost because Liberals who abstained from voting in 1886 now went to the poll—an explanation which calmly ignores the fact that not only did the Liberals poll more votes than in 1886, but the Unionists 400 less. But "the demon of inaccuracy" haunts the Unionist journals even when they try to be fair, and the *Observer* puts the Liberal increase at 100 above its correct figure. "No conclusions," we are told, " can be drawn from by-elections." Certainly not, if you do not know your facts, or cannot correctly add your figures. Persons who make twice two amount to five cannot draw any conclusions in mathematics; nor those who make black white, in optics. But the explanations of the defeated side are merely childish folly—of no interest to sensible folk, except as emphasizing the significance of the victory. What sensible and scientific persons do is to look at the facts, and the simple fact is this, that the largest Unionist majority in Scotland has been clean wiped out. The following are the seventeen seats in Scotland carried by Liberal Unionists at the last election, the figures giving the majorities :—

Ayr Group	1,175	Greenock		697
Ayrshire, North	Unopposed	Inverness Group		273
„ South	5	Inverness-shire		Unopposed
Dumfries-shire	854	Lanarkshire, Partick		801
Edinburgh, West	650	Peebles		50
Falkirk Group	20	Perth, West		940
Forfarshire	407	Roxburgh		428
Glasgow, Rollox	119	St. Andrews		416
„ Tradeston	704			

Of these seventeen seats, West Edinburgh has been won already; and now Ayr Burghs—with one of the smallest of the electorates but with far the largest Unionist majority—has gone too. That means that, with the possible exception of the two uncontested seats, there is not a single Liberal Unionist in Scotland who will hold his own next time, and who would not be turned out by his constituents to morrow if they had the chance. The parliamentary application of this electoral moral is very clear. Already the Government was one which was in on false pretences. To-day it is one whose false pretences have been found out and repudiated by the country. It is as such that the Opposition must deal with it—showing it no respect, and granting it such respite only as may be necessary to give it time to finish working out its own undoing.

A GREAT VIOLINIST "AT HOME."

He is *chez lui*, when in London, at the snug and quiet Hôtel Dieudonné, in Ryder-street, St. James's. But he is quite as much "at home" in Paris, St. Petersburg, Moscow, Berlin, Vienna, Madrid, or any other city in Europe. There are three persons living, and only three, who can set foot in almost any city in the world, announce a concert, and be certain of drawing a full house. They are Patti, Rubinstein, and Sarasate. Sarasate has been doing this in London during the brilliant little season which he has just brought to a close. He will be doing it by and bye in his native town of Pamplona, in Spain. And when he takes up the bow again, after his long summer holiday, he will do the same thing in whatever city of France, Germany, or Russia it may please him to commence afresh. And it is all so easy to him ! He never toils, and he never needs to exert himself. What is glibly and often rather absurdly talked of as the "natural gift" of the artist, is his indeed. It is extraordinary, but it is true, that from one year's end to the other

SENOR SARASATE.

WAR OR PEACE ?

(FROM OUR SPECIAL COMMISSIONER IN RUSSIA.)

I.—AT COUNT TOLSTOI'S, JASNAIA, PAULIANA.

I AM in the heart of Russia. It is more than a month since I crossed the frontier at Wirballen, and as yet I have not ventured to write more than a passing sentence on the primary subject of my visit. When I left London Lord Wolseley told me that my first duty would be to discover whether the Cossacks would be in Bucharest in May. May has come and gone, and never a Cossack has been moved towards the Roumanian frontier. I have spent three weeks in the capital of the Empire which in London seems to be regarded as the disturbing centre of European tranquillity, seeing every one who was likely to be able or willing to enlighten me as to the probable course of events. I have visited Moscow, and now I have retired to the country seat of Count Leon Tolstoi, far from the hubbub and turmoil of the great cities, to write at the desk of the author of " War and Peace" the net result of my observations as to the chances of War or Peace.

COUNT TOLSTOI.

I have been exceptionally favoured in the opportunities alike of collecting information and of summing up the net result of my investigation. I am at a loss to express my sense of the cordial kindness with which I have been welcomed everywhere. From the highest to the lowest I have to acknowledge gratefully the same simple, hearty friendliness which has made my stay in this country a period of intense and almost unmingled enjoyment. And now, after living as it were in oxygen for a month

in St. Petersburg and Moscow—after spending night and day in the midst of the immense stimulus that is afforded by a perpetual recurrence of new scenes and the incessant intercourse with the ablest and most interesting men and women who are gathered together in the capital of a great Empire—I have fled away into a secret place apart, to write down in the midst of the solitude and tranquillity of nature, far from the hum and stir of cities, the judgment which I have formed on all I have seen and heard. Here we are in the full splendour of the early summer. All day long the air is tremulous with the song of larks, and at night, when the stars begin to glisten and glitter in the beautiful blue of the sky after the gloaming, the nightingales fill the woods with plaintive music. The lilacs are in full bloom, and the yellow acacia, the plantations are fragrant with the heavy scent of the lily of the valley, which grows everywhere wild among the trees. Great silver birches, with trembling leaves, bend and bow in the pleasant wind, and down the long avenue of elms you catch glimpses of the ponds wherein the frogs keep up that curious chorus so strange to English ears. Everywhere the ground is covered with vegetation, green and rank. Nature overflows with verdure, and the bees in the acacias keep up a

The display of Stead's "War or Peace?" article, which brought on a crisis at the *PMG*. (See page 241)

In addition to the leader and follower, three and one-half pages of Thursday's issue were devoted to "Public Feeling on the Subject" —extracts from letters from peers, M.P.'s, public men, ordinary citizens, and clergy, along with the comments of some religious and provincial journals. Most of the published extracts praised the *PMG* venture, but there were nine letters of protest, which Stead claimed represented all the signed letters received with three exceptions: one from W. H. Smith, another from a London correspondent, and a third from a Liberal M.P. "whose name out of charity and mercy we withhold." Other articles told of the prosecution by the City of London of *PMG* vendors, who were freed on four pounds bail, and described the riotous scene outside the office under the heading "The Siege of Northumberland Street." The previous day's apology to disappointed readers was repeated, as all editions had again been sold out.

Even while these stories were coming off the presses, Wednesday's mob violence was being reenacted in front of the *PMG* office. Once more the police responded tardily and in insufficient numbers. The crush was so great that for three hours the Thursday issue was virtually suppressed, and again damage was done to the building. That afternoon during the question period in Commons the Home Secretary was asked if he knew that the street and footpaths leading to the *Pall Mall Gazette* offices were blocked, and whether he had made any arrangements for dispersing the crowd and securing "safe and adequate access." Cross replied that the police had their customary instructions to keep streets clear. Later that evening the Criminal Law Amendment Bill came up again for the second reading, which had been adjourned in May. Perhaps because the *PMG* had put him on the defensive, Cross opened by stating that the government intended to take up the bill at the earliest possible time and push for its enactment. After a brief debate, during which Samuel Morley praised the character of Stead—whom he did not know personally at that time—the bill easily passed its second reading.[7]

In the leader for Friday, July 10, "Of Good Cheer Indeed," Stead gloried in the storm he had raised and declared that public opinion was on his side. He welcomed the word that Samuel Morley and Cardinal Manning had agreed to sit on the committee which he had proposed to investigate the truth of his disclosures and prom-

7. *Hansard's Parliamentary Debates*, 3d ser., vol. 299 (1885): pp. 126, 197-211.

ised that the "Maiden Tribute" series would be vindicated as completely as "The Truth about the Navy." The leader also admonished the police for their failure to cope with the previous day's
demonstration, and hoped they would have a strong enough force
on hand to permit the final "Maiden Tribute" report to be circulated "without having our office taken by storm by those who
yesterday were shot headlong through windows with reckless disregard of the safety of life or limb." The final report of the commission, which ran as a follower of over five pages on Friday,
included Stead's strongest attack yet on the police. It denounced
certain aspects of the Criminal Law Amendment Bill as it now
stood, which, according to Stead, were designed less to raise the
age of consent and check vice than to increase "the arbitrary
power of the police in the streets." Their power was already ample,
not only to check vice, "but also for the purpose of levying blackmail upon unfortunates." Stead repeated the point made earlier
that most prostitutes felt it was necessary to make payments to
police to avoid arrest and that brothels paid as much as fifteen
hundred pounds per annum in police allowances. He was careful
to state that there were many on the police force who were not
guilty of such practices, but cited several examples of "The Black
Sheep of the Flock." Among these was one officer, recently in a
high position on the Metropolitan police, who was guilty of incest
with his daughter, of using police intimidation to prevent the girl
from exposing him, and of persecuting his daughter's fiancé. The
report conceded that the story might not be true, but offered to
turn over the name of the man to the Home Secretary. "We publish
it merely in order to challenge the most searching inquiry, and if
possible, to secure its immediate contradiction." [8] Stead ridiculed
the argument that if the criminal activities described in the report
had really been taking place, the police would have discovered
them; during his own apparently evil transactions with procuresses,
which were being carried on even after the "Maiden Tribute"
series had begun, he was never in any way molested by the law.

Returning to his old theme of the "responsibility of the disolute
rich for the ruin of the daughters of the poor," he indicted "certain
great drapery and millinery establishments" wherein hundreds of

8. This sordid story might have been the one with which Stead had
promised on the previous day to "astound the world." But it provides another
example of a sensational revelation which had no direct bearing on the objective of the crusade.

thousands of girls were ruined yearly (Stead was never guilty of excessive caution in his estimates); a theater at which, so he had heard, "no girl ever kept her virtue more than three months"; and other business houses which were "little better than horrible ante-chambers to the brothel," such as employment agencies and servant registries. He added that "London, say those who are engaged in the white slave trade, is the greatest market of human flesh in the whole world." One other recurring theme in the report—one which again offended some Victorian sensibilities—was Stead's obvious sympathy for the prostitutes themselves. While admitting that there were exceptions, he claimed that "nothing can be more absurdly exaggerated than the usual talk about the state of the streets" and the extent of "impertinent solicitation" by streetwalkers. From his own nocturnal wanderings "the deep and strong impression which I have brought back is one of respect and admiration for the extraordinarily good behavior of English girls who pursue this dreadful calling." With a typical flourish he concluded, "The publicans and harlots are nearer the Kingdom of heaven than the scribes and pharisees who are always trying to qualify for a pass-port to bliss hereafter by driving their unfortunate sisters here to the very hell of police despotism."

The veracity of the revelations published from July 6 through July 10 was later questioned, and certain inaccuracies in the Lily story which came to light during Stead's trial for the abduction of Eliza Armstrong cast doubt over the whole series, but in its broader outlines the picture painted of the horrors of juvenile prostitution in London in 1885 was painfully true to life. Still, in reading some of the more lurid stories and descriptions, it is hard to avoid the suspicion that some of Stead's madams and prostitutes were em-bellishing their stories to impress the fervid, eccentric-looking, and somewhat unworldly interviewer.

The Northumberland Street crowds apparently were more orderly on Friday afternoon—or the police more efficient—for Stead had no additional complaints to make. But, if the violence subsided, the demand for the paper did not, and once more all editions were soon sold out. That night, during the question period in the House of Commons, Cavendish-Bentinck was moved to ask why the Metro-politan police had not stopped the sale of "very undesirable publi-cations," as had the City police.[9]

9. *Hansard's Parliamentary Debates,* 3d ser., vol. 299 (1885): p. 289.

The first phase of the campaign which gained for Stead and the *Pall Mall Gazette* their greatest notoriety was now ended. It might be said that his name became a household word, except that many a righteous family head banished both the name and the paper from the house. Some of Stead's critics questioned his motives, and others his methods. Some denounced him because they believed that his stories were exaggerated, while others felt that even if they were true, they should never have been printed in a respectable newspaper. Not that the Victorians were unaccustomed to sensationalism in the press, but they did not expect that kind of journalism in the *Pall Mall Gazette*. Even those papers which did show a lively interest in crime, scandal, and gossip avoided a subject like prostitution; and it must be remembered that at this time the *PMG* itself would not print the word "syphilis." [10] Stead, by tearing aside the veil of secrecy from sexual immorality and criminality, had exposed English women, girls, and young men to a view of depravity which they should never have seen. He had not just mentioned the unmentionable; he had bellowed it. And, of course, some of Stead's opponents—although fewer than he sometimes implied—were upset because they partook of the pleasures he was proscribing.

The "Maiden Tribute" crusade had its defenders as well, particularly among religious leaders. It is one of the paradoxes of this episode of Victorian journalism that the libertine Frank Harris attacked the *Pall Mall Gazette* in the name of decency and morality, while numerous churchmen and their journals defended it. During this first week of the crusade the *Christian*, the *Tablet*, the *Church Review*, and the *Methodist Times* all came out in Stead's favor. The *Church Review* argued that to charge him with "pandering to the bad passions of men is a little too preposterous," and the *Methodist Times* was so far carried away as to state, "The editor of the *Pall Mall Gazette* has done what we believe Jesus Christ Himself would have done in his place" (July 11). The bulk of the mail received by the *PMG* consisted of letters of praise and encouragement, and on Thursday Stead printed samples under such crossheads as "Peers," "Bishops," "Members of Parliament," "The Clergy of all Denominations," and "Public Men." On Friday, July 10, Lord Shaftesbury, whom Stead was pleased to call "the greatest Christian Philanthropist of our time," provided an influential

10. Scott, *Life and Death,* p. 126 n.

endorsement. In a speech at a Mansion House meeting of the Society for the Prevention of Cruelty to Children he spoke favorably of the *PMG* crusade and called for governmental action on the matter (July 11).

One area in which the response to the "Maiden Tribute" campaign was not all that Stead wished was in the "coward press" (July 11). Except for the *Evening News*, the London daily papers ignored the *PMG's* revelations. Without mentioning them, the *Times* did carry an article on the Criminal Law Amendment Bill which suggested that the age of consent not be raised beyond fifteen, since the law "must not go beyond public opinion" (July 11). On Saturday, July 11, the *Weekly Times* followed the *Evening News* in attacking what it called a "public outrage." It conceded that in a city of four million a few of the crimes described in the revelations might be committed, but "that is no reason that unspeakable things should be proclaimed from the housetops." As for Stead's motive: "Obscurity is *Pall Mall's* hell; notoriety its heaven. It has now become notorious with a vengeance—so notorious that it will be kicked ignominiously out of virtuous homes." As usual, the provincial press was more willing to grant the *Pall Mall Gazette* recognition, and while the *Western Daily Mercury* questioned whether the end justified the means (July 9), most of the papers seemed to agree with the London correspondent of the *Sheffield Observer* that the good would outweigh any evil resulting from the revelations (July 11). Few would have disagreed with the *Reading Observer* that "the *Pall Mall Gazette* has fully earned the right of claiming for itself that it has created the greatest sensation of modern journalism" (July 11).

Throughout the controversy Stead was generous in his praise of the *PMG* staff members for their assistance and support, although there were differences of opinion over the campaign within the *Pall Mall* family itself. Although Stead later wrote that he did not remember "having any serious difference of opinion with Milner upon any question that was handled in the Pall Mall," this recollection does not quite square with the developments after the launching of the crusade, and Stead did admit that the whole affair "tried Milner severely." [11] In a letter to Cook while Milner was out of London in July, the assistant editor complained of the embarrassments he was suffering and lamented that "it was bad

11. Stead, "Character Sketch: Milner," p. 22.

enough while one agreed more or less with Stead, but . . . it is
rather too much to suffer for one's supposed approval of what one
hates." [12] Soon after Milner resigned to begin the more successful
and noteworthy phase of his career, but his disenchantment with
the "Maiden Tribute" campaign did not affect his loyalty or his
personal regard for Stead, whom he supported during the Eliza
Armstrong trial. Cook left no record of how he felt about the
"Maiden Tribute" revelations, but J. Saxon Mills thought it impossible that he "should have wholly approved of Stead's methods."
However, Mills may have been ascribing his own feelings to Cook,
for although Mills admired Stead and applauded the objective of
the crusade, he strongly questioned the methods Stead employed.
In any case, Cook, like Milner, remained loyal to Stead throughout his subsequent troubles, and Mills thought it "a tribute to the
sterling qualities of Stead's character that even the experiences of
the 'Maiden Tribute' Crusade" did not alienate his staff. [13]

Stead himself seems to have had no doubts, no second thoughts,
once the crusade was under way. During the first week, while the
revelations were being printed, the Archbishop of Canterbury wrote
to him, "Opinions are more divided than on anything I have ever
known. You have sent a sword on earth. I only trust it will cut the
right knots." [14] Stead could have taken his answer from a leader
which he wrote on the same day (July 8). He applied to his own
crusade, "with all humility," a paraphrase of the exclamation of the
martyr Hugh Latimer: "Be of good cheer, for we have this day
lighted up such a flame in England as I trust in God shall never be
extinguished." On Saturday, July 11, Stead asked, "In the opinion
of the pulpit are we deserving of support or suppression?" He
appealed to all readers attending church or chapel the next day to
send the *Pall Mall Gazette* a postcard telling how the nation's
clergy were reacting to his crusade. The battle was far from over,
and Stead was preparing to stay on the offensive.

II

Stead soon made it quite clear that the conclusion of the reports
by no means meant the end of his crusade. His leading article for
Monday, July 13, "To Our Censors," proclaimed that the revelations

12. Mills, *Edward Cook*, p. 66.
13. Ibid., pp. 55, 64-65, 68.
14. Whyte, *Life*, 1:162 n.

were being printed in every capital on the Continent as well as by the "purest journals in the great American Republic." The paper had been "simply overwhelmed" by the response to his poll of churchgoers, and had not yet heard of a word of protest from the pulpit. On the other hand, "all the forces of wickedness in high places" were against the crusade, and Stead mentioned the attempts at suppression by W. H. Smith and Son, the stopping of delivery of the *PMG* to the Prince of Wales, and the attempts of Mr. Cavendish-Bentinck to extinguish the paper with a pose of outraged morality. "But on our side," he continued, "there stand arrayed with hardly any exceptions the best and purest and noblest men and women in London." Much of the rest of this issue was devoted to other aspects of the controversy. The follower spelled out the changes and additions which the "Chief of our Secret Commission" wished to see in the existing laws on the subject. Stead repeated his belief that "the bill should be aimed, not at the repression of vice, but at the suppression of crime," taking the position that two adults should be free to practice immoral acts if both were willing and they did not disturb their neighbors. An Occasional Note quoted the reactions of the French and German press, another column was devoted to news of various societies, leagues, and social organizations which had passed resolutions praising the *PMG*, and a feature was inaugurated which for a time appeared regularly—a column or so of articles under the general heading "Modern Babylon." Two full pages were devoted to "The Pulpit on the Question of the Hour," with quotes and summaries from various sermons delivered the previous day which indicated a virtually unanimous endorsement of Stead's activities. All told, over six pages of Monday's *PMG* dealt with some part of the "Maiden Tribute" crusade, and this pattern was to be followed for weeks to come. Indeed, the pages of the *Pall Mall* are repetitious after the second week of July, and the way in which Stead's causes monopolized his paper was another source of Milner's irritation.[15]

On July 14, Stead announced in the leading article, "Put to the Test," that the truth of his revelations was going to be judged by a committee composed of the Archbishop of Canterbury, the Cardinal Archbishop of Westminister (Cardinal Manning), the Bishop

15. Late in July, Milner wrote to Cook, "Stead talks, writes and thinks of nothing else but his virgins, . . . and I do comfortably and with ease what little reference to the world in general the paper still condescends to make" (Mills, *Edward Cook*, p. 67).

of London, and Samuel Morley, M.P., with the possible addition of the Lord Mayor and the City recorder. This group came to be called the Mansion House Committee from its place of sitting. An invitation was extended to any public figure who wished to serve on the committee, with a hopeful mention of Gladstone, who would certainly have been a fine catch. Indirectly associating the Liberal leader with the crusade, Stead asserted that despite the virtual suppression of the *PMG* outside of London, the provinces were taking up the cause, and he predicted a great agitation comparable to Gladstone's Bulgarian atrocity campaign of 1876. On pages 11 and 12 of the issue a summary of press comments on the crusade carried a subhead which announced, "The Conspiracy of Silence Breaking Down"; but the breakthrough was limited. The usual complaint was registered that the London morning journals were still silent "on the one topic which at this moment holds the attention of the world." The provincial press was praised for having spoken out "boldly," but it was admitted that many of the more important provincial dailies were as mute as their London counterparts. Still, some twenty of the smaller papers were quoted, most of which lauded the *PMG* and assailed its critics.

That afternoon during the question period in the Commons, Cross was asked by R. N. Fowler, the Lord Mayor, what legal steps were going to be taken against the *PMG*, and he replied that he had been advised that it would not be desirable to take any such action.[16]

On July 15 for the first time in ten days the "Maiden Tribute" disappeared from the *PMG's* first page, but the inside pages carried letters, features, press summaries, parliamentary debates, and straight news stories relating to the campaign. It was also announced that the independent commission to investigate the revelaitons, expanded to six members by the inclusion of the Lord Mayor and the City recorder, had held its first meeting.[17] On the next day the leader dealt with another of Stead's perennial concerns: minimizing the seriousness of renewed trouble with Russia over the Zulfikar Pass. However, "The Maiden Tribute" was back in

16. *Hansard's Parliamentary Debates,* 3d ser., vol. 299 (1885): p. 661.
17. These two officials did not remain on the committee, but the original four were joined by Robert T. Reid (later Earl Loreburn), Queen's Counsel and M.P. for Dumgries. Reid later became attorney general (1894) and lord chancellor (1905-12).

the follower, "More Proof—If Needed," wherein Stead declared that even while the Mansion House Committee was sitting he was able to get a girl delivered to him—as the "Chief Director of the Secret Commission"—willing to sell her virginity for five pounds.

On July 17 the first breach in the "conspiracy of silence" by London's morning papers occurred when the *Standard* took note of the "Maiden Tribute" crusade in a leader over a column in length, which began:

> We venture to say that no other capital in Europe would tolerate for an hour the spectacle presented in the main thoroughfares of London at the present moment of men, women, and children offering to men, women and children copies of a newspaper containing the most offensive, highly-coloured and disgusting details concerning the vicious ways of a small section of the population.

The *Standard* denounced the *PMG*'s contents bills, as well as its contents, and regretted that neither the Home Secretary nor the Lord Mayor had put a stop to its sale. Comparing the recent issues of the paper to the "surreptitious wares" sold in back rooms, the leader singled out what it regarded as the real motive behind the revelations: "The profit thus made by denouncing vice is literally made out of the vices denounced." The *Standard* itself was eager to extirpate vice, but only by legal means. "The sewer that runs underground may need cleansing; but the zeal that makes a handsome profit by turning it into the street will hardly be appreciated." The "Maiden Tribute" articles could only be condoned if they were the work of "disinterested enthusiasts" who distributed, rather than sold, them "in carefully selected quarters." The leader concluded:

> We protest the streets being turned into a market for literature which appeals to the lascivious curiosity of every casual passerby, and excites the latent pruriency of a half-educated crowd . . . we decline to admit that such a crusade is a legitimate subject for journalistic speculation, or a fitting tool for commercial advertisements.

In his response that evening Stead asked why the protest hadn't been made ten days earlier and denied the charge of making profit out of the campaign. He recalled that when the first article was

published the almost universal opinion, expressed by "legal, journalistic, literary and political experts," was that the *PMG* would be
ruined. However, "those more immediately concerned with the
conduct of the paper" were convinced of the truth of the reports
and considered it a duty to publish them. Stead declared that any
proceeds from the sale of "Maiden Tribute" pamphlets were going
into a fund started by the secret commission to continue the fight
against London vice, and also made some cogent points about the
phenomenal sale of the *PMG* during the week of the revelations.
The paper itself received no benefit from the inflated prices, and
the general chaos and disorganization, along with the cost of getting emergency paper supplies, nullified the slight gains made on
the increased sales. "The profit on the sale of a penny newspaper
is very trifling," and the commercial department of the *PMG* ended
up out of pocket by the whole enterprise. Stead's further observation, that if the crusade was undertaken for profit the editors were
fools, undoubtedly would have been supported by that same commercial department. Near the conclusion of his rebuttal Stead made
some observations which, although they would have been more
relevant a decade or so later, genuinely reflect the difference between Stead's application of the New Journalism and that of others
who adopted his techniques: "There are plenty of journals published in London whose owners frankly confess that their object is
solely commercial. They look upon their newspapers simply as a
money producing machine, and their estimate of the commercial
danger of touching the subject which we had to handle so freely
is shown by their persistent silence." Stead did not believe that in
the long run the paper would be hurt by the revelations, but insisted that at the moment, considering the expense of the investigations, the balance sheet would show "a small but appreciable mone-
tary loss."

In the inside pages of this issue there were the usual notices of
meetings about the Criminal Law Amendment Bill and excerpts
from other newspapers, including a long one from the *Standard*'s
leader. One of the most favorable of the press reports was taken
from the *Methodist Times,* which declared that "the battle is already won" and predicted that with the publication of the pamphlet based on the "Maiden Tribute" series there would come "a
burst of Holy Christ-like rage before which the Bulgarian Atrocity
agitation was a very little thing." And, in fact, as the second week

of the crusade drew to a close, public opinion seems to have been roused to the point where its pressure was about to help push the Criminal Law Amendment Bill through the House of Commons.

In the leader for July 18, Stead gave a hint that the passage of the bill would not end his campaign. He described the circulation of a petition in Liverpool to hold a town meeting on the protection of young girls and praised it as the right type of action. He also denied that there was no longer any need to maintain the public outcry because further agitation was needed to prevent Home Secretary Cross from weakening the version of the Criminal Law Amendment Bill approved by the House of Lords. Most of the second page was taken up by "Two Views of the 'Maiden Tribute.'" The first, "From a Saunterer in the Labyrinth," made the interesting suggestion that lustful passion for young girls was stimulated by the introduction in London of public roller skating. The second, "From a Study Armchair," was largely sympathetic to the crusade, but hinted at a profit motive behind it and chided Stead for making it a class matter. "To talk about the vices of the rich," the writer said, "is sheer claptrap. . . . The theory of the rich young man leading the poor man's child astray is rubbish." Elsewhere in the paper, Stead reprinted a bitter blast from the *St. Stephen's Review.* This Conservative weekly called the *PMG* "The Common Sewer of Northumberland-street" and deplored "that an English journal should drag our good name through the mud, and enable the revolutionary *Canaille* of Paris to point the finger of scorn at us." To destroy Stead's class thesis, it pointed out that the House of Lords had passed the bill before the *PMG* had even thought about it, and that it had first been shunted aside in a House of Commons controlled by Gladstone's Liberals (July 18).

Although the enormous demand for the *PMG* moderated considerably during the second week of the crusade, copies of the earlier issues continued to sell, at "every price from a shilling to a sovereign" (July 14). To reach a broader audience outside of London the entire series was published in pamphlet form, and the *PMG* frequently referred to the reception of the articles in foreign countries, where in some cases the entire series was reprinted. Stead apparently did not understand—or care—that his efforts to promote his cause on a worldwide basis gave more ammunition to those who felt his real motive was notoriety or profit rather than the amending of the laws of England. This danger was noted by those not necessarily antagonistic to the crusade. The *Sheffield Independent,* for example, praised the campaign but saw "some little danger of the imposing personality of our evening contemporary overshadowing the work it set itself to do; and of its head being turned by the adulation it is so careful to collect from the four corners of the earth" (July 16).

On Monday, July 20, Stead printed a message "To Would-Be-Subscribers" which well illustrates his occasional egocentricity and his insistence upon blind faith from his disciples. After describing the progress to date in the collection of subscriptions to the special fund for "Investigation, Prevention and Rescue," Stead stressed that new funds would be accepted only if they came with no strings attached, no conditions, no requests for any accounting of how the money was spent. "I will not," he thundered, "receive a sixpence which I am not free to spend . . . as if it were my own pocket money. So far as subscriptions to the Secret Commission are concerned subscribers must trust me all in all or not at all." Stead also flatly rejected the idea of setting up a committee to supervise rescue work, since he did not want to be trammeled in his personal operations in any way.

On July 21 the attack on the *Pall Mall Gazette* was resumed in the House of Commons by Staveley Hill, who asked, "For how much longer is it intended to acquiesce in the sale by men, women and children of this indelicate literature in the streets of London?" He added that "The namby-pamby word 'indelicate' is not my word. The word I used was 'filthy'; but if that is thought inadmissible I choose to describe the literature as obscene." Home Secretary Cross assured the house, "If obscene literature is spread abroad the persons who spread it do it at their peril." Staveley Hill and Mr. Onslow then brought up the matter of the illustrated version of the revelations being sold in pamphlets, which were described as "vile" and indecent, and Onslow notified Cross of his intention to put the question down for the following session's question period.[18]

Stead was unconcerned about such denunciations and the leader for the next day's paper outlined his latest tactic. "An Appeal to the People" called on the working classes to put pressure on Parliament and asked for "spontaneous" agitation, not just in London, but throughout the country. "There should be town's meetings every-

18. *Hansard's Parliamentary Debates,* 3d ser., vol. 299 (1885): pp. 1408-9.

where, from the Mansion House in the City down to the humblest village green in the three kingdoms." He could not believe that the common people could be held back from joining his crusade; and page 6 carried almost two columns of notices of rallies held and town meetings scheduled, sample petition forms, and lists of contributors to his Secret Commission Fund under the grandiose heading "The National Awakening."

During the Commons question period of July 22, Onslow asked whether the executive had no power to halt the sale of the various *PMG* publications dealing with the "Maiden Tribute." Cross's reply hinted that legal trouble might be brewing for the paper:

> I said yesterday that the publishers of obscene publications published them at their own peril. Whatever may be said for the motives of those who made the first publications, nothing whatever can be said but evil about these pictorial illustrations; and the police have had special instructions to watch these publications and take such action as they may be recommended to take under proper legal advice.[19]

On Saturday, July 25, Stead, still anxious to see England's greatest city in full cry behind his cause, asked in his follower, "What Is London Going to Do?" He described with satisfaction the way in which the agitation was growing in the provinces, with other large cities following the example of Liverpool. But, although there had been meetings on the matter, with more scheduled, "there has been as yet no stirring of the depths" in London itself. Then, doing some spadework for the next phase of the campaign, he printed a letter from "the north" which suggested a Hyde Park demonstration for London.

The question of prosecuting the *Pall Mall Gazette* was raised again on the following Monday, July 27, and the hopes of doing so under existing law were finally laid to rest. In the Commons that night P. A. Muntz asked whether the law officers of the Crown thought that the *Pall Mall Gazette* had violated the law against obscene publications, and, if they did believe an offense had been committed, why the journal had not been prosecuted. Cross, in reply, reiterated his statement of the fourteenth that the Law Officers felt it would not be desirable to take proceedings against the

19. Ibid., p. 1561.

editor of the paper. "I have never swerved from that conclusion," Cross added, "and the matter remains as before." [20]

Meanwhile, more and more of the provincial journals and periodicals were taking notice of the crusade. A few denounced it and many praised it, although approval was often tempered by reservations about Stead's methods. But still most London newspapers continued to ignore the agitation. On July 28 Stead unleashed a barrage at his silent competitors in a long leader, "The Press and the Public," in which he reaffirmed his own faith in the "growing power of the press" and expressed his satisfaction with the soundness with which it had been used in recent years. But, he added, this power entailed certain duties, of which the most important was "to give its readers full, constant, and impartial information about all events of national importance." When news was suppressed, the guilty newspapers were jeopardizing the influence of the press, and "it is this dangerous game which the metropolitan and a certain section of the provincial press are playing at this moment." Stead once more invoked the hallowed memory of 1876 and asserted that twenty-seven provincial towns had held public meetings, which were packed despite the hot weather. There had also been "simply innumerable" meetings of workingmen's clubs, benevolent societies, and other such groups. "Yet the London press has taken less notice of all these events than it did of the abortive attempt of the London publicans to get up an anti-beer tax demonstration in Hyde Park some months ago, and not a tithe of the notice which it has accorded to the silly exhibition of an Oxford crew in rowing across the channel." [21] He was quick to insist, "We have no anxiety at all on account of the movement," which, with the aid of the provincial press, was now too strong to be denied. But he was alarmed at the prospect that members of the press and Parliament might undermine their own "legitimate and useful authority" by their indifference to this great crusade. The majority of the people would infer that journalists and politicians who spurned the cause were in sympathy with the evil itself. "If there is a social revolution in this country," he said ominously, "it will be over this very question," and the one thing which could bring about an explosion would be the attempt to hush up the matter.

---

20. *Hansard's Parliamentary Debates*, 3d ser., vol. 300 (1885): pp. 51-52.
21. It might be mentioned that the *PMG* also gave the event full, and not unfavorable, coverage.

On July 29 the Mansion House Committee issued its report, which was published in next evening's *PMG* as the first news article on page 8. The report stated in full:

> We have been requested to investigate the truth of the statements contained in the Pall Mall Gazette of 6, 7, 8 and 10 July, 1885, under the title "The Report of Our Secret Commission."
>
> In doing so we decided from the first to exclude any inquiry into charges against particular men or classes of men or into the conduct of police officers.
>
> We have strictly confined ourselves to inquiry into the system of CRIMINAL VICE described in the report.
>
> After carefully sifting the evidence of witnesses and materials before us, and without guaranteeing the *accuracy of every particular we are satisfied* that, taken as a whole, The Statements In The Pall Mall Gazette on this question are SUBSTANTIALLY TRUE.

Stead's leader, which covered most of the first page, was headed simply: "True." He exultantly proclaimed that "these five competent investigators" had confirmed the existence of the system of vice which he had exposed, "and the whole world knows that the terrible story of the Maiden Tribute is substantially true." The fact that the Mansion House Committee did not guarantee every particular was brushed aside with the observation that "trivial errors in points of detail were unavoidable." After reprinting some of the serious charges made by the *Pall Mall Gazette* which the committee had apparently accepted as true, Stead then broke forth with one of his purple passages: "We stand here in the belfry of the world, ringing a tocsin whose peal clashes discordant upon the ear of civilized mankind." The huge sale of *PMG* reprints, "authentic and pirated," in England was said to have surpassed the one-and-one-half-million mark; and although it is difficult to see what possible effect it might have had in cleansing London of its cesspools of vice, Stead also boasted of large sales of the pamphlet in France and America and of translations made, or being made, of the revelations in Denmark, Germany, Russia, and Poland. Predictably, he concluded his leader by lamenting the refusal of certain newspapers and political leaders to enlist under the banner of his crusade. Such crimes of omission, he said, were comparable to those of the "Minotaur" himself.

On this same day, July 30, the debates on the third reading of
the Criminal Law Amendment Bill opened and during the next
two weeks Stead could hardly have complained that the House of
Commons, at any rate, was ignoring him, his crusade, or his newspaper. Some members fulminated and raged at him; others—
usually with reservations—defended him, but he was not ignored.
It is rare, indeed, for a newspaper editor or his paper to receive
the attention given to Stead and the *PMG* during the various
phases of the debate. The oratory—which upon occasion could only
be described as impassioned—tells us much of the motives ascribed
to Stead by his detractors; the virtues recognized by his supporters;
the unfortunate aspects of his crusade as seen by both groups; and,
perhaps most important, the effect which the agitation seems to
have had on the nation and its legislative chambers.

The Home Secretary opened the debate by remarking that it
dealt with questions of a very grave nature, and he expressed regret that so much time had lapsed since the second reading. His
statement that "this is a question which has stirred England from
one end to the other" brought an expression of disapproval from
a member, and Cross continued in a vein that Stead himself might
have used in a *PMG* leader: "Our hon. Member expressed dissent;
but . . . there is nothing more sacred to the English people, and
there is nothing which they are so determined to maintain, as the
purity of their own households." Cross said he was surprised that
Mr. Hopwood wanted to introduce an amendment which would
have postponed consideration of the bill, and, with an apparent
reference to those who were opposed to it, he concluded, "They
will have to answer to their constituencies for their action in this
case." The thinly veiled threat in Cross's remarks ensured a measure of acrimony from the outset of the debates. In moving his
amendment Hopwood denounced the "sensational statements of a
filthy character" which had been made during past weeks, and
angrily resented that those who opposed the current Criminal Law
Amendment Bill found their reputation blackened by implication.
He reminded the House that he had himself introduced the last
act which Parliament had passed for the protection of children, and
questioned the innocence of those who claimed that the revelations
had been made in the service of humanity. In the course of his
tirade he denounced not only the *PMG*, but also the Salvation
Army, which had taken up Stead's cause. Hopwood suggested the

possibility that under the bill designing women might take advantage of young men, and denounced as inflammatory a statement by Samuel Morley "that with reference to this matter there was one law for the rich and one for the poor." He concluded his lengthy and rambling discourse with a call for a parliamentary inquiry on the truth of the *PMG* charges and asked why Stead could not reveal the authority for his statements to the public, as he had done for "a so-called Commission of Prelates and Cardinals."

Other members then rose to denounce the commission, the *PMG* and its editor, the crusade in general, and its class implications. As one member put it, there was "nothing more congenial to the ill-conditioned Democrat than to cast foul slanders and aspersions on the higher orders of society." Mr. Cavendish-Bentinck, by now a symbol of opposition to the crusade, said that the Commons was being asked to legislate under the influence of panic. He denied that he objected to the Criminal Law Amendment Bill as such, but he felt that it was being exploited for electioneering and used as an instrument of class warfare. As for the *Pall Mall Gazette*, "the conduct of the Government in allowing abominable newspapers to be sold about the streets was a disgrace to civilization—it was a disgrace to the Home Secretary." What he wanted was a full discussion of the bill, without the pressures of "the reprehensible agitation which had been going on out-of-doors." Sir Frederick Milner replied to the assertion that the government had only taken up the bill because of the agitation. He insisted that "it was the intention of the present Government, as soon as it came into office, to pass this Bill into law." As far as the *Pall Mall Gazette* was concerned, it might have exaggerated in its revelations, "but if one-tenth part were true, it was necessary for the House to deal with the evil." Hopwood then withdrew his motion and the House proceeded to go into committee for its debate with occasional further references—usually derogatory—to the "Maiden Tribute" campaign.[22]

The resumption of the debate on the Criminal Law Amendment Bill, along with the publication of the Mansion House Committee report, helped to widen a little the crack in the London press's wall of silence. On Friday morning, July 31, the *Daily News* admitted the necessity of the bill, but saw little relation between it and recent "astonishing statements which . . . have been improperly,

22. *Hansard's Parliamentary Debates*, 3d ser., vol. 300 (1885): pp. 578-90.

or at any rate prematurely, described as revelations, disclosures, and exposures." Its leader writer refused to accept as conclusive the type of inquiry held by the Mansion House Committee. That evening the *St. James's Gazette,* which up to this time had noticed its leading rival's campaign only obliquely,[23] was more direct in its approach. Its first leader said the Criminal Law Amendment Bill would probably do more harm than good, and contained a blistering indictment of "certain most eminent prelates" who had sat on the Mansion House Committee. The "so-called revelations" published by "a too-notorious publication" had been written in such indecent language that if those clergymen had ever read fifty lines of them in public "they would deserve to be stripped of their priestly vestments and flogged at Newgate." Yet they did not condemn them, nor did they condemn Stead for deceiving and corrupting young girls. The *St. James's Gazette* also scoffed at the value of the committee's report, since it excluded consideration of everything important and qualified its conclusions with such vague terms as "on the whole" and "substantially."

In the same evening's *PMG* Stead answered the *Daily News* in an Occasional Note in which he declared that "the fickleness, the half-heartedness, the general wishy-washyness of the Daily News" was the despair of all "true liberals." By denouncing "The Maiden Tribute" it forfeited its role of Liberal leadership, just as it had lost its chance to lead the Bulgarian agitation in 1876. "And now," Stead continued, "as a crowning demonstration of its imbecility, it is writing about the crimes brought to light by our Secret Commission in just the same spirit in which United Ireland, for instance, speaks of reports of outrages on landlords." English Liberalism, he concluded, needed a better London spokesman "than this exponent of namby-pambyism in politics and indifferentism in morals." The parliamentary report for this issue (July 31)—much more extensive than the usual summary—took up almost two pages and gave great attention to the comments on the *PMG.* In addition, Stead wrote a personal report on the previous day's debate, in which he contrasted the crowded House sitting until 2:00 A.M. with the nearly

23. It had reprinted part of the *Standard's* attacks (July 17), published a letter from Lewis Carroll which denounced the popular outcry (July 22), and in a leader, "Legislation for Vice," expressed its contempt for "the man who seeks notoriety for himself and his moral sentiments by filling the public ear with plain speech" on the subjects involved in the Criminal Law Amendment Bill (July 28).

empty chamber that had assembled for the second reading in May. He also made one unfortunate comment which was to be used by his enemies as further proof of his lack of sincerity in posing as a champion of womanhood: he declared that for the time being the age limit should not be raised beyond sixteen, as some members had proposed, since it would cut off the means of livelihood for girls over sixteen without offering them compensation. In the leader, Stead—whose labors during this period were staggering— again tried to stimulate more action on behalf of his crusade in London. He began with the now tiresome account of meetings being held all over the nation, making the customary analogy to the "Bulgarian Atrocity" campaign, and complained that London had yet to speak. He frankly admitted that a City meeting summoned by the Lord Mayor, or a Hyde Park demonstration, could no longer influence the decision of the House of Commons. Thus there can be no question that Stead was looking beyond his original goal and, for whatever reason, determined to keep alive the movement which he had fostered. He concluded the leader with the announcement that a conference was to be held at the Canon-street Hotel the next night, open to all persons interested in organizing a Hyde Park demonstration.

The House of Commons on the evening of July 31 engaged in another lengthy debate on the Criminal Law Amendment Bill as it entertained a further series of proposed amendments. There were no direct references to the *PMG* in this session, although Mr. Hopwood obliquely expressed his view of the influence of the newspaper on the matter before them. "Though the right hon. Gentleman the Home Secretary might have no choice but to yield to the popular cry," it was reported, yet Hopwood "thought they were putting on the statute book a heap of matter that they could well do without."

The next day the debate was given three full pages in the *PMG* —one of the most extensive parliamentary reports of Stead's editorship. In his leader, "Progress Indeed," Stead retraced with obvious satisfaction the development of his crusade and its influence on the legislation now being debated. "Next Monday is Bank Holiday," he wrote. "Last Bank Holiday our Secret Commission began its investigation. What a transformation has been wrought in the interval!" The saving of the bill was the most remarkable illustration "of the power of a simple recital of facts in the columns of a newspaper" since the Bulgarian campaign. He attacked the prudery of those who objected to exposing the sins of society and who "would apparently deliberately prefer that the daughters of the poor should suffer these atrocities for ever rather than that the daughters of the well-to-do should hear of them." He concluded with a discussion of what he considered to be the weaknesses still in the bill, particularly the clause which would prohibit a court from accepting the testimony of a girl too young to understand the nature of the oath. With typical Steadian hyperbole he maintained that those who supported this feature of the bill were saying, "If a child is too young to understand the nature of an oath, let her be outraged with impunity."

By Monday, August 3, the struggle over the passage of the Criminal Law Amendment Bill entered its final stage. Stead's follower for the day was mostly concerned with the need to improve several of its features before the final version was accepted. Meanwhile, progress was also being made toward his next objective. In the *PMG's* "New Crusade" section it was reported that the organizing conference for the proposed Hyde Park demonstration had met on Saturday night. The meeting had been "characterized by great earnestness and enthusiasm" and had passed a resolution to hold the demonstration on some Saturday afternoon in the near future.

In Monday evening's parliamentary session the Criminal Law Amendment Bill finally passed through the committee stage of the House of Commons. During the course of the debates, which were again lengthy and at times acrimonious, the *PMG* was once more the target of some caustic criticism. One of the most heated exchanges came when Mr. Stansfeld[24] moved a clause to make it illegal for a doctor or a midwife to ascertain the virginity of a girl, if it was believed that such examination was being conducted for immoral purposes. The sweeping—not to say unenforceable—nature of the proposal was worthy of Stead himself, and there was no question that the revelations of the *PMG* had convinced Stanfeld that such legislation was desirable. The attorney general, Richard Webster, opposed the clause, and also denied, on behalf of the government, the influence of the newspaper which had obviously inspired it. However, he refused to "pass any criticism upon the action of *The Pall Mall Gazette*." Webster's good will was not

24. Sir James Stansfeld (1820-98) had a connection with Stead because of his long-standing dedication to the repeal of the Contagious Disease Acts.

shared by several of the members, and the debate on the proposed amendment included attacks on the Mansion House Committee, the *PMG,* and Stead, who was described by Staveley Hill as a "filthy editor of a filthy production." One of the few to defend the "Maiden Tribute" series was Samuel Morley, but like so many of Stead's supporters in the House, he made it clear that he had some reservations. "No doubt," he admitted, "as a matter of taste, most serious objections might be raised to the *Modus operandi* of the newspaper in question." When the attention of the house was finally directed back to the amendment being considered, it was defeated easily. Other amendments were then brought forward, and most defeated, before the bill was reported out of committee, to be presented for its third reading on Wednesday.[25]

The press of other business delayed the final consideration until Thursday. During the interval Stead's clarion was, of course, not silenced, but he did permit more news and comment on other matters to intrude on the *PMG's* preoccupation with what Milner called "his virgins." [26] The leader for Tuesday, August 4, celebrated the latest step in the progress of the bill, but for the two days after that the crusade actually disappeared from the first page of the paper. Both leaders for these days dealt with the prosaic matter of politics, including a mostly favorable analysis of Joseph Chamberlain's "unauthorized programme." [27] On August 6 a small news item in the "New Crusade" section, which gave assurance that Eliza Armstrong was safe and well, was a portent of later difficulties for Stead of which he was probably unaware at the time.

In Parliament the debate on the Criminal Law Amendment Bill resumed on the night of Thursday, August 6, with another series of proposed amendments. The attack on the *PMG* became more direct, and even threatening, when Staveley Hill moved a new clause to the bill which would have called for imprisonment and a fine for anyone selling or publishing "any matter or thing calculated or tending to debauch." Hill claimed that such a measure

25. *Hansard's Parliamentary Debates,* 3d ser., vol. 300 (1885): pp. 876-86.
26. Mills, *Edward Cook,* p. 67.
27. The *PMG* gave this program considerable attention as Chamberlain revealed it in various speeches throughout the year. A moderate, and often vague, series of proposals, it seemed like dangerous radicalism to many of that day. It called for such things as free education, giving local authorities the power to acquire land at a fair price for the building of artisans' dwellings, revision of local and national taxation, and agrarian reforms to stimulate the growth of a peasant proprietorship.

was necessary because during the tenure of Home Secretary Cross the nation had witnessed "the Augustan era of obscene literature. Just recently a newspaper failing in its circulation, and having a very great difficulty to maintain its own in the world, thought by a very sensational report to regain its circulation." At this point Mr. Bryce interrupted to ask if the remarks were relevant, and with the ruling by the speaker that they were, another full-scale parliamentary discussion of the *Pall Mall Gazette* was underway. Hill continued his justification of the proposed amendment in an emotional and angry discourse, charging that the *PMG* had invented stories, in order to boost circulation, which would debauch the minds of the young and that "this filthy literature" had permeated almost every household in the nation. Thus, he reasoned, while placing on the statute book a law to purify the bodies of young people, Parliament should also try to purify their minds. Since Cross had not suppressed "this filthy paper," he could only assume that the existing laws were insufficient and that his amendment was necessary. Hill also directed the House's attention to the *Pall Mall Gazette* of July 31, which he said had been shown to him by a friend.[28] Pointing out Stead's recommendation there that the age of consent not be raised beyond sixteen, he observed that "this was the view taken by a journal professing to be shocked at immorality." Hill also discussed the implications of the widespread sale of "Maiden Tribute" pamphlets in other nations and spoke approvingly of American laws against obscene publications. The penalties called for in his own proposal (up to two years imprisonment and a fine of two hundred pounds) were, he felt, not too severe—in fact "if the 'cat' were added it would be an improvement."

In response to what he termed the "somewhat impassioned speech" by Hill, Attorney General Webster said that it was unnecessary to read the law officers of the government a lecture on the law, and took full responsibility for advising Cross not to act against the *Pall Mall Gazette*. He also stated that the existing laws were strong enough and concluded that the proposed amendment would not solve the problem of the sale of obscene publications. This scarcely slowed down the debate on Hill's proposal, which he probably never expected would be adopted, but provided another

28. Several opponents of the crusade, when mentioning an item in the *PMG,* would stress that they ordinarily never read such a paper but that someone else had shown them the relevant passage.

springboard for those M.P.'s who wished to assail the *PMG* and its editor. There was obviously considerable difference of opinion in the House on the question of whether or not the Criminal Law Amendment Bill would have been introduced but for the "Maiden Tribute" furor. Most of those who gave credit to the *PMG* for this legislation also evinced some qualms about the tone and nature of its articles. George Russell came closer than any of the other members to an unqualified defense of Stead, emphatically denying that the editor's motives were mercenary. Stead's primary idea was to carry out a much needed reform, and, Russell explained, "it was a work which it was impossible to conduct without certain departure from journalistic rule and style of language usually adopted in newspaper literature." This view was not shared by others who spoke on the issue. Thorold Rogers, although he opposed Hill's amendment because it was obviously directed at a specific newspaper, fired a volley at the *PMG* and its editor. Explaining carefully that he had not read the "odious journal" for a long time because of its sensationalism and vulgarity, he stated that the *PMG* had done what it might have thought was its duty "in the worst possible manner." Whatever benefits might have resulted from the campaign, "he did not think any honest man could sit in the House whilst these matters were being discussed without denouncing the paper." When the debaters had exhausted the issue—and the House —Hill rose to withdraw his motion with the statement that "after the complete repudiation they heard of the course taken by *The Pall Mall Gazette*, he would not put the House to the trouble of a division." Following further debate, from which the *PMG* was mercifully omitted although several of the amendments proposed reflected material which had appeared in its pages, the weary members rose at 3:00 A.M. but deferred the final vote until the next meeting.[29]

When the object of all of this attention appeared on the streets the next day, August 7, "The Maiden Tribute" still had not regained its position as a subject for the leader, but the follower, "The Church and the New Crusade," described a manifesto by the Archbishop of Canterbury which was circulated at a meeting of the Church of England Purity Society. It consisted of a general denunciation of the vice exposed by the *PMG* and included the admonition "The evil-doing is confined to no one class in the com-

29. *Hansard's Parilamentary Debates*, 3d ser., vol. 300 (1885): pp. 1407-19.

munity." Stead could not ignore the attacks on him and his paper made during the previous night's sitting of the House. His rebuttal, contained in the first two paragraphs of the Occasional Notes, was, considering the temperament of the editor and the provocation he had been given, dispassionate and brief. In the first Note he flatly branded as "absolutely false" Hill's charge that the proprietors of the *PMG* had made ten thousand pounds from the "Maiden Tribute" crusade. They had, according to Stead, "not made a single penny." As for the further charge that the campaign had been designed "to galvanize into life a declining journal," the editor pointed out that his paper's circulation had been rising steadily during the past two years and that "the daily sale for the half year ended June 30 was more than any previous six months in the whole course of the somewhat eventful history of the journal." In the second paragraph Stead replied to the charge of obscenity, declaring, "We are much more anxious to suppress the circulation of obscene literature than the honourable members who denounced the course which we have taken." All of the *PMG* stories were true, and their publication was necessary to achieve a moral purpose, "two characteristics which differentiated our tragic revelations from the ordinary smoke-room stories in which so many honourable members find such unclean delight." Stead concluded by thanking those members who had spoken forth in behalf of the *PMG* and reminded Cross that the bill really would not have had a chance of passing without the newspaper's action. Most of the parliamentary report described that part of the previous night's debate in which the *PMG* had figured so largely.

In the session of August 7 the House of Commons finally, to the delight of Stead and his supporters, reached the moment of the third reading. As everyone by this time knew it would, the bill passed, and was thus ready to be returned to the Lords for the approval of various amendments which had been added.[30]

The *PMG* of Saturday, August 8, again gave Parliament full coverage, with a three-page article on the debate. Stead, with the immediate triumph now in hand, felt compelled to justify the continuation of his crusade in a leader entitled "Why a Demonstration Is Necessary." He noted that the bill would undoubtedly receive the royal assent the next week, but "the mere printing of words on paper" would not change things. "Everything will depend in turn,"

30. Ibid., pp. 1461-1511.

he continued, "upon the spirit with which it is regarded by the people at large. That is why, especially in London, it is so important to maintain the agitation which has so auspiciously begun." He described how the opportunity to improve the moral tone of the nation had been seized in the provinces, while warning that even here there was danger that it might dwindle away. Thus, a national conference for people active in the movement was scheduled at St. James's Hall on August 21. It was true that the Hyde Park demonstration had caused some differences of opinion, but it would be in London that the law would be most difficult to administer. Furthermore, "the ordinary organs of public opinion are dumb," and no one newspaper, "least of all an evening newspaper," could hope to reach the population. Finally, in what might have been a hint of some dissension in the Purity ranks, Stead rather strongly upbraided those who made excuses for inaction. The arguments advanced for continuing the agitation were not completely without merit, yet, given Stead's character and temperament, and considering his obvious delight with the campaign, it is difficult not to assume that the crusader in Babylon was at least partly motivated by the desire to remain still longer at what he firmly believed was the center of the national stage.

Ironically, it was in this same issue of August 8 that the *PMG* reported the first news story of the petition for divorce filed against Sir Charles Dilke. Stead had defended his "Maiden Tribute" articles by contrasting them to the sensational divorce reports in other newspapers, but the Dilke case called forth one of the *PMG's* rare headline displays, including a top head in boldface: "Great Social Scandal." Stead later was to conduct a less praiseworthy crusade against Dilke because of this scandal, leading many people to consider him vindictive and petty.[31]

On Monday night, August 10, the House of Lords considered the amendments which had been added to its original Criminal Law Amendment Bill. As in the Commons, the debate brought up the question of the "Maiden Tribute" campaign. The Earl of Milltown, while favoring the bill, "complained of the obscenity through which they had been compelled to pass, and that boys and girls of tender years had been allowed to sell such a filthy and obscene publica-

---

31. For a balanced treatment of the Dilke case, as well as Stead's involvement, see Roy Jenkins, *Sir Charles Dilke: A Victorian Tragedy* (London: Collins, 1958).

tion under the nose of the public, without the authorities taking any action whatever." In his view other publications which had been suppressed "were comparatively pure to this publication." Lord Mount-Temple replied that the publicity given to the criminal activities in London had definitely influenced the passage of the bill, which had earlier been given a cold shoulder by the Commons. After further discussion of amendments, the Bishop of Winchester concluded the debate with a speech in praise of the bill, although like so many others he believed "that the obscene literature referred to was doing an infinity of mischief." The Lords then proceeded to accept the Criminal Law Bill as amended, and Stead had won his most notable victory.[32]

32. *Hansard's Parliamentary Debates,* 3d ser., vol. 300 (1885): pp. 1553-57. The basic provisions of the bill as passed were: the age of consent was raised to sixteen; brothels could be searched on the basis of information sworn before a magistrate by any parent, guardian, or person acting in the bona fide interest of a missing girl; young girls could be taken from immoral parents; proceedings could be taken against any person procuring a girl under sixteen or any girl or woman by force; special protection was given to idiot or imbecile females.

CHAPTER SIX

Triumphant Imprisonment

oIIIoIIIoIIIoIIIoIIIoIIIoIIIoIIIoIIIoIIIoIIIoIIIoIIIoIIIoIIIoIIIoIIIoIIIoIIIoIIIoIIIoIIIoIIIoIIIoIIIoIII

The book on "The Maiden Tribute" was not closed. Yet to come was Stead's "New Crusade," with his cherished Hyde Park demonstration. Also ahead lay the editor's trial and conviction for an act committed during his investigations, an act which demonstrated his lack of judgment if nothing else. To some men this might have been a tragic climax to the campaign—to Stead it was a great moment of personal triumph.

I

The *PMG* leader for Tuesday, August 11, "Why We Are Going On," reiterated Stead's thesis that the real work of the crusade had just begun. "We entirely agree with the *Times*," he said, "and those excellent people who are constantly decrying our efforts, when they say that the law after all can only deal with the fringe of evil." Answering those who felt that the crusade should now end, Stead stressed the need to generate sentiment for purity reforms, to spur individual actions, and to form "Vigilance Committees in every town in the land."

On August 12 the *PMG* reprinted in its follower a letter by the Archbishop of Canterbury which had appeared in the *Times* that morning. Dated August 10, it was addressed to a correspondent who had asked if he had approved or condoned the recent activities of the *Pall Mall Gazette*. The archbishop replied that he had expressed no such approval, but that without some public movement in its behalf the Criminal Law Amendment Act probably would not have passed. He strongly deprecated "the modes of inquiry

169

adopted in some instances" and trusted that Stead would "himself feel that there can be at least no need for further publication." However, he also called for parents, clergymen, and employers to form vigilance committees, and, in defending the Mansion House Committee, by implication endorsed the truth of the "Maiden Tribute" disclosures. Stead's response was predictable. He could not agree that there was no need for continuing publication of the "Maiden Tribute" pamphlets and in any case he could not prevent the sale of pirated editions. Furthermore, it was necessary to keep the story alive to rouse the people of England to organize the very committees the archbishop was calling for. An even blunter reply took the form of a notice over the first column on page 8 which announced that the only copyrighted edition of *The Maiden Tribute* was on sale for twopence, and that a four-page leaflet with condensations of the reports of the secret commission and the Mansion House Committee would be sold for ten shillings per thousand for general distribution.

Over the next week and a half the new crusade dominated the *Pall Mall Gazette* much as had the campaign to pass the Criminal Law Amendment Bill. Stead did not ignore other news, and there was even time for some of his minor crusades, such as woman suffrage and new factory legislation. But the major theme was sounded again and again in Occasional Notes, news items, press summaries, and announcements dealing with the next stage of the "Maiden Tribute" campaign. Between the passing of the Criminal Law Amendment Bill and the Hyde Park demonstration on August 22, only the August 18 issue did not discuss the subject on the front page. As the day for the demonstration approached, the news stories grew longer and showed little more objectivity than the leaders themselves. An August 19 story mentioned that "owing to the general exodus from town, a list of speakers has been found with great difficulty"; and the next day's leader reported that the Bishop of Bedford, who would move the first resolution at the pre-demonstration conference to be held in St. James's Hall on August 21, would be the single, solitary bishop in London. Most of the others had written either that they would be out of the country or were too engrossed in diocesan work to attend. According to a letter from the Archbishop of Canterbury, the primate saw the need for vigilance committees, but "I do not myself see how a Hyde Park Demonstration can help this administrative question," although "a wise, good representative Conference of thinking, able men, could help it enormously." Despite the difficulty of rounding up clergymen and other distinguished persons, however, the committee in charge of the demonstration predicted in the same issue that "the gathering . . . will be the largest ever seen in London; one estimate is that nearly half a million people will assemble in Hyde Park."

The reaction of most of the London press to the proposed meeting and demonstration provoked the *Methodist Times* into taking up the cudgel again in defense of the cause:

> We are not surprised that the newspapers, when their puerile conspiracy of silence ignominiously failed, turned with savage rage upon the *Pall Mall Gazette*. It is, however, rather too outrageous for them to pretend that their rage is dictated by a love of chastity. They wantonly publish the details of the divorce court; they ardently defend the indelicate nudities of Royal Academicians; they write admiring reviews of novels which debauch the minds of boys and girls; they advertise and applaud the painted harlots that disgrace the theatres of London. . . . No one can stop the movement now, for God is in it. If the wicked suggestion of the *Times* that it should be stopped by force were adopted there would be a revolution. . . . Let every God-fearing Londoner make his way to Hyde Park next Saturday. [August 20]

On August 21, Stead wrote in his leader, "Today in St. James's Hall, tomorrow in Hyde Park, the great popular movement which took its rise in the publication of the 'Maiden Tribute of Modern Babylon' will be brought to a climax." He characteristically gave thanks to God for the popular uprising of the past seven weeks, and rather uncharacteristically added, "But far too much has been made both by friends and by foes of the part we were compelled to play in this matter." Previously the *PMG* had been vague about what purpose the gatherings might serve other than providing inspiration to the participants. Stead now indicated that the practical program of the Friday conference was to organize the Vigilance Association of London. With such an objective his crusade was moving further afield from what many people would have considered to be the legitimate functions of journalism. To expose an evil or to campaign for the passage of a law was one thing; to assume the responsibility of acting as a watchdog over public morality was quite another.

On Saturday, August 22, the *Pall Mall Gazette* published a special morning edition of sixteen pages, devoted entirely to the morning, afternoon, and evening sessions of the previous day's Protection of Girls National Conference at St. James's Hall. The regular afternoon edition enthusiastically proclaimed in its leader the emergence of the "New Factor in Politics." In the story and analysis of the conference we find Stead the visionary—the optimistic prophet of momentous change in English society. To him, the most notable feature of the conference was that "Bishops and atheists, Methodists and Malthusians, Capitalists and Socialists, members of Parliament and working men, met on a common platform to discuss what can be done to staunch a running sore in the body politic." He noted the "respectful attention" with which the Social Democratic spokesmen were received when they "repeated their familiar impeachment of society," opining that "if ever the Socialists are able to induce English people to break the eighth commandment, it will be because of the revulsion of horror produced by breaches of the seventh." English politics had gone to pieces because of the timidity of its leaders, and he called for bold men willing to "essay great and hazardous experiments in social reconstruction," who had "proved their popular sympathy." But Stead did not see such leaders rising from the Socialist ranks.

In a sense, the Hyde Park demonstration was a test of the influence of the *Pall Mall Gazette*. For weeks it had gone all out to convince the "God-fearing" citizens of London that it was their duty to attend. But how many Londoners, God-fearing or otherwise, were likely to be reached by Stead's paper? The phenomenal leap in sales during the "Maiden Tribute" revelations was ephemeral and the paper's regular readers by no means represented a cross section of London society. For all of his appeals to the people, Stead viewed the *PMG's* role to be that of influencing the makers and shakers, not the masses whose attendance was necessary to make any "popular" demonstration a success. And for the most part the interest of the lower classes in this "cultured" evening paper was only passing. Most of the other London papers either ignored or decried the demonstration. The *Spectator*, for example, hoped that the Hyde Park meeting would not multiply the crimes it was designed to combat and claimed that a recent increase in such crimes was apparent from news stories throughout the country, an increase it attributed to the "morbid excitement" stirred up by the *PMG*'s agitation. The *Spectator* affirmed the position of Dr. Basil Jones, Bishop of St. David's, who refused to attend the Friday conference lest it indicate "indirect approval of the recent action of the *PMG* (which I regard as, perhaps, the gravest offense against public decency and morality which had been committed in any even nominally Christian country)." While the bishop agreed "whole-heartedly" with the aims of those holding the conference, he did not think they could be achieved at a public meeting.[1]

Monday, August 24, brought another *PMG* special morning edition of sixteen pages with a headline running the width of the page and a large illustration on page 1.[2] The accompanying story acknowledged that it was difficult to estimate the size of a crowd, but gave the paper's own estimate at 100,000 to 150,000, mentioning that some estimates ran as high as 250,000. It was certain, at any rate, "that there has been no such gathering of Londoners since the Park railings went down in 1867." The rest of the special issue was filled with descriptions of the ten processions to the gathering place, commendations of the good behavior of the crowd, and accounts of the speeches, including Stead's, at the different platforms which had been set up.

The leader of the regular afternoon editions also featured "Saturday's Success," stating that "the first London Town's Meeting surpassed the most sanguine expectations of its promoters." In an apparent contradiction of the claim made in the morning edition, the crowd was said to be slightly smaller than that which gathered in July, 1884, to demand county franchise. However, Saturday's demonstration, unlike the 1884 meeting, had the backing of no political party and included only Londoners; moreover, "it was bitterly opposed or altogether ignored by all the daily papers." Stead noted with disappointment that Cardinal Manning had failed to take part and that, surprisingly, the Salvation Army was "conspicuous by its absence." Still, according to the editor, despite gloomy prophecies the meeting was a success. No obscene literature was sold and the speeches were on a high moral plane—"There was no setting class against class, there were no disgusting details,

1. "News of the Week," *Spectator*, August 22, 1885, pp. 1089-90.
2. There were five other sketches to illustrate the special issue; this journalistic innovation was used more frequently than ever during the "Maiden Tribute" months.

no inflammatory and sensational demagogues." The meeting proved that even without recognized natural leaders the masses were responsive "to a straightforward appeal to their nobler instincts."

The estimates of the size of the crowd in the other London papers were, as an Occasional Note commented, "what they choose to make it." The most depreciatory estimates were those of the *Standard* ("some thousands of idlers") and the *Telegraph* ("[the crowd] did not seem to exceed 15,000"). The *Times* reported that the gathering was sizable, but, as the *PMG* remarked, "it has a whole column full of reasons to explain the ugly fact away." The *PMG* said that other estimates ranged from 40,000 to 100,000, and observed, "When it is remembered that all these are the grudging confessions of men who have done their worst to make Saturday's demonstration a failure, our readers will have no difficulty in taking our word for it that it was a magnificent success." The appraisals of the meeting were as varied as the guesses about the attendance. Some papers dismissed the whole episode as irrelevant; others saw it as contributing to a positive evil. Perhaps the most sympathetic account in the London press appeared in the *Daily News*, which called the attendance good and declared that despite the sale of some obscene literature the overall tone of the meeting was high. The *Sunday Times* report also was favorable, speaking well of both the size and spirit of the crowd.[3] The evening papers tended to be more derogatory than the mornings, although the *Echo* described the crowd as large and referred to the good intentions of the sponsors. The religious papers, which came out later on, were mostly sympathetic to the Hyde Park meeting, as they had been to the original crusade.

From the myriad of conflicting accounts, a few observations might be drawn. Without trying to make an impossible—and unrewarding—estimate of the numbers involved, it would seem that the crowd was, indeed, relatively large. To that degree, then, the crusading editor had triumphed over what he saw as the forces of darkness and evil, and the power of the press had been shown again. Stead's message had been spread, and it must be assumed that a large part of any sizable mass demonstration would represent the working classes. The question which cannot be answered is, Why did they come? To give or receive inspiration for the con-

3. The editor of the *Sunday Times* wrote a letter to Stead pointing out that his paper had publicized the demonstration in advance and had given a five-column report of it on the day following (*PMG*, August 26, 1885).

tinuance of the crusade? To be entertained? To satisfy curiosity, prurient or otherwise? No one can say, of course, and Stead's analysis would obviously differ from that of other reputable observers and journalists. But despite the hagiographic accounts of this episode presented by some of Stead's admirers, there is no evidence, and no real reason to assume, that the Hyde Park demonstration had any noticeable effect on the improvement of public morality or the enforcement and implementation of the Criminal Law Amendment Act.

After Hyde Park the new crusade began to taper off, although the demonstration was certainly not the end. For a time there was a clamor for the repression of the sale of indecent literature, in which the *PMG* joined. Many blamed the *PMG* for having inspired such literature, and the paper duly printed these comments, along with accounts of meetings at which the *PMG* was heatedly attacked and defended.

Meanwhile, the final and perhaps most dramatic chapter of the "Maiden Tribute" crusade was beginning to unfold. By his own later account, when Stead, at the outset of his investigations, purchased Eliza Armstrong, he made two mistakes: he failed to secure the consent of the girl's father and he had not asked for a written receipt for the purchase price from her mother.[4] He might have added that another mistake was accepting Rebecca Jarrett's testimony that Mrs. Armstrong was aware her child was being procured for immoral purposes. It did not occur to him that others might see as unpardonable arrogance his assumption that, because his motives were good, he had the right to abduct a girl from her parents.

On Saturday, July 11, more than five weeks after Mrs. Jarrett had taken Eliza, Mrs. Armstrong appeared at the Marylebone police court to report that her daughter was missing. She said that the girl had been offered a "nice situation" at Croydon, but that she had tried in vain to locate her. The next day *Lloyd's Weekly Newspaper*, which played a leading role in publicizing the Armstrong case, carried a long story under the heading "A Mother Seeking a Lost Child." On Monday, July 13, several other London papers, including the *Pall Mall Gazette*, reported the episode.[5] Nothing

4. Scott, *Life and Death*, p. 128.
5. The mother's name was not given in the stories, most of which seem to have been written by the same court reporter. It is possible that Stead was not even aware that the woman in question was Mrs. Armstrong.

more was heard of the matter publicly until July 31 when Mrs.
Armstrong renewed her application for the return of her child. On
this occasion she told the court that her suspicions had been
aroused when someone sent her a copy of the *PMG* which told of
the purchase of Lily. The *St. James's Gazette* now picked up the
story and observed, on August 1, "Either a clever lie has been con-
cocted in order to produce a sensational story, or the child has
been exposed to treatment of a character to demand a strict magis-
terial investigation." It pursued the matter in articles on August
4 and 5, suggesting that the Salvation Army was primarily responsible for the girl's disappearance. On August 6 Stead assured his
readers that the authorities knew all the facts about Eliza Armstrong, who was safe, happy, and in good hands, and said angrily,
"If ignorant and misdirected philanthropy incites journalistic jealousy to insist on the return of the child to her old surroundings the
change will be in every way for the worse." Meanwhile *Lloyd's*
had sent representatives to interview the principals and to try to
locate the girl. In its weekend editions of August 9, 16, and 23,[6]
it described the progress of its investigations—which were often
frustrated by Bramwell Booth of the Salvation Army—and campaigned with a tenacity worthy of Stead himself to have Eliza
returned to her parents. On August 11 Stead's old antagonist,
Cavendish-Bentinck, brought the case up in Parliament, asking
Cross if he had read *Lloyd's* and if he had initiated any inquiries.
The Home Secretary replied that he had done so and was now
seeking the opinion of the attorney general.[7]

On August 21 Stead spoke at the St. James's Hall Conference, on
the eve of the Hyde Park demonstration. He was interrupted by
a cry of "Armstrong," and replied, "I will tell you about Armstrong." He absolved General Booth and the Salvation Army from
any blame, accepting full responsibility himself for taking Eliza
away from drunken parents and a home "that was steeped in vice"
(August 22). Stead, along with Booth, had been trying to convince Mrs. Armstrong that her daughter would be better off not
returning to her old life, but on Saturday, August 22, he wrote to
the mother saying her child would be handed over the following
Monday. Eliza arrived back from France on Sunday and was, as

6. Like most Sunday newspapers of this period, *Lloyd's* had both Friday
and Saturday editions; the Armstrong stories varied from one edition to the
next as the case developed.
7. *Hansard's Parliamentary Debates*, 3d ser., vol. 300 (1885): p. 1739.

promised, returned to her home the next day. Ou August 25, Stead wrote a follower on "The Case of Eliza Armstrong." For some reason—probably to protect the girl, and possibly to protect himself—he was at this stage denying that Lily and Eliza were the same girl. He claimed that the events described in the revelations had happened to another thirteen-year-old, and that he had merely taken Eliza through the same procedure to show that it could have happened. Eliza was now, he reported, safe and sound. Unfortunately, the details of the Lily story, as well as the dates given, made it clear that it was really Eliza Armstrong he was talking about. Thus he not only hurt his personal reputation, but cast doubt on the rest of the revelations as well.

Shortly after this Stead left for the Continent and a much needed rest, but his holiday was destined to be cut short. After communications with General Booth and the police, the government decided to prosecute Rebecca Jarrett and she surrendered herself to Scotland Yard on the night of September 1. On September 2 she was charged at the Bow Street police court with abduction and assault, and on the same day Stead cabled his paper from Frindelwold, Switzerland, protesting the arrest and reiterating that he was solely responsible for the Eliza Armstrong incident. His message was printed in the *PMG* leader for September 3, "A Welcome Prosecution." The leader writer praised the "Chief Director's" behavior throughout his investigations, and reminded readers that he had asked for public investigation of the revelations from the outset.

Stead had no cause to complain about a "conspiracy of silence" during the hearing and trial of the Eliza Armstrong case. The *Standard* for September 3 said it was unwilling to prejudice legal proceedings, but then launched into a long denunciation of Stead and his actions. It once more decried the "Maiden Tribute" series as "thrusting upon the public all the mass of semi-moral, semi-prurient, and wholly sensational details which had been burning in the editor's pocket." The *Morning Advertiser*'s attack on Stead the same day was, if anything, more scathing. The editor was accused of deliberately taking advantage of a poor, ignorant family and the episode described as "one of the most horrible enormities which has been perpetrated in modern times." On the other hand, the provincial press showed, in the *PMG*'s words, "less readiness to prejudge the question." On Monday, September 7, Stead; Sampson Jacques, a journalist who had helped him with his investigation; Bramwell Booth; Mrs. Combe, a Salvation Army worker who had accompanied Eliza to France; and Louise Mourez, the abortionist who examined Eliza and sold Stead the chloroform, joined Mrs. Jarrett under charge at the Bow Street police court. Stead felt he could not expect fair reporting of the hearing from the rest of the London press, and announced that evening that beginning on September 8 the *PMG* would issue a special morning edition giving an acount of the previous day's proceedings. The *PMG* reports of the hearing and trial which followed were usually written in a very subjective vein, frequently including statements which could only be described as editorial. Still, if these articles were not always objective, neither were they grossly distorted. At the same time, for all of Stead's innuendos about biased reporting, the other London papers—although many of them did make it clear where their sympathies lay—were generally accurate, if selective, in their accounts.

The Bow Street hearings were held on September 7, 8, 12, and 14, after which there was an adjournment until September 26. At every session the courtroom was packed with spectators and reporters, as most of the London dailies sent three or four men to cover the event. The crowds outside the building were large, boisterous, and extremely hostile to the defendants. On Monday, September 14, a lady was seen distributing rotten eggs, and that evening the police had to provide an escort for Stead and his companions to ensure their safety as they left. The *PMG* leader the next day, "A Short Breathing Space," denied that the "ragtag and bobtail which has gathered from day to day outside in Bow-street" reflected the views of the British people. It was true that the paper claimed to have the support of public opinion, but "we have never asserted that the pickpockets and *Maquereaux* of London and their hangers-on were on our side."

On Saturday, September 26, the hearing was concluded with the defendants bound over for trial at the Central Criminal Court. Stead had not been allowed to speak about his motive in the affair, which led the *PMG* to observe in an Occasional Note the next Monday that, from the defendant's viewpoint, "the conduct of the magistrate was almost ideal, so thoroughly was it in keeping with the character of the prosecution." The same issue reprinted from the special morning edition "Mr. Stead's Suppressed Defense," which covered three full pages. According to an introductory paragraph, W. H. Smith and Son refused to sell this morning edition, although it had sold the previous ones which reported the case against Stead. The "Defense" began with a summary of the failure of Parliament to pass a Criminal Law Amendment Act prior to 1885, and then gave a step-by-step account of Stead's personal involvement in the cause, his investigations, the purchase of Eliza, and the "Maiden Tribute" campaign.

While waiting for the trial, Stead revived the new crusade on a tour of England, in which he spoke to public meetings summoned to demonstrate the support of the community for the Criminal Law Amendment Act. Needless to say, the *PMG* gave full coverage to these meetings and assured its readers of their success in terms of the size and enthusiasm of the crowds. For ten days Stead, who seems to have developed into an able and convincing public speaker, addressed at least one and sometimes two meetings every day. He returned to London to speak to a gathering at Exeter Hall on October 15. The *Times, Standard, Post,* and *Daily Telegraph* did not mention the affair at all, and the *Daily News* and *Chronicle* ran only a bare outline story. The *PMG* itself gave more than a page to an account of the meeting, which apparently was well attended, and of Stead's tour of the North—an acount which amounted to a eulogy of the editor.

On Monday, October 19, the *PMG* leader, "The New Chivalry," spoke glowingly of the great moral revival in England brought about by the new crusade, and called Stead "a humble and remote nineteenth-century representative of PETER THE HERMIT." It denied that the new crusade departed from the original lines of the "Maiden Tribute" campaign and that it wished to set class against class or "to make men compulsorily virtuous by Act of Parliament." The curbing of vice required not just legal, but moral, weapons, and these were being forged by the crusade. In effect, the leader writer was proclaiming, presumably for Stead, that one of the functions of a newspaper was to stimulate the improvement of the public morality of a nation.

Stead and his codefendants appeared at the Central Criminal Court on October 19, and on the next day a grand jury found a true bill against them on separate charges of abduction and indecent assault. The first trial opened at Old Bailey on Friday, October 23, with all the defendants in the dock except Louise Mourez, who was not charged with the abduction.[8] Justice Henry Lopes

8. Booth and Combe were charged with abduction but not with indecent assault.

presided, with Attorney General Richard Webster prosecuting, and on November 7, after twelve sessions of the court, the trial concluded. Since Stead never denied the basic charge—that he had taken Eliza Armstrong from her parents without the permission of her father—the result was a foregone conclusion. However, certain other points of interest emerged from the testimony. It was apparent that Stead had put too much faith in Rebecca Jarrett, who proved to be a most damaging witness for the defense. Perhaps because she did not want to incriminate old friends from her earlier life, perhaps because the sharp questioning of the prosecutor confused her, she contradicted Stead, contradicted herself, and all but broke down on the stand. It will never really be known how much of the first part of the Lily story, which described the transactions with Mrs. Armstrong and a neighbor and the attitude of the mother to her daughter, was true. It was ascertained that, despite Stead's earlier denials, Lily was Eliza Armstrong. On November 2, during the eighth day of the proceedings, Stead said that the Lily article was a literal transcript from memory of what he understood Mrs. Jarrett to have told him. On the next day he made another statement which, although it had no real bearing on the trial, cast a slight cloud over his other revelations. He admitted that he was in a state of "intense excitement" while conducting his investigations, and that, although a teetotaler and nonsmoker, he had indulged in champagne and cigars in order to pass as a veteran participant in the world of vice. On November 7 the jury returned the verdict of guilty of abduction against Stead and Mrs. Jarrett, while General Booth and Sampson Jacques were found not guilty. (The charges against Mrs. Combe had been dropped earlier.) In rendering the decision the foreman stressed that the jury believed that Stead had been misled, and recommended that the government "secure the efficient administration of the Act recently passed for the protection of children."

On the next day the Sunday *Lloyd's,* which had a proprietary interest in the case, was jubilant. In a first-page leader it said, "Happily . . . the jurymen have done their duty in a way that establishes—we trust once and for all—the inviolability of English homes, be they ever so humble." The verdict proved, as *Lloyd's* had maintained all along, that Eliza was not sold but abducted, and the evidence given showed that the stories of other dreadful crimes were "no more truthful than the alleged sale of Eliza by

her mother." The comments of the *Observer* on the same day high-
light one of the differences between the old journalism and the
new: "Our conception of the duty of journalism differs entirely
from that on which Mr. Stead has based his defense. It is not the
duty of the journalists to act as a literary knight errant, and to
undertake a crusade for the redress of every wrong, whether real
or imaginary. Journalism, after all, is not a mission, and editors
are neither missionaries nor evangelists."

On Monday, November 9, the chief London dailies, in reflecting
on the trial, were unanimous in their denunciation of the "Maiden
Tribute" campaign, although some were willing to acknowledge its
good motives. On the whole they applauded the verdict as a vindication of the good name of the English people, and several felt
that there must now be doubts about the other revelations. The
provincial papers once again tended to differ from their metropolitan contemporaries. They made much of the purity of Stead's
motives, of the fact that the charge against him was a technicality,
and of the general support which they all seemed to think he had
from the public. Perhaps the *Western Morning News* summed it
up best when it stated, "Stead has erred because he is so good a
man." Yet there also appeared in some of their commentaries the
underlying conviction that for all of the purity of his motives, he
had indeed erred, and the *Leeds Mercury* questioned the truth
of the other "Maiden Tribute" stories.

As "The Chief Director of the Secret Commission," Stead wrote
the *PMG*'s leader for Monday. "I had a fair trial," he began, "a
full hearing, and on the evidence before the court a just verdict."
He had no desire to appeal "either to the mercy of the judge or
to the tribunal of public opinion," since barren controversy about
an isolated incident should not divert attention from the real campaign. After praising the judge, the attorney general, and the jury,
Stead admitted that legally there was no alternative to the verdict.
Rebecca Jarrett, "with her muddled brain and defective brain," had
misled him, intentionally or not; his consolation would come from
the good which he had done in protecting young girls. This same
issue published what was really another editorial on the case,
although it was presented as a straight news story on page 8. Under
the heading "The Verdict and the Revelations," the article objected
to attempts to discredit all of the revelations on the ground they
had been based on Rebecca Jarrett's evidence. It was pointed out

that she had been the source of only three of the total of fifty-seven columns of the "Maiden Tribute" series, and that of those three columns, less than half actually had any bearing on that part of the Lily case at issue during the trial.

The other Monday evening papers showed more acerbity than the mornings in their consideration of the issues involved in the Armstrong case and the "Maiden Tribute" crusade. One of the most brutal of these accounts, and the most antagonistic to Stead personally, appeared in the *Globe*. It accused him of posing as a martyr in the interest of personal profit, which he increased by touring the provinces and "sending round the hat." It suggested that since the sum collected must be considerable, the editor should use it to make provision for Eliza Armstrong and her parents. The *St. James's Gazette* was also vitriolic in its analysis of Stead's character, declaring that he "was probably intoxicated when he took into his mind certain details worked into this story. . . . There was no truth in it, and nobody was better aware of it than the man who arranged and carried out a most cruel imposture. . . . Now we see in what condition the inquirer was sometimes when he was gathering revelations." The *Echo,* in turn, stressed the profit motive in Stead's venture and asserted that there could be no other explanation.

Stead and Mrs. Jarrett were not sentenced until they, along with Jacques and Mourez, had been tried on the charge of assault. The trial began on Tuesday, November 10, before a new jury, which gave its verdict the same day. Louise Mourez was found guilty of indecent assault and the other three defendants of "aiding and abetting." In passing sentence, Justice Lopes told Stead that his motives were good, but that he had experimented with a child and used a "person of alleged reformed character" who had deceived him. The result was "that your experiment, instead of proving what it was intended to prove, has absolutely and entirely failed." The publication of the "Maiden Tribute" series supposedly had no bearing on the case, but the judge saw fit to lecture Stead about it. He accused the editor of publishing a distorted account of Eliza Armstrong's story and deluging "our streets and the whole country with an amount of filth which has, I fear tainted the minds of the children that you were so anxious to protect, and which has been . . . a disgrace to journalism." Stead was sentenced to three months and Rebecca Jarrett to six months on the two charges, Sampson Jacques to one month and Louise Mourez to six months on the single charge of assault.[9]

The sentencing brought forth a new spate of commentary in the *PMG* and other journals. The *PMG* leader for Wednesday, November 11—presumably written by Cook—dealt with the subject of "The Sentence—and After." It began, "With the sentences which Mr. Justice LOPES passed yesterday on the several defendants in the ARMSTRONG case we have no fault whatever to find." The sentence was what Stead had told his friends to expect, and he had no more intention of flinching from it than he had of flinching from his crusade. The leader writer did question the propriety of Justice Lopes's allusion to the *PMG* articles, for which Stead was not being tried, since it might tend to support the charges being made by some of the provincial newspapers that the sentence was a vindictive one. The article also emphasized that the Jarrett testimony in no way discredited the revelations as a whole; that in fact, since Stead's only error in the Armstrong case was the belief that Eliza's mother had sold her knowingly, it was more than ever clear that the Criminal Law Amendment Act was necessary to protect the children of women who could so easily be duped.

The rest of the Monday London papers regarded the sentence with approval, except for the *Daily Chronicle,* which credited Stead with the best of motives and suggested that his sentence should be shortened. Several had caustic comments to make about Stead's character. The *Times* referred to his fanaticism and pointed out that his only response to the charge was to glory in his cause. "The zealot bows to the law," it said, "but is not less a zealot." The *Standard* wondered "that it should ever have been possible for a moment to conceal such atrocious proceedings under the mask of holy purpose," and thought that the recital of the abominations perpetrated by Stead suggested monomania. The *Globe* took much the same tack, expressing the conviction that the "self-constituted saint" got off too lightly. In the provincial press there was somewhat more diversity of opinion, with the balance weighing heavily on the side of Stead and his campaign. However, some of these papers were as critical as their London brethren; the *Scotsman,* for instance, saw the revelations as "the excited productions of a brain heated by champagne in common stews" (November 12). Of all

9. Stead was pleased that the length of his sentence seemed to confirm another of his premonitions. The three months he received was to start with the opening of the session, which meant he would actually serve only a little over two months in jail; before the sentencing he had been "certain I was going to prison for two months" (Whyte, *Life,* 1:185).

the analyses made of Stead and his character, probably none was
wider of the mark than that of the *Sheffield Independent*. In denouncing the sentence imposed on the editor, it asserted that "three
months' imprisonment to a delicate, highly-nervous and sensitive
spirit will be a torture too hard to bear. He ought not to be left
quietly to endure this infliction" (November 14).

At the end of the week the *Spectator,* which had more than once
expressed its dislike of the "Maiden Tribute" campaign, now decided that "the public will welcome the leniency of the sentence."
It also accepted the verdict of certain other journals that Stead's
judgment during his investigations had been muddled by "drinking champagne with women of bad character." This led him to
exaggerate the horrors with which he was dealing, and it was
"obvious that the whole procedure which led to this Armstrong
case was the conception of an over-excited brain." The *Spectator*
did grant Stead a desire to do good, but saw it "mingled with the
vainglory of posing as a hero and martyr in the case." [10]

Without question Stead gloried in his martyrdom and, as he
often acknowledged, he enjoyed his stay in Holloway prison. He
lived in relative ease, relieved of many of the daily pressures which
had so greatly increased in recent months. He had frequent visits
from friends and family, and, in effect, continued to edit the *PMG*
from prison. In his diary, in letters to friends, in later books and
articles, Stead made it clear that it was a thoroughly pleasant experience, and his annual celebrations of the date of his jailing—at
which he would dress in his prison uniform—suggested that he was
recalling a festive occasion. Not the least important source of his
pleasure was the conviction that the recent publicity had lifted
him to a new pinnacle of fame and influence. As he told Morley
when his former chief visited him at Holloway early in 1886, "As
I was taking my exercise this morning in the prison yard, I asked
myself who was the man of most importance now alive. I could
only find one answer—*the prisoner in this cell.*" [11] Although he
promised Yates Thompson that there would be no more "Maiden
Tributing," [12] he only meant it in a narrow sense. Stead's tenure
as editor of the *Pall Mall Gazette* had about four more years to
run, and while nothing again would match the excitement and

10. "The Armstrong Verdict," *Spectator,* November 14, 1885, pp. 1508-9.
11. Morley, *Recollections,* pp. 209-10.
12. Scott, *Life and Death,* pp. 143-44. Stead wrote to Thompson from the
dock at Old Bailey on November 10, offering his resignation, but it was
refused (p. 142).

public attention stirred by the articles of July, 1885, there were new campaigns to come and fresh dragons to slay.

Stead's release from prison on January 18, 1886, was the occasion for an enthusiastic meeting of friends and well-wishers at Exeter Hall, and some qualified praise in the next day's *Daily News*. Remarking on the irony that Stead's release coincided with the sentencing for a mere month of a man convicted of attempted assault on a little girl, the morning paper acknowledged that Stead had made mistakes in his campaign and that "the particular course he pursued . . . was conducive to evil effect on public morals," but that the permanent good of the Criminal Law Amendment Act was more important. "Mr. Stead is an enthusiast," the *News* observed, "and enthusiasts have ever affronted the wisdom of the worldly wise." On the evening of January 18 the *PMG* printed the first of five illustrated articles by the editor on "My First Imprisonment." The last installment appeared on January 27 (a day on which much of the issue was devoted to Salisbury's resignation and the formation of Gladstone's ill-fated third ministry), and was subtitled "Happy Holloway." Stead's whole retrospective attitude toward his imprisonment is best summed up by his concluding sentence: "I have ever been the spoiled child of fortune, but never had I a happier lot than the two months I spent in Happy Holloway."

Stead's trial and imprisonment provided a dramatic climax to the "Maiden Tribute" campaign, of which Eliza Armstrong's story became—somewhat to his regret—a symbol. But what did the bizarre events of the summer of 1885 mean to Stead, to the *Pall Mall Gazette,* and to the history of British journalism? The editor himself and some of his contemporaries would insist that the whole campaign had demonstrated the power and influence of the press; it had shown what a newspaper could achieve, both in terms of arousing public opinion and in pressuring a reluctant legislature. Stead had believed in this power since his days with the *Northern Echo.* The passage of the Criminal Law Amendment Act, the Hyde Park demonstration, and the excitement at Old Bailey in October merely confirmed his belief. These events undoubtedly helped to shape the grandiose and far-reaching scheme for the newspaper of the future, which he was to outline later in the *Contemporary Review.*[13]

13. See p. 204 ff.

It is impossible to answer categorically the question of whether or not Stead, through the pages of the *Pall Mall Gazette,* actually was responsible for the passage of the Criminal Law Amendment Act. But in spite of the denials made by certain M.P.'s and Home Secretary Cross's insistence that the ministry had always intended to pass the bill,[14] the "Maiden Tribute" agitation at the very least ensured that it would be passed at this time. Those who believed Stead's cause to be righteous were in no doubt about the importance of his role. Benjamin Scott referred to the act as being "wrung from a reluctant legislature" and said that "we are mainly indebted [for its enactment] to Mr. W. J. *[sic]* Stead, an energetic denouncer of criminal vice, and of the system of regulated prostitution." [15] Millicent Garrett Fawcett, who, like Scott, was connected with Stead in his fight against the Contagious Diseases Act, wrote in 1912 that the "chivalric campaign" of 1885 had been responsible for the Criminal Law Amendment Act, and declared that "all who care for justice to women and who desire to see the law and its administration make sure that, as far as possible the world shall be a place of happiness and safety for children, have lost a stalwart friend in the death of W. T. Stead." [16] But the verdict need not depend upon the testimony of friends. The debates in the House of Commons over the *PMG* series are significant. Understandably, many members denied the influence of the newspaper agitation on their deliberations—who would want to admit that his views were shaped by a press campaign led by an eccentric sensational journalist?—but the constant references to the *PMG* during the sessions dealing with the bill as well as the jam-packed House while the new amendments were being hammered out, attest to Stead's influence. The archenemy of the "Maiden Tribute" campaign, Cavendish-Bentinck, tacitly acknowledged this influence during the debates when he said that "but for the publications to which reference had been made, he did not believe that the House would have been so full as it was on the present occasion." [17] Among the

14. Lord Granville was quoted as saying that he and Harcourt had been determined to steer the bill through long before the *PMG* agitation began and that Cross had promised full assistance in getting it passed regardless of cost in time and effort ("News of the Week," *Spectator,* November 21, 1885, p. 1538).

15. Benjamin Scott, *A State Iniquity: Its Rise, Extension and Overthrow* (London: Kegan Paul, Trench, Trübner, 1890), p. 290.

16. Millicent Garrett Fawcett, Henry Scott Holland, and E. T. Cook, "W. T. Stead," *Contemporary Review,* May 1912, p. 609.

17. *Hansard's Parliamentary Debates,* 3d ser., vol. 300 (1885): p. 589.

observers of the press, too, many who objected to the campaign itself were willing to acknowledge its effectiveness. This attitude was perhaps best summarized in an article on Stead which appeared in the *Speaker* a few years later. "Nothing," it declared, "could have been more unfortunate, nothing more reckless or reprehensible, than the methods by which he started that agitation; but in itself the object at which he aimed was entirely good, and we have to thank him for a great improvement in the law of the land." [18] As the progress of the bill is reviewed, from the apathy evinced toward it by the Commons before July, to its passage in August, it is difficult to quarrel with the later judgment of the *Times* that "whatever may be thought of his methods, it cannot be denied that his crusade did, in fact, carry the Criminal Law Amendment Act and give impetus to international efforts towards checking the 'white slave trade.'" [19]

As far as rousing the nation is concerned, there can be no doubt that, for better or worse, because of the revelations, the Hyde Park demonstration, and the Armstrong case, tens of thousands of Englishmen were made aware of a problem which had never entered their consciousness before. The attention given to the campaign by provincial newspapers and various periodicals, the enormous sale of the *PMG* and of the "Maiden Tribute" pamphlet, the debates in the House of Commons, and, finally, the extensive newspaper coverage of the trial all ensured this result. Indeed, it was the widespread publicity given to Stead's exposés which formed the basis of a great deal of the criticism directed at him. There is no way of measuring how much of the public interest thus created reflected a prurient interest in sexual vice—a factor stressed by Stead's critics—and how much a sincere desire to correct a great social evil. However, the indignation of the articulate sector of the nation seems to have been directed more at the crimes exposed than at the man responsible for their exposure.

Many continued to denounce the "Maiden Tribute" campaign after its conclusion. In 1886 the *Spectator*, in an article deploring that scandalous trials seemed to have become more numerous and publicized, observed that they were doing "nearly as much mischief as the discussion on the Criminal Acts Amendment Bill and its resulting trial, which we believe, will be found, like Queen

18. [Wemyss Reid], "The Modern Press: IV.—'The Review of Reviews,'" *Speaker,* January 28, 1893, p. 100.
19. *Times,* April 18, 1912.

Caroline's trial, to have tainted the taste, and the morals too, of a whole generation." [20] Henry Fox Bourne, a contemporary of Stead, in his well-received history of the British press which appeared in 1887 viewed darkly the activities of the men behind the *Pall Mall Gazette*.

> They claimed to have procured or hastened an important change in the law for the protection of young women and children by an elaborate combination of very ugly facts and specious fabrications in a set of articles, unexampled in their way, entitled "The Maiden Tribute of Modern Babylon." As self-constituted censors of public morals and reckless pursuers of private objects, they . . . were lavish in insinuations and innuendos when the scandalous details they sought were scanty or had no existence. [21]

For many who came to believe that Stead's "revelations" were largely fabrications, the Eliza Armstrong case was pivotal. To some, Stead's prosecution amounted to an injustice, and they rallied to his side as Milner did; to others the incident seemed proof that Stead had built the edifice of his crusade on fraud and fantasy. Bernard Shaw, who had been won over to the cause by the revelations, was among those convinced that the trial had proved that Stead had lied. In 1922 he wrote to Frederick Whyte, "Nobody ever trusted [Stead] after the discovery that the case of Eliza Armstrong in the Maiden Tribute was a put-up job, and that he himself had put it up. We all felt that if ever a man deserved six months imprisonment Stead deserved it for such a betrayal of our confidence in him." [22] A similar view of the Armstrong case and the "Maiden Tribute" revelations was taken some years later by Hugh Kingsmill, who explained Stead's unreliability on the ground that he was "far too emotionally exasperated for exact inquiry into so delicate a matter." Kingsmill suspected that the women interviewed were only too ready to tell Stead whatever he wished to hear; and he felt that it was "difficult to find any excuse for the part in the drama thrust upon Mrs. Armstrong," whom he thought was tricked into appearing as a mother who would sell her daughter to a brothel. Yet he admitted that "without such methods, half cal-

20. "The Scandal of Recent Trials," *Spectator*, December 4, 1886, pp. 1621-22.
21. Bourne, *English Newspapers*, 2:343-44.
22. Whyte, *Life*, 1:304.

lous, half hysterical, Stead would hardly have forced the Criminal Law Amendment Bill through Parliament. The taste of the times required to be stimulated with monsters of depravity and helpless victims." [23]

In addition to the attacks on Stead's tactics and unreliability, there were doubts about the value of the results produced. In May, 1887, the *Saturday Review* claimed that in the two years since the passage of the Criminal Law Amendment Act, the number of crimes against women and children with which the amendments dealt actually increased. The very trials brought about by charges pressed under the terms of the act were an evil, for "there can be no doubt that every one of these trials does great harm. No one who has ever watched the demeanour of an uneducated audience on such occasions can doubt it for a moment. . . . there can be no doubt that the alteration in the public morals hitherto effected by the passing of the Act of 1885 has been principally for the worse." The article concluded, "The fact is that two years ago the body politic allowed itself to be poisoned, and now it must allow the poison to work itself out." [24] A more elaborate criticism of the act was offered in the October, 1885, issue of the *Law Quarterly Review*. H. A. D. Phillips, a justice of the peace in the Bengal civil service, discussed at length various weaknesses of the act and assaulted the *Pall Mall Gazette* and its "open sale of such garbage." He found it particularly objectionable that the *PMG* had "shown how pure girls may go and earn £5 and then *return to service as if nothing happened!*" He told of seeing a *PMG* placard which read, "£5 for a virgin warranted pure!"; and of two fifteen-year-old girls accosted outside the Charing Cross station by a hawker crying out, "Come on, Miss, 'ave a copy. This'll show you 'ow to earn five pounds!" According to Phillips, such a remark would have been punishable by a fine and imprisonment in India. He ended his article with a tirade against Stead, his crusade, his character, and his class bias, and vowed that "a sentence of penal servitude for life would not be too severe for him." [25]

It must be admitted that the denunciations of Stead and his crusade were not wholly unwarranted. The "Maiden Tribute" rev-

23. Kingsmill, *After Puritanism*, pp. 188-92.
24. "Outrages against Women," *Saturday Review*, May 28, 1887, pp. 769-70.
25. H.A.D. Phillips, "Offenses against Marriage and the Relations of the Sexes," *Law Quarterly Journal*, October 1885, pp. 471-84.

elations were sprinkled with exaggerations; the "Secret Commissioner's" sources were by no means unimpeachable; innocently or not, Stead did malign Mrs. Armstrong and was less than candid about other aspects of the case; by inference, he unfairly presented sexual immorality as peculiar to the rich; and the whole series exemplified journalism of the most sensational kind. Moreover, there seems to have been no dramatic diminution of criminal vice in London as a result of the act. Yet, on balance, the more praiseworthy aspects of the campaign outweigh the criticisms. The overall picture painted in the articles seems to have been reasonably accurate, and it is hard to quarrel with Stead's contention that even if Mrs. Armstrong was innocent of any culpability, the case still showed that young girls could be procured for immoral purposes. The sexual appetites of the wealthy might be no more base than those of the poor, but it was primarily the upper classes who had the opportunity to indulge such appetites. And although one distortion does not justify another, Stead's polemics were no more inaccurate than those of some of his opponents who seemed equally convinced that immorality was primarily an attribute of the masses. Stead would not deny that the "Maiden Tribute" crusade was sensationalism, but it was in the category of what he termed justifiable sensationalism. It was not the *fact* of shouting that mattered, but *what* was being shouted. If Stead's newspaper crusades did not have the impact of *Uncle Tom's Cabin* (to which he compared them), if the passing of the Criminal Law Amendment Act of 1885 did not end sexual vice in London, if some of the provisions of the act were unfortunate or unworkable, still it was no mean achievement to raise the legal age of consent to sixteen. Finally, the fears that Stead's revelations would breed lust and vice among impressionable readers seems to have been grossly exaggerated. It is still an open question whether outright pornography exerts the evil influence often ascribed to it, and "The Maiden Tribute of Modern Babylon" was not pornography, though labeled as such by many in its day.[26]

Although it can be persuasively argued that Stead's cause was noble and his motives just, in terms of the history of British journalism this is not the main issue. Regardless of its motivation or justness, the "Maiden Tribute" series was a key event in the develop-

26. An interesting, though uncritical, fictionalized account of the "Maiden Tribute" crusade is given by Stuart Cloete in his novel *The Abductors* (London: Wm. Collins Sons and Co., 1970).

ment of the modern British press. It is true that in the long run
the *PMG* was financially hurt by the crusade. As a result of it,
according to Scott, "the Pall Mall lost most of its advertisements and many of its readers." In a letter written early in 1886
(misdated February, 1885), Greenwood, the editor of the rival *St.
James's Gazette,* said that his paper's circulation had gone up many
thousands, "our new subscribers, of course, being the best of theirs."
Greenwood also remarked that "the railway readers of the *PMG*
try to hide what they are reading; how queerly ashamed they
look." [27] In fact, the desertion of the *PMG* by its older readers
never reached catastrophic proportions, but there was enough drop
in advertising to cause Yates Thompson some soul-searching about
his editor's crusades.[28]

However, it was not the long-run loss but the sensational spurt
in sales while the revelations were being published that intrigued
most observers. In December, 1886, the *Saturday Review* saw the
"Maiden Tribute" precedent as already encouraging imitators in the
field of unwholesome sensationalism. Since, so it was claimed, the
amount of indecent reporting was rapidly increasing, it "must be
presumed that editors and managers believed that this sort of publication does not materially diminish the number of their customers,
and does materially increase it." [29] Bourne also emphasized the
gains enjoyed rather than losses suffered by the *Pall Mall Gazette's*
directors. He disapproved of their campaigns and crusades but
admitted that they "secured for 'The Pall Mall' a considerable reputation which, whether the general effect was good or bad, evidently
answered the purposes of the producers." [30] Kennedy Jones,[31] whose

27. Scott, *Story of Pall Mall Gazette,* p. 281.
28. The total number of columns of ads for the first week in July, before the
impact of the "Maiden Tribute" series, was fifty-two and a half. By the first
full week in August it had dropped to thirty-nine columns. It rose only slowly
after this and never exceeded forty-five columns for any week during the
remainder of the year. Some of this fluctuation, of course, might be attributable
to other factors. For more on Yates Thompson's displeasure, and Stead's reaction, see Scott, *Life and Death,* pp. 143-45.
29. "A Question for Editors," *Saturday Review,* December 11, 1886, pp.
774-75.
30. Bourne, *English Newspapers,* 2:344.
31. Kennedy Jones was already an experienced newspaperman who had
worked in Glasgow and Birmingham as well as London when he persuaded
Alfred Harmsworth to buy the declining *Evening News* in 1894. As editor
(1894-96) Jones helped to revive the paper. In 1896 when the Harmsworth
brothers founded the *Daily Mail,* he contributed financially, as well as being
second in command to Alfred on this remarkable enterprise.

close association with Alfred Harmsworth made him one of the leading practitioners of the "later" New Journalism, offered the most revealing analysis of all. After recounting how Stead had introduced new fashions into nineteenth-century journalism, Jones turned to the "Maiden Tribute" campaign:

> His battalions of readers were recruiting quickly, but not quickly enough for him. This keenly perceptive Northerner had noticed that the Londoner, busy about his own affairs, is singularly unobservant. He will walk through a popular thoroughfare twice a day five or six days of the week for the greater part of his working life, and never raise his eyes to the first-floor level. The simplest way to collect a crowd in London is to shout loud enough from a top-floor window "Murder! Fire! Thieves!" So to an upper casement Stead went and raised the old scream at the top of his voice:
>
> "Babylon! Babylon! The Mother of Harlots! The Great City of Babylon!"
>
> He got his crowds.[32]

That Jones misread Stead's motives is beside the point. What is important is that the man who made his name in journalism as editor of the *Daily Mail* recognized the significance of Stead's crusade in the development of the modern newspaper. For all the reservations Kennedy Jones expressed about the ends of this particular sensation, his own career shows that he was one of those who were impressed by the means. "The Maiden Tribute" had demonstrated how well sensationalism could succeed in a daily newspaper.

32. Kennedy Jones, *Fleet Street and Downing Street* (London: Hutchinson, 1919), pp. 114-15.

CHAPTER SEVEN

Stead on Journalism

For more than a year after Stead's release from prison the tempo of life on the *PMG* slackened perceptibly from the frenetic pace set in "Maiden Tribute" days, although there were news stories of the first importance to be covered: the defeat of Gladstone's first Home Rule Bill, followed by the breakup of the Liberal party and the great 1886 electoral victory of the Conservatives; the deepening economic depression, which brought on demonstrations, mass meetings, and riots; the two divorce trials involving Sir Charles Dilke, which saw the *PMG* changing from a supporter to a determined opponent of the former Liberal cabinet member; new developments concerning such perennial favorites of Stead as imperial federation and housing and naval estimates; and, overseas, the annexation of Burma and more of the recurrent upheavals in the Balkans. The *PMG* also undertook to crusade for women's rights and relief for the unemployed, but the campaigns were carried on in subdued tones and evoked no great reaction. During this period of relative calm Stead continued to comment freely on the British press, praising, deploring, encouraging, needling, and, on at least one occasion, imitating. He also presented to the public his most comprehensive analysis of English journalism in terms of the present and the future.

I

On several occasions during the early months of 1886 Stead praised rival newspapers for adopting *PMG* innovations. On February 3, the *Times* was congratulated for including an alphabetical index like that which the *PMG* had been using since 1884. On March 3, the *Morning Post* was commended for printing an interview; to Stead's delight "the first interviewee selected by the Conservative and Courtly organ of English society is none other than the Nihilist 'Stepniak'—who if all that his enemies say be true is not only a dynamitard and revolutionist, but an assassin to boot." The *Daily News* had changed editors [1] in January and soon began to introduce modest innovations which the *PMG* duly noted. On March 12 the *News* printed an interview and on March 27 began using inset titles for its leading articles. Stead admitted that these changes were not earth-shaking, but "any recognition in English journalism that a newspaper is not a stereotyped (we use the word metaphorically) inflexible thing . . . calls for prompt recognition. *Nos compliments fraternels*" (March 27).

On May 20, under the heading "Popular Papers That Pay," Stead ran an interview with George Newnes. During the years that Stead was exerting his influence on the daily newspaper, Newnes, a Manchester businessman, had introduced into periodical journalism a style which was to affect the press as a whole. In 1881 he had founded a penny weekly, *Tit-Bits*, consisting of brief stories, or snippets, culled from the news. Dealing in anecdotal style with subjects of interest to the apolitical readers of limited literacy who had been spawned in part by the Education Act of 1870, *Tit-Bits* was much more appealing to the mass audience than a newspaper like the *PMG*. It was a type of journalism which was to have great influence on such later newspapers as the *Daily Mail* and the *Daily Express*. (The apprenticeship *Tit-Bits* afforded to Alfred Harmsworth was not its least important contribution to popular journalism. Harmsworth contributed to it when he was seventeen; later it provided a model for his *Answers to Correspondents*, established in 1888.) By 1886 *Tit-Bits* was flourishing, and because of its role in the history of English popular journalism the comments of both Newnes and his interviewer are worthy of attention.

In his introduction to the interview Stead classified *Tit-Bits* and *War Cry*, the organ of the Salvation Army, as unquestionably "the two most remarkable successes of the last half-dozen years." *War Cry* was not a commercial enterprise, but *Tit-Bits* was "a great commercial property, and from the point of view of pounds, shilling, and pence may be regarded as one of the most remarkable in-

1. Sir Henry Lucy succeeded Frank Hill amid speculation that Hill had not made the paper bright enough, which in itself suggests Stead's impact on the London journalistic scene. In a *PMG* interview Lucy said his policy would be to make the *News* more "lively and readable" (January 11).

stances of journalistic success that has been achieved in our time."
Newnes, like Stead, was the son of a Congregationalist minister and
had attended Silcoates; and he had no journalistic experience prior
to the founding of his weekly. "He knew what he liked," Stead
wrote, "and generalizing from his own taste, he one day hit upon
the vein which has brought him to his present position of influence
and affluence." Stead noted the enormous growth in the *Tit-Bits*
circulation, "sustained by constant resort to novel expedients which
have helped at once to advertise the paper and attract fresh
readers," and he made a point both of its wholesomeness and of
Newnes's rule of never allowing "a word, an expression or a sentence to appear . . . which a lady could not explain to a child who
would ask its meaning in the presence of a room full of people of
both sexes." Since *Tit-Bits* appealed to a different audience, it was
"possible that the majority of the readers of the *Pall Mall* . . . have
never had a copy in their hands," and Stead was at pains to correct the impression that *Tit-Bits* still consisted entirely of snippets
from other papers: they now accounted for only a third of its forty-
eight columns. Original contributions brought a guinea a column,
and among the regular features in 1886 were "Answers to Correspondents" (whose popularity so impressed the young Harmsworth), legal information, translations from foreign journals, and
an inquiries column. *Tit-Bits* supplied "a great deal of information
in the form in which it can be best assimilated by the desultory
newspaper reader," but the emphasis was on human interest and
it ignored politics. As Newnes explained to his interviewer, "You
with the *Pall Mall Gazette* had great influence, and help to make
Acts of Parliament, but I am content . . . with the issue of salutary
literature without attempting to change opinions." [2]

Prize contests were one of Newnes's early innovations. When the
circulation of *Tit-Bits* leveled off, he decided that "something must
be done to make a sensation and to make the paper better known."
He hit upon the idea of giving away a seven-room house for the
best Christmas story, and succeeded in attracting twenty-two thou-

2. Newnes to Stead in 1890: "There is one kind of journalism which directs
the affairs of nations. It makes and unmakes Cabinets. It upsets governments,
builds up navies and does many other great things. It is magnificent. That is
your journalism. There is another kind of journalism which has no such great
ambitions. It is content to plod on, year after year, giving wholesome and harmless entertainment to crowds of hard-working people craving for a little fun
and amusement." (Quoted in Reginald Pound, *Mirror of the Century: The
Strand Magazine, 1891-1950* [New York: A. S. Barnes and Co., 1967], p. 29.)

sand competitors for a building which had cost him six hundred pounds. The prize for another contest was a one-hundred-pound-per-year job on *Tit-Bits*. It was not as risky a proposition as it might seem, Newnes said, because the competition was a stiff one requiring enough ability to ensure that "anyone who could win the prize would be worth £100 a year. . . . The gentleman who was victorious is still with me, and has received a large increase in salary."[3] In a vein reminiscent of Stead, Newnes complained that on the Continent and in America his competitions had received a great deal of attention, but in England "the press practically boy-cotts *Tit-Bits*, and rarely, if ever, favorably mentions it."

In July, Stead paid *Tit-Bits* the high compliment of imitating its prize-giving competitions, although on a much more modest scale. A twenty-pound prize was offered in a plebiscite to determine the merit of paintings at the Royal Academy exhibit. Contestants voted on twelve different categories—for example, best picture of all, best classical picture, and worst picture of all—with a prize going to the person who agreed with the majority in the most categories. Stead, who liked to mock art critics, announced that the paper would give "an analysis of this great critical vote, which would serve picture-painters and picture-dollars as a very faithful gauge of the artistic tastes of the British public" (August 4). Some two thousand *PMG* readers responded to the challenge.[4]

In a September 30 article on prize competitions the *PMG* stated that the response to the academy competition proved the popu-larity of puzzles, and defended them as providing a mental chal-lenge to jaded society as well as the stimulus of an honorarium. While a daily puzzle would be out of place in a morning paper, "it is the duty of an evening paper not only to instruct and advise but also to amuse," and in consequence the *PMG* would devote a column once a week or oftener to a contest. First prize would be two pounds, second prize one pound. "Puzzle Number One," which followed, called for suggestions for an original contest to be used later. The winning proposal was that contestants should rate members of the House of Commons in twelve categories, in-

3. The man was Arthur Cyril Pearson (1866-1921), who founded *Pearson's Weekly* (1890) and started the *Daily Express* in 1900 as a rival to Harms-worth's *Daily Mail*.
4. In a sense the contest promoted "culture," for to enter it contestants had to purchase a sixpence guide to the exhibition. The winner was announced on August 16.

cluding best orator, best debater, most unpopular, and most accomplished. The results indicate something of the character of *PMG* readers: Gladstone won five of the favorable categories, while the freethinker Charles Bradlaugh topped the list as most unpopular. The obstreperous Irish Nationalist Joseph Biggar narrowly defeated Parnell in the race for most obstructionist (October 13). In all, the *PMG* ran thirty-three contests before announcing on May 25, 1887, that it was ending the feature "for a time." However, the contests were not revived during Stead's editorship.

In a contest announced on November 3, 1886, competitors were asked to vote on newspapers in nine categories (the *Pall Mall Gazette* and the *Pall Mall Budget* were excluded from the voting). According to the results reported on November 15, the *Times* was regarded as the best English newspaper and the best daily, the *Spectator* as the best weekly. Other winners and their categories were the *Daily News,* best Liberal paper; the *Standard,* best Conservative newspaper; *Punch,* best comic newspaper; *Truth,* best society newspaper; *Christian World,* best religious newspaper; *Police News,* worst English newspaper. The *Times* won in its two categories by an "overwhelming majority, while *Lloyd's* was very close to the *Spectator,* with the *Saturday Review, Graphic,* and *Illustrated News* close on the heels of their more austere rival." The *Daily News* and the *Standard* were "far ahead of all competitors"; *Punch* was a virtually unanimous choice for the best comic paper; and *Truth* was "far ahead of its elder brother, the *World.*" The *Christian World's* chief competitor was not mentioned, but the *PMG* was careful to note that "the *Police News* and the *Evening News* ran a hard fight in Class No. 9, the *Police News* just winning." The results were not particularly surprising, and no less than fourteen competitors pegged them accurately enough to share the prize. The vote for the worst paper prompted Stead to interview the proprietor of the *Police News,* George Purkess, "in order to learn something as to its character, career and circulation, and to discover what points its conductors could plead in defense of the publication." Purkess, who took the results of the *PMG* balloting complacently, "urbanely volunteered much interesting information as to the history and position of his weekly illustrated calendar of crimes, casualties, and curious incidents," and cheerfully acknowledged "that good fortune had been meted out to him in a very generous measure." But Stead made it obvious that the *Police News* provided a type of sensationalism which he considered beyond the pale.

Late in the year 1886 Stead was given an opportunity to lecture his contemporaries when the Colin Campbell divorce suit became a cause célèbre.[5] The case revealed a double standard practiced by much of the press. It also provided further illustration of the distinctions which Stead drew in determining what was acceptable newspaper fare and it revived memories of the "Maiden Tribute" campaign. The *PMG* gave the trial full coverage, although not to the extent or with the same detail provided by some of the other London papers. Beginning on November 26 with a two-column account accompanied by four sketches and a double headline, the *PMG* reported on the case every day that it was in progress and continued to comment on its implications after its conclusion. Indeed, the verdict occasioned a leader entitled "Whitewashed All Around," which, while expressing sympathy for Lady Colin Campbell for having to endure what she did during the trial, strongly implied that her acquittal was not called for by the evidence (December 21).

Still, throughout the period that the Campbell case was in the spotlight Stead maintained a running attack on the reports which were appearing in other newspapers. On December 2 an Occasional Note observed, "The deliberately detailed reports of the Campbell case which are published every morning and evening by nearly every paper in the country must have somewhat surprised those who did not at the time see through the hypocrisy of these same papers when they condemned the mere mention of certain topics as prejudicial to the public morals." Over the next few days the *PMG* concentrated its fire on the "revolting" and "injurious" coverage given by the *Evening Standard* (December 3), which, it later claimed, "easily distances every competitor" in its detailed and copious stories on "the filthiest case ever reported" (December 6). However, when on December 11 the *PMG* carried the first of a series of summaries of the space allotted by various London dailies to the Campbell case, the breakdown showed that the *Daily*

5. Lady Colin Campbell already had secured a legal separation from her husband, a younger son of the Duke of Argyll. The divorce trial consolidated her suit against her husband, on grounds of adultery with a housemaid, and his suit against her, on grounds of adultery with four men—the Duke of Marlborough, the chief of the Metropolitan Fire Brigade, a high-ranking army officer, and a surgeon. On December 20, after deliberating for three and a half hours, the jury returned a verdict of not guilty in each case.

Chronicle, not the *Standard,* led the way.⁶ In the same issue Stead
answered the *Saturday Review,* which had charged that because
of the "Maiden Tribute" series newspapers had been tempted to
report divorce cases in "revolting" detail. He described the weekly
as an apologist for the upper classes and predicted that "after this
we may expect to be told some fine Saturday that it was the means
taken to secure the passing of the Criminal Law Amendment Act
which led to the destruction of the Cities of the Plain." Three days
later Stead zeroed in on a new target. "The interest felt by the
wealthier classes in the Colin Campbell case," he said, "is set in high
relief by the recent conduct of our expensive contemporary, the
Observer." This Sunday paper had greatly reduced its usual long
list of church services "to make room for the details of the filthiest
divorce case on record," yet few dailies or weeklies had "surpassed
the *Observer* (editor, Mr. Edward Dicey, C.B.) in denunciation
of the efforts which the *Pall Mall Gazette* made last year to check
some enormities of London vice" (December 14). In the *PMG*
leader for December 16, "Pecksniff and Poison," Stead further distinguished between types of sensationalism. He had never been
one to remain silent on ugly subjects when speaking out was necessary, but the time had come to protest "the extent to which the
newspapers flood the town with all the fetid filth that exudes under
the pressure of cross-examination in the Divorce Court." There was
no gain to be realized from such stories except the "filthy pence"
made by editors who prostituted the press by pandering to prurient curiosity and debauching the public mind. The diatribe was
strikingly reminiscent of those directed at Stead in 1885; probably
intentionally so. He observed that the *Chronicle,* "another mighty
purist last year," had published about 180,000 words on the trial,
and "by a curious coincidence there are 181,258 words in the New
Testament." Why was it, he wondered, that the "eloquent and impassioned moralists" of July, 1885, were now so silent about "this
deluge of obscenity." An Occasional Note in the same issue ex-
plored another facet of divorce court reporting, perhaps as a justification for the *PMG*'s own coverage of the Campbell case. It
stated that two witnesses who provided important evidence in the
trial had not been subpoenaed, but had come forward in the interests of justice after reading the story in the newspapers. This was

6. The column totals were *Chronicle,* seventy-four; *Standard,* forty-six;
Daily News, forty-four; *Telegraph,* forty-three; and *Times,* twenty-six.

seen as an argument against the complete suppression of divorce court news, which some people had been suggesting, but did not excuse the verbatim reporting of indecent testimony.

During the furor over the press coverage of the trial the National Vigilance Association applied in the Queen's Bench Division for a rule nisi to file criminal information against the publishers of Frank Harris's *Evening News*, on the grounds that the detailed reports of the Campbell case were an obscene libel. On December 18 Justice Denman gave a ruling that although it was a serious matter, the legal argument could not be taken up before the next sittings, and since the Campbell case was now finished, "it would be better to leave the parties to proceed otherwise" (December 18). Commenting on the failure of the application in an Occasional Note two days later, the *PMG* hoped that the action of the National Vigilance Association would act as a check on other newspapers. It felt that reports should be carefully sub-edited in the interests of public morality, but opposed any restriction on the freedom of the press. "If all reports had been suppressed," said the Note, "Sir Charles Dilke would have probably been sitting for Chelsea to-day." [7] On that same evening, December 20, the *Evening News* carried a rather tortuous explanation of its treatment of divorce news. It defended such coverage on the grounds that it exposed the fearful consequences of wrongdoing which were "the chief foundation of all true morality." The next morning the *Standard,* edited by W. H. Mudford, ran a pious article on the Campbell case, lamenting that such a sad tale, exposing the meanness of human nature, "should have been dinned into the public ear from day to day." That evening the *PMG* printed the statements from the *News* and the *Standard* over a large cartoon showing a news vendor from each paper in conversation, with the following legend:

> First Newsvendor (Mr. H——s' agent): What cheer, Billy? This 'ere Colin Campbell licks Chawlie Dilke into smash, don't 'e?
> Second Newsvendor (Mr. M——d's agent), slapping his pocket: 'E do just. (A fact).

Stead's interest in the double standard followed in reporting divorce cases, and a related issue of class inequities, carried over

7. Dilke lost his seat in Parliament after being named correspondent in the Donald Crawford divorce case. The scandal, in effect, forced him out of politics.

into the early months of 1887. On January 3 the *PMG* reprinted on a news page a circular letter sent to the controllers of the press and "signed by many men of eminence," including Gladstone, Cardinal Manning, the Archbishop of Canterbury, Henry James, and Arnold Morley. It asked newspapermen to minimize unnecessary details in the reports of divorce cases and warned of the dangers of familiarizing young people with vice. Perhaps the best answer as to why newspapers were not likely to comply was provided on another page under the heading "Sixteen Years of the Kerbstone and the Gutter." In an interview, two women newspaper vendors who had recently won dismissal of charges of obstruction made the point that the contents bills were what sold newspapers and that the two biggest recent windfalls for the vendors had been the Dilke and Campbell divorces.

The *PMG* renewed the debate in an Occasional Note on January 6, complaining that the day before most papers had suppressed the account of a trial of a supposedly respectable man who was convicted of outrages against eight small children. Asserting that there were "many like him still at large," the *PMG* argued that newspaper publicity might frighten such people or encourage their victims to bring them to justice. Yet there was not "even a paragraph to expose his crimes, while a hundred columns can be spared to chronicle all the libidinous imaginings of servants and blackmailers who crowd like carrion round a scandal in high life." Stead continued to make it clear he did not favor the complete censorship of divorce cases. On January 18 there were three Occasional Notes on the attempt of magistrates at Liverpool to stop the publication of divorce suits and other "indecent cases." The *PMG* saw this as "a powerful stimulus to vice," since publicity was the only security for justice in the courts. Without authorized reports, there would be "secret, exaggerated" ones of every sensational divorce case, which would hamper justice and lower public morality. "So certain and so serious is this that if there were no alternative between no reports of indecent cases and full reports we should elect unhesitatingly for the latter." The difference between the stories on the Campbell case in the *Evening News* and the *Times*, it continued, illustrated the alternative of expurgated reports. If a newspaper pandered to prurient taste with excessively detailed accounts, the law of obscene libel should be adequate; if it was not, it should be amended. The conclusion was that the "true way of meeting 'the injury done to public morals,' is not to suppress public reports, but to insist on their subserving the public interests."

A week later another Occasional Note called attention to an article by Mrs. Josephine Butler, published elsewhere in the paper, which opposed the idea of prohibiting newspaper reports of divorce cases. Such a policy of regression would, according to the *PMG*, be suicidal. "Better a bad smell once in a while when the sewer is flushed than to allow it to generate undisturbed and unnoticed for ever its poisonous gas" (January 25). On another page the *PMG* printed an extract from a pamphlet by Mrs. Butler, "The Revival and Extension of the Abolitionist Cause," in which she opined that the upper classes feared the reporting of divorce cases, since such stories tended to lower respect for the rich and extend the idea of democracy. A law prohibiting such reports would be against the ideals of those who had long suffered from the "Conspiracy of Silence." She did deplore the recent publication of horrible details of cases, but these simply proved that "the vicious example of the rich and great is a curse to a nation." The best way to correct the conduct "of the *Evening Standard,* the *Evening News,* and other papers" would be for the public to stop buying them. "The object of the journalist is to make money, neither more nor less," she said, "and if his circulation was decreased, his object would be thwarted."

On February 3 the Home Secretary, Henry Matthews, suggested that the president of the Divorce Division could deal with the matter of divorce case reporting "by way of Rule of Court, . . . to check the daily publication of offensive reports without impairing the important advantages of the public administration of justice in such cases" (February 4). Stead registered his objections in the next evening's leader, "Should Scandals in High Life be Hushed Up?" According to Stead, Matthews's real purpose was to make it impossible for papers to report fully on upper-class cases, for the Home Secretary's statement was "simply a euphemism for a proposal to hush up scandals in high life." Stead warned that covering up the vices of high society instead of utilizing legal remedies already available to control obscene publications was a remedy worse than the disease. The *Times* had supported Matthews's proposal, as well as the suggestion that divorce reports should not be published until the cases were decided, and Stead found its arguments for "this latest nostrum" extraordinary. A de-

layed report would be considered biased, reporters would put a
sensational gloss on suppressed material, and "the condensed report
must of necessity be much more concentrated filth than the daily
reports, where the objectionable matter is diluted by an immense
quantity of perfectly innocuous and often most highly instructive
detail of social life." To buttress this last point Stead spoke of a
future Macaulay getting material for a study of late Victorian society from the press reports of the Dilke and Campbell cases.

The divorce court judges were, at any rate, cool to Matthews's
proposal, and on February 18 the *PMG* was pleased to report that
the Home Secretary "will not introduce a Bill for Hushing up Scandals in High Life." The issue was not dead, however, and was the
subject of Commons debate on April 22. During an exchange over
a motion by Samuel Smith to increase the government's powers of
censorship the *PMG* once more found itself under attack for its
revelations of 1885. Sir Richard Webster, the attorney general,
spoke with particular harshness of the "outrageous articles" through
which Stead "under the assumed pretense of doing good" had introduced disgusting details—many of them invented—and lastingly
stained the future of his paper.[8] The *PMG* rebutted "the Attorney
General's sneer" in its April 23 issue by recalling that at the Armstrong trial, when the Archbishop of Canterbury and other witnesses were available to "prove the character" of Stead's motives,
the same attorney general had said, "*I have never questioned from
the beginning to the end Mr. Stead's desire to do good.*" The leader
for this same issue was addressed "To the Attorney-General and
Others." Terming Smith's motion "ill-advised," Stead acknowledged
that "Mr. SMITH has been scandalized, as many others have been,
at the extent to which some newspapers have abused the right of
reporting divorce cases." However, Stead agreed with the attorney
general (whose speech was praised except for that "uncharitable,
not to say unjust" remark) that there was no need to alter indecent
publication laws since a judge could order a case heard in private,
and reporting of obscene details could be punished under existing
laws.

Stead recalled the controversy "between the classes and the
masses two years ago," when the *PMG* took a course which he
admitted could be defended only because there was no alternative
and because of the urgency of the matter. He declared that he was

8. *Hansard's Parliamentary Debates*, 3d ser., vol. 313 (1886): pp. 1669-71.

certain Smith had no intention of preventing publications designed
for public good, and "the only difference between the *Pall Mall
Gazette* and the contemporaries who had constantly assailed us
for action" was that the *PMG* had a moral end, while its opponents
did not. "So long as it is merely ministering to a prurient curiosity
there is literally no limit to the space they are willing to devote
to the publication of scabrous matter." The leader also insisted
that the only means of public exposure of infamous persons was
through the press, although the press was often not very zealous
in this matter. In fact, Stead claimed, in crimes where the victim
was "only a woman" over half of the press would be found shield-
ing the culprit and hounding anyone who tried to expose him.
"Their favorite weapon is the cry of indecency," he averred, and
suggested—with little reason—that muzzling the *PMG* (at this time
in the midst of a new crusade)[9] was the real motive of many seeking to gag the press.

The subject was to reappear from time to time in the months to
come, but the furor gradually diminished, as did the *PMG*'s fear of
censorship. No legislation emerged, and the coverage of divorce
cases by the press did not noticeably change, but Stead had been
given a further opportunity to refine and present his thoughts on
the proper functions of the newspaper press.

II

During the respite from strenuous crusading in 1886 Stead gave
a more explicit account of his journalistic ideals in two articles in
the *Contemporary Review*. The first, published in May,[10] revealed
just how sweeping his ideas about the power and influence of the
press were. "Government by Kings," it began, "went out of fashion in this country when Charles Stuart lost his head. Government
by the House of Lords perished with Gratton and Old Sarum. Is
it possible that government by the House of Commons may equally
become out of date?" For Stead this was a rhetorical question, for
already "the trend of events is in that direction." The tendency in
the nation was to convert representative government into government by delegate and to be impatient with any intermediary.
Science, particularly in the guise of the telegraph and the printing
press, had resurrected the Witan days, in which the entire com-

9. See p. 212 ff.
10. "Government by Journalism," *Contemporary Review* 49 (May 1886):
653-674.

munity was within hearing and could participate in governmental discussion. The House of Commons, under the Septenniel Act (which established a seven-year maximum period between general elections), was often out of harmony with the nation, and its tendency toward despotism was tempered only by "the Press and the Platform." The growth of the power of these two political instruments was "indicative of the extent to which the nation is taking into its own hands the direct management and control of its own affairs." Whereas the M.P., upon election, leaves his constituency and plunges into a new and different world, the editor "must live among the people whose opinions he essays to express." Since he will lose his readers if he does not keep in touch with them and reflect their views, the newspaper is always up to date. "The editor's mandate is renewed day by day, and his electors register their vote by a voluntary payment of the daily pence." As for the platform, its power was "largely the creation of the Press." Statesmen now made their important speeches not in Parliament, but on the stump, where they would be more fully reported. Thus Stead saw the press becoming to the Commons what the Commons was to the Lords—a "Chamber of Initiative." Here, in "this first tribunal of popular opinion," bills were debated into final shape and reforms first threshed out. The fourth estate, free and open to all, showing great diversity and, in its columns, affording the most democratic debating place, was becoming more powerful than all the other estates of the realm. Statesmanship and leadership in the Commons was diminishing, and the member of Parliament "turns eagerly to the journalists for light and guidance." The importance of the press as a gauge of public opinion was already immense, but Stead believed it could be enormously increased, since other instruments were flawed in various ways. By-elections were helpful but too infrequent; private letters from constituents were "a most untrustworthy test" (although Stead inexplicably put a high value on letters to the editor); caucuses represented only a minority; and although public meetings better expressed public feeling than even newspapers, they could not always be sitting. Thus M.P.'s perforce had to depend upon newspapers to judge public opinion.

Stead quite obviously viewed the British politician as one who, whether he admitted it or not, was already subordinate to the press and thus should be more cooperative with it. Instead of denouncing newspapers, statesmen should take them into their confidence and

explain policies so as to avoid uninformed criticism. The prime
minister, Stead pointed out, reported every day to the queen—who
had much less real power than the press—on what happened in
Parliament.

In Part Two Stead was even bolder in his assertion of the power
and influence of the newspaper, as it existed and as it could be.
Although journalists did not think of journalism as an agency of
government, "the editorial pen is a sceptre of power," for the newspaper must be more than "a peepshow, through which men may
catch glimpses of the great drama of contemporary life and history."
He compared editors to the ancient Hebrew prophets, "whose
leaders on the current politics of Judaea and Sūmaria three millen-
niums ago are still appointed to be read in our churches." But
Stead was more concerned with the journalist as a ruler than as a
preacher. "To rule—the very idea begets derision from those whose
one idea of their high office is to grind out so much copy, . . . yet
an editor is the uncrowned king of an educated democracy." One
secret of the power of the press was that it could swing the balance
in a divided cabinet, and "there can be no doubt that the influence
of the Press upon the decisions of Cabinets is much greater than
that wielded by the House of Commons." He attacked the old
notion that journalists should not exercise civic responsibility; to
the contrary, it was their duty to combat evil and use their power
for public good. "The duty of a journalist is the duty of a watch-
man," he proclaimed, and no one could doubt his sincerity on that
score.

After offering his customary defense of "justifiable sensationalism," Stead returned to the question of the "direct governing functions of the Press." Among the most important was "the Argus-eyed
power of inspection." The newspaper was an always alert inspector whose daily reports were submitted to the whole people, and
its sphere of investigation should be increased to include jails,
asylums, and other official institutions. In fact, Stead suggested
that editors be granted the same official rights as a justice or representative of the Home Office, with the privilege of making unexpected visits. And he echoed the age-old lament of the newsman
when he called for modification of the laws of libel "to permit a
newspaper much greater liberty to publish the truth than the Press
at present possesses." In conclusion Stead predicted that newspapers would exercise even greater powers "when all our people

have learned to read, and the Press is directed by men with the instinct and capacity of government."

In his second article, published in November,[11] Stead's ideas were even more grandiose, not to say alarming. He began by attacking impersonal journalism, for "the personality of the editor is the essential centre-point of my whole idea of the true journalism of the governing and guiding order." A competent editor with the right personality "might, if he wished, become far the most influential Englishman in the Empire." Such an editor—and few could doubt whom Stead had in mind—would attain his position by knowing all the facts and determining what the people really thought. Editors should not gauge public opinion more accurately only to follow it blindly but, rather, to change such opinion when it was thought to be wrong. Thus, the first step was to get genuinely in touch with the people, and Stead had audacious ideas about how this could be accomplished. First, the editor and his assistants should know personally anyone whose opinion on a given subject was of any weight. Although it was unlikely that the editor could be intimately acquainted with all the cabinet members, for example, he should be able to ascertain their views on any subject within twenty-four hours, "not of course for publication, but for his own guidance and the avoidance of mistakes." At present, this was impossible because ministers were trained in the old school and because most journalists did not try to cultivate their acquaintance. The situation was even more difficult in respect to "ambassadors, judges, generals and great financiers," yet it was the editor's duty to know the thinking of all important people, from the Queen on down. For legislative matters, the ideal newspaper should have a whip in the House of Commons to determine the opinions of members on both sides of the aisle, and similar systems of informed representatives should prevail in important foreign capitals as well. In addition to these official and administrative contracts, there should be a close association with people of all levels of the social system. Only when all victims of injustice came with their complaints to editorial offices could newspapers "justify their claims to be tribunes of the people." If all this was visionary and utopian, wrote Stead, "it is something to have an inspiring ideal," and furnishing one was a responsibility that went with the power of the journalist.

11. "The Future of Journalism," *Contemporary Review* 50 (November 1886): 663-679.

Stead still hoped that one of the great newspaper proprietors would be content with a "reasonable fortune" and "devote the surplus of his gigantic profits to the development of his newspaper as an engine of social reform and as a means of government." If no such selfless publisher existed, some millionaire should emulate the medieval builders of cathedrals and schools and found such a journal. But if it were to be established, merely circulating the paper would not provide the editor with a pipeline to the views of the masses. Stead's plan for securing their views foreshadows in some respects present-day public-opinion polls. It would be necessary, he said, for the paper to establish close personal relations with "the right individuals in every town and village," perhaps by means of a system of "major-generals" reminiscent of the Cromwellian Protectorate. The country would be divided into districts, with a man or woman to act as the editor's alter ego in each such division. Among their other duties the district leaders were to keep the editor informed of everything that was going on, "either for encouragement, or for repression, or merely for observation and report." Each district leader would recruit volunteers from all walks of life to serve as his assistants—men and women sympathetic to the editor's ideals, who would be satisfied with a free copy of the newspaper as compensation. They would stand ready to report immediately their own and their neighbors' views on any disputed matter. Their reports were to be filled in on printed forms and sent to their editor, who would have them tabulated and would thus be able to speak authoritatively on the subject within three days. In times of crisis the deputy major-generals would be able to ascertain the true feelings of the people; this had been demonstrated during the "Bulgarian Atrocity" and Criminal Law Amendment Bill campaigns. Indeed, Stead saw them acting as propagandists who could "secure public expression of popular feeling" by arranging a series of open meetings at which information from the central office could be furnished to the people. "Under the proposed scheme," he said, "the local deputy would be the live coal which sets the place ablaze, and he would be able to have at command exactly the kind of information needed for the locality." Stead did recognize the dangers inherent in such a scheme, for he mentioned that the deputy would have neither the funds nor the machinery to force opinion. Yet he also spoke of his newspaper of the future sending "a three-line whip" to its field representatives when it was "convinced that the Government was pursuing a policy contrary to the general wishes of the community." Of course, the line between collecting and directing public opinion can be a fine one.

To keep the organization together and instill "the personal sense of common interest" Stead would have the personnel involved periodically visited by a "journalistic traveller." He cited the similar use by commercial firms of travelers to their retail houses and deplored that no newspaper used this valuable system "to ascertain the social and political fashions in vogue in great centres like Nottingham and Glasgow." The newspaper of the future should have two alter egos of the editor on the road at all times, visiting the associates in each town and making them feel important, exchanging ideas, and dropping the "indifferent" ones. In answer to the expected charge that his scheme of unpaid associates was utopian, Stead replied, "I believe it is quite possible to evoke on the part of Englishmen and Englishwomen at least one-tenth as much self-sacrificing zeal for the welfare of the commonwealth as is now called out as a matter of course in the service of a municipality or in the interest of a sect." With the example before him of Oliver Cromwell enlisting in his New Model Army "men who put a conscience to their work," Stead asserted that the men and women who served his ideal newspaper would be enrolled in "the greatest spiritual and educational and governing agency which England has yet seen." He conceded—with conscious modesty—that the editor to manage this newspaper might not yet be on the English scene, "but unless our race is destined to decay, both the editor and the occasion are certain to arrive."

Stead's article did not receive the widespread attention that he probably thought it would and should. Perhaps this was partly because of the journalists' creed of ignoring their rivals, and partly because the author was that wild man at the *PMG*.[12] Among those who did take notice of Stead's vision of the journalist's role in society was his old friend Mme Novikoff. After the appearance of the first of his articles she wrote a criticism of it which appeared

12. Early in the next century a considerably greater outcry was raised against Alfred Harmsworth's presumed threat to secure political power through the press, and the leader of the denouncers was the editor of the *Review of Reviews*, William T. Stead; but it is true that Harmsworth's commercial success made him appear more of a menace. See, for example, "The Battle of the Trusts," *Review of Reviews*, December 1906, p. 568, and "Bleaching of the Yellow Press," *Review of Reviews*, August 1907, pp. 122-23.

in the *PMG* as a follower on July 13. Her objections reflected the aristocratic biases of a loyal daughter of Russian czardom. She was dismayed at the very thought of a government belonging to "popular meetings of journalism" and at the growth throughout Western Europe of the power of orators, mobs, and journalists. She chided Stead for saying that an editor must strive to interest his readers, because this meant pandering to the ideas of the masses at a time when people were dominated by "Socialist dreams" and "hatred of wealthy minorities." But Mme Novikoff's criticism did not so much refute Stead's prophecy of the growing power of newspaper editors as reveal that she was appalled by its truth. After the publication of Stead's second article, another attack on his ideas appeared in the professional weekly the *Journalist.* In "'The Future of Journalism': A Reply to Mr. Stead," Robert Dennis summed up some of the chief objections to Stead's proposals.[13] He ridiculed the idea of an omniscient editor, with spies in every parish, to whom no politician, statesman, or ruler would refuse to confide secrets. He believed that the *PMG* editor did not foresee the mischief which could arise from his proposal—an impossible scheme in any case— "but it is the common defect of Mr. Stead's enterprises that they involve consequences of which he does not dream." Nor did he think that important men would answer inconvenient questions or unnecessarily take journalists into their confidence and risk having their plans divulged.

On the other hand, J. W. Robertson Scott did not seem particularly alarmed by the implications of Stead's articles. Writing in *Sell's Dictionary* for 1888,[14] he expressed his belief that England had already reached the state of "Government by Journalism" which had been discussed by a "particularly 'live' editor" sometime earlier. "The immense powers possessed and daily exercised by the editors of our morning and evening newspapers," he wrote, "can scarcely be overestimated. And yet, in the whole Kingdom there are only some 170 of them." In 1889 in his defense of New Journalism as "the Journalism of the Ideal,"[15] Scott cited with approval and quoted extensively from Stead's two articles. He also emphasized the steady growth of press influence in recent

13. Robert Dennis, "'The Future of Journalism': A Reply to Mr. Stead," *Journalist,* November 26, 1886, pp. 101-2.
    14. Scott, "Some Newspaper Men," pp. 118-27.
    15. Scott, "The 'New Journalism,'" pp. 48-59. See p. 30 ff.

decades, as newspapers multiplied, became cheaper, and began to reach men of every class.

Whatever his peers may have thought of the *Contemporary Review* articles, only William T. Stead could have written them; they were the culmination of his thinking on the subject of the power of the press. Stead had long been convinced of his God-given mandate to play a significant role in English journalism, and from the time of the "Bulgarian Atrocity" campaign, events had seemed to bear out his conviction. A tale has been told of Stead's discussing with Gladstone a problem of state which had been worrying the cabinet, and saying to him: "Look here, Mr. Gladstone! If you and I were to put our heads together, we could settle this business in half an hour, without troubling any of those fellows." [16] Apocryphal or not, the story is not out of character. Stead undoubtedly considered himself the editor of the Newspaper of the Future, and his self-confidence and impracticality did not allow him to see the perils inherent in his plan. He was willing to sacrifice himself for a righteous cause, and he could see no reason why his major-generals and their unpaid deputies would not be similarly motivated. He saw no danger in the vast potential power that the head of such an organization could wield, because he himself would be at the helm and he, of course, would use his power only for public good. For Stead the Newspaper of the Future was far from an impossible dream, and in the light of his career his illusions are understandable. True, his evaluations of the importance of some of his campaigns were exaggerated; but was it not also true that the naval estimates had been increased, that Gordon had been sent to the Sudan, that the dispute with Russia had been settled without war, that the Criminal Law Amendment Act was on the statute books, that many of his innovations were being adopted, however reluctantly, by the respectable press? In 1886 he was on the crest of the wave, and if personal notoriety had been one of his goals he had certainly achieved it as well. Among all the editors of the metropolitan newspapers, as a fellow journalist pointed out, only William T. Stead was known to the general public.[17]

16. [Wemyss Reid], "The Modern Press. 'Review of Reviews,'" *Speaker*, January 28, 1893, p. 100. Stead denied having made the statement (See Whyte, *Life*, 1:311).

17. Demos [pseud.], "To the Metropolitan Editors," *Journalist*, October 22, 1886, p. 30.

CHAPTER EIGHT

Justice by Journalism

For more than a year the *PMG* had muted its trumpeting and Henry Yates Thompson presumably was able to breathe easier, but in 1887 Stead showed that his crusading days were not behind him. In his best-remembered campaign of the year he played a favorite role—the champion of a woman wronged—and received much applause and fewer jeers than usual. The Lipski crusade, which followed, was well publicized at the time, but has been given surprisingly little attention by biographers and press historians—perhaps because it resulted in a resounding and mortifying failure.

I

The crusade for Mrs. Langworthy was one of Stead's more unusual campaigns, although it had some of the old familiar ingredients: protection of womanhood, distaste for the upper class, and anger at those who did not exhibit the same zeal in righting a wrong. The story had begun four years earlier when a millionaire named Edward Langworthy apparently had tricked a young lady, Miss Mildred Long, into an illegal marriage ceremony. After fathering her child, he filed for bankruptcy and fled the country, leaving her destitute. Mrs. Langworthy's efforts to retain legal redress got nowhere until Stead heard of her plight. On Monday, April 18, 1887, *PMG* readers were introduced to her story in a follower headed:

212

Strange True Stories of To-day
The Langworthy Marriage
Prologue

The prologue opened with a bizarre tale of an "immensely rich"
Englishman on his honeymoon at Lisbon amusing himself by tor-
turing and killing cats, and then proceeded to recount the story
of his marriage and the cruel sport he was having with his bride,
"a refined and cultured lady." To date, the authorities had regarded her plight with an indifference which, if it persisted, would
enable her husband to defy the law and treat court orders with
contempt. Having deserted his wife and driven her to destitution,
Langworthy might also drive her to her grave, and it was in order
to "thwart this conspiracy of wealth and power" that the *PMG*
was publishing the story. Although it sounded incredible, it was
"already familiar to at least half-a-dozen English judges"; and "for
such offenses where the law is powerless, and the High Court of
Justice is contemned, publicity is our last and only resource." The
story of the Langworthy marriage was told in chapters, the first
four taking up most of pages 2 and 3. There were seventy-five
chapters in all, the last published on May 11.

On April 27, in a follower headed "Notice to the Public," it was
announced that the disbelief which had greeted the series had
given way to indignation, and that a committee was being formed
to raise funds so that Mrs. Langworthy could prosecute her claims
in Argentina, where her husband now lived. The case was a complicated one, eventually involving an annulment, a breach of promise suit, a claim for child support, denials of both marriage and
paternity by Langworthy, and, after the original settlements were
made, battles over the amounts. Stead championed Mrs. Langworthy throughout and solicited public support and contributions
to assist her in her court fights. Once more the response was
gratifying, though at times not massive enough to satisfy the *PMG*
editor. On April 30 he told his readers of the avalanche of letters
about the "strange true story"; none were favorable to Langworthy
(hardly surprising in view of the way the story had been covered);
many expressed indignation at his conduct and suggested forms of
punishment. Some correspondents already had sent contributions
to be used to bring Langworthy to justice and to succor the
wronged wife, and Stead promised more details about the fund

later on. As usual, he was piqued at the metropolitan press for paying no attention to his crusade; indeed, on May 3 the entire installment of the Langworthy story (chapters 45 through 48) was devoted to the way the *Times* had hushed up the facts.[1] Stead's main point was that although usually much publicity was given to proceedings in the law courts, the public was kept largely in ignorance of the Langworthy affair. The *PMG* blamed this mostly on Messrs. Bircham, Langworthy's solicitors, who had even put pressure on the *Times* to prevent its running an advertisement from Mrs. Langworthy. Stead saw a clue to the *Times*'s behavior in the fate of the fortnightly *South American Journal*, which had been threatened by the Birchams with a law suit after it had published a comment on the case.

On May 11, the day that the serialized "Strange True Story" came to an end, Stead wrote a leader under the heading "How to Help Mrs. Langworthy." The *PMG*, he said, had "never printed any narrative concerning any individual" which had "excited so deep an interest and commanded so sustained an atention" (although later on in the same piece he complained of public apathy). All who wished to help were invited to subscribe to the Langworthy Defense Fund which had been started by a hundred-guinea subscription from the *PMG*. Within two days there was £550 in the fund.

On May 12 the claim that false statements had been used to defeat Mrs. Langworthy's original application for alimony was brought up in the House of Commons.[2] This news was recorded in the next evening's *Pall Mall*, which also noted that the *Times* had "suppressed" all mention of it in its parliamentary reports. By this time the customary pattern of press response to Stead's campaigning was beginning to emerge. For the most part, the London papers were silent. But at least none were hostile, as in some past cases, and a number of the provincial papers and some weekly and monthly journals were sympathetic. Matthew Arnold recently had published the article which popularized the term "New Journalism,"[3] and early in May the *Tablet* noted that "its leading repre-

---

1. The chapter headings were: XLV. "Muzzling the 'Times' "; XLVI. "How It Was Done"; XLVII. "The 'Times' Boycotts Mrs. Langworthy"; XLVIII. "'If You Say Anything More about Mrs. Langworthy, We'll Make It Hot for You.'"
2. *Hansard's Parliamentary Debates*, 3d ser., vol. 314 (1887): pp. 1666-67.
3. See p. 29 ff.

sentative, the *Pall Mall Gazette*," was justifying the New Journalism by its efforts to redress the wrong done to Mrs. Langworthy.[4] The *Methodist Times*, long a staunch ally of Stead, observed that "the 'New Journalism' may not suit Mr. Matthew Arnold, but it fills plain practical Christians with great delight." It hoped that readers would contribute to the Langworthy fund, and asked the *Times* to explain why it had made no mention of the reference to the case in the House of Commons.[5]

In a May 24 leader, "The Lady, the Lawyers, and the Public," Stead announced "The Langworthy Marriage" would be published the next day as a pamphlet.[6] He praised the response to the fund, which had now swollen to thirteen hundred pounds, and rebuked those who, he felt, were derelict in their responsibilities. The legal profession had not shown sufficient interest; indeed, poor clergymen had been much more generous than lawyers, whose whole profession had been "stained" by the case. Also, "those keepers of the ears of King Demos, the editors of our newspapers," with only a few exceptions had ignored the story of a woman wronged, of the law's delay, and of the advantages of wealth in court. "Journalistic jealousy," Stead believed, "is surely out of place in a case such as this." The *Law Times* disagreed, and commented sardonically on Stead's suggestion that lawyers should contribute to the fund: "A novel theory has been started by the new journalism. If a suitor fares badly in the courts, if there is a delay and injustice at the hands of the law, when a subscription is raised for the sufferer let lawyers be well to the front." [7]

Meanwhile, more and more of the provincial newspapers were lining up on the side of righteousness, including some not noted for their support of Stead. Thus the *Birmingham Times* admonished its colleagues to get over their "journalistic jealousy" and publicize the case. It pointed out that it had "no sympathy with the political views of the *Pall Mall Gazette* nor with the style of journalism it represents," but believed that the Langworthy case overrode such considerations (May 28). The *Northern Echo*, on the other hand,

4. "Notes," *Tablet*, May 7, 1887, pp. 727-28.
5. "Notes of Current Events," *Methodist Times*, May 19, 1887, p. 317.
6. A *PMG* extra, the pamphlet sold for sixpence, "With a Cabinet-Size Photograph of MRS. EDWARD M. LANGWORTHY, AUTOGRAPH, and NUMEROUS PORTRAITS." According to J. Saxon Mills, the Langworthy pamphlet was the most successful, in terms of sales, of all the extras (*Edward Cook*, p. 72.)
7. "The Law and the Lawyers," *Law Times*, May 28, 1887, p. 55.

approved of both the cause and the way it was being championed, declaring it to be "a production worthy of the New Journalism" (June 13).

On July 5 the *PMG* printed "Mr. Langworthy's Reply," with "Notes and Comments by Another Hand." Actually, Langworthy's letter was reprinted from the Argentine *La Nueva Epoca,* a clipping of which had been sent from Buenos Aires. In it Langworthy denied having presented "that woman Long" as his wife and having gone through a false marriage ceremony. He explained that he had been too busy with his business affairs in Argentina to defend himself in a law suit in England. As for the *Pall Mall Gazette,* it was "a filthy paper (*papelucho*), without either capital or importance, whose editor has recently been let out of prison . . . [for] having been found guilty of publishing a series of highly immoral articles." Langworthy also claimed that before publishing this latest series Stead had gone to Langworthy's mother, "asking her whether the matter could not be arranged." In answer to the Langworthy letter, the *PMG* declared that this "insolence and slander" justified all it had printed. It denied the insinuation of blackmail and castigated Langworthy for referring to the mother of his child as "that woman Long." Each of the other charges in the letter was convincingly answered, although the slurs on the *Pall Mall* and its editor were ignored.

With the help of the *PMG* fund—and perhaps the *PMG* publicity —Mrs. Langworthy won her suit; on July 14 she was granted twelve hundred pounds alimony and her child five hundred pounds per annum for maintenance. The next day in a follower, "Mrs. Langworthy's Triumph," Stead bestowed laurels on the lawyers for their skill and the public for its support but strangely claimed no credit for the *PMG.* A follower on July 18 denounced Langworthy's "absurd" appeal to have the sums reduced, and rejoiced that scandal had fallen on him "like a thunderbolt," once his hapless wife, "betrayed, deserted and all but killed had . . . found utterance for her wrongs." On July 19 a breach of promise suit in which Mrs. Langworthy asked for twenty-eight thousand pounds damages opened before the London Bankruptcy Court, and on August 9, shortly after seven o'clock in the evening, Stead received the telegraphed news he had been awaiting: "Verdict twenty thousand pounds, fifteen hundred costs, child secured, Langworthy." [8]

8. Whyte, *Life,* 1:244.

After reporting this happy result in the *PMG*'s news pages the next day, Stead took another look at the case in the leading article on August 11. He complimented Mrs. Langworthy, her solicitor, Theodore Lumly, and the "real heroes of the story," the English judges who had heard the case in its various phases and who, with "unswerving integrity and sound judgment," decided in Mrs. Langworthy's favor all down the line. As for Edward Langworthy, "not until he was publicly hooted along the platform of a railroad station in the Argentine does he seem to have realized the immensity of scorn which his conduct has excited throughout the civilized world. . . . To him, and to similar evil doers, publicity is of all things the most appalling." Stead also thanked the public for its contributions to Mrs. Langworthy's "war chest." Not all of the money collected had been spent, and Mrs. Langworthy would decide whether it would be returned pro rata to contributors or used to establish a new new fund "for the assistance of those who may hereafter find themselves in a similar evil plight."

Although there were additional articles, letters, and followers related to the Langworthy affair and to the final disposition of the fund (which had reached £1,680), the crusade was over and once again Stead had triumphed. Most of the London press took no more notice of the case's dénouement than they had of its development. There were some exceptions: the *Morning Advertiser* and the *Evening Standard* went so far as to express their satisfaction with the outcome; and the *Globe,* which, as the *PMG* did not fail to point out, had "never said a word or moved a finger to help Mrs. Langworthy," congratulated both the principals and the public. But the *Globe* regretted "the way in which this case has been carried on. There has been far too much sentiment about it from start to finish." In a more direct assault on Stead it warned, "Government by journalism would land us in sufficient straits, but justice by journalism would open up a never ending vista of muddles and mistakes." [9] From the provincial papers, as usual, Stead received more favorable comment. The London correspondent of the *Western Daily Mercury* not only praised the *PMG* editor but took his metropolitan contemporaries to task for their persistence in jealously ignoring "one of the most brilliant exploits of modern journalism" (August 15).

Compared to some of Stead's other causes, the Langworthy case

9. *Globe,* August 11, 1887.

may appear to be a minor episode in his career, but it did not appear so to his admirers. Canon Wilberforce applauded the way the *PMG* "chivalrously supported and caused justice to be done to a woman cruelly deceived," [10] and Sir Wemyss Reid later told Mme Novikoff that he considered it Stead's greatest achievement as a journalist.[11] Stead's perennial champion, the *Methodist Times*, called it "one of the most brilliant and glorious events in the history of journalism," bringing "new hope to the human race"; [12] and Stead himself ranked it high in the list of his crusades. He wrote in his personal journal, "The fact that Langworthy was hissed off a platform in the interior of the Argentine because of what we published abides with me as one of those permanent consolations with which a man can comfort himself in the days when he is depressed and disheartened." [13] Some years later, in an article on the importance of London newspaper editors, Stead wrote that they "may be with . . . truth regarded as the unsworn honourable members of the King's Public Council, or they may be treated as Public Councillors of King Demos." In his view the functions of this public council to the king closely resembled those of the Privy Council as defined in the reign of Edward I, and he cited the Langworthy case as an example of a situation in which journalistic power "was used as the resort of those who failed to obtain justice in the ordinary course." [14]

Perhaps it was his success in the Langworthy case, then in its final stages, which persuaded Stead to act again as a "Public Councillor"—to try once more to provide justice by journalism—but this time the result was disastrous. The only thing that prevented Stead's crusade for Israel Lipski from being the most humiliating experience of his career was that he simply refused to be humiliated.

At first, the *PMG* had treated the trial and conviction of Israel Lipski for the willful murder, by poison, of one Miriam Angel as a straight news story. It was given no more prominence than most murder trials, and less than some. On July 20, as the trial was

10. Whyte, *Life*, 1:238.
11. Reid, *Memoirs*, p. 315.
12. "Notes of Current Events," *Methodist Times*, August 18, 1887, pp. 548-49.
13. Scott, *Life and Death*, p. 125.
14. William T. Stead, "His Majesty's Public Councillors: To Wit, the Editors of the London Daily Papers," *Review of Reviews*, December 1904, pp. 593-94.

drawing to a close, the story received scarcely more than a column-inch—about the same space given on the same page to an account of the International Chess Congress competition in Germany. On August 1 another brief notice reported that the jury had brought in a verdict of guilty after being out only a few minutes, that Lipski had protested his innocence, and that Justice James Stephen had sentenced him to death. However, an Occasional Note commented that the trial had left several points unresolved—for example, although two ounces of nitric acid were used in the murder, Lipski had bought only one—and concluded that the case "call[ed] for consideration at the hands of the authorities before the death sentence is enforced." A full page of "Sketches at the Lipski Trial" appeared in the August 3 *PMG*, and then the case dropped from sight until August 12, when a short news article, "Will Israel Lipski Be Hanged?," told of the efforts of Lipski's solicitor, John Hayward, to obtain a respite. The previous night he had talked for more than an hour with Justice Stephen and the prosecuting counsel, Mr. Poland, and convinced them that he had a case good enough to lay before Home Secretary Matthews. The appeal was rejected and on August 13 the *PMG*'s Lipski campaign got under way, with a first-page leading article, "A Legal Murder," and a follower, "The Case for Lipski Restated." [15]

Stead asserted in the leader that the execution of Lipski would be an act of murder. He recalled the conduct of the Home Secretary in a recent case in which a Miss Cass had been unjustly charged with prostitution. The *PMG* and a number of other papers had given the Home Secretary and the police a bad time over the incident, and Stead now referred sarcastically to "the infallible MR. MATTHEWS," who "is now quite as sure that the unfortunate LIPSKI committed murder in Whitechapel." Since Miss Cass had not been sentenced to death she had been able to vindicate herself, but Matthews would be safe from Lipski and was quite willing to hang an innocent man. Stead maintained that the trial judge, Justice Stephen, "is haunted by a terrible doubt that after all Lipski is innocent." If this belief happened to be true, the consequences would be terrible. Prime Minister Salisbury should insist on at least a week's respite: "That is not too much to ask when a life is at stake. The Prime Minister must know by this time that he cannot

15. Technically the crusade began in the latest edition of the previous night's paper.

trust the judgement of his Home Secretary." Although Stead was not asking for a pardon, he made it dramatically clear that he had already personally judged Lipski innocent. He painted a chilling picture of Lipski sleeping twice more, after which "an innocent man will be strangled to death—strangled in the name of the law and the will of the Home Secretary!" His blood, Stead declared, would be on the heads of both Matthews and Salisbury. "One word from Lord Salisbury, and ——— ——! Surely that word will not be left unspoken?"

As Stead restated Lipski's case in the follower, there indeed appeared to be some weak points in the case for the prosecution. These included the facts that Lipski had been found under the murdered girl's bed, covered with bruises, and that his slight physical build made it difficult to understand how he had been able to overpower his victim. At the same time, Stead paraded his naive assumption that the charge of rape was particularly unlikely, since the accused was engaged to be married.

On an inside page he explained the genesis of his articles on the affair. Hayward had told him of Justice Stephen's conversion, and the story had "made a deep impression on the editor of this journal." In order to rouse public opinion against the execution, some striking fact, hitherto unknown, had to be discovered and "obviously the only fact which would convince the public was the conversion of the judge." Hayward, who protested to Stead that the interviews with Justice Stephen had been confidential, refused permission to have them publicized, but Stead believed he had to make a choice between ethics and duty. For a long time he debated the question and at press time received a letter by messenger from Hayward, again imploring him not to report the private conversation. To do so, Hayward said, would ruin him professionally, "and, what is of more consequence, it would be adverse to the interest of my poor client." This might have ended the matter for a less self-confident—or arrogant—man, but for Stead it meant more soul-searching, and then a decision to publish. "How can it injure [Lipski] to convince the public that the judge who tried him is no longer certain of his guilt? In any case, we take the responsibility of our decision." The crusade was launched.

The immediate goal was achieved over the weekend when Matthews stayed the execution for a week. In the *PMG* article on the reprieve on Monday, August 15, great importance was attached to the missing nitric acid bottle and the whereabouts of a man called Schnuss, who Lipski claimed was one of the two real murderers. In his leader, "A Life for a Bottle," Stead spoke of "the growing conviction in the public mind" that to hang Lipski while any doubt existed as to his guilt would be murder. He was careful to place the whole responsibility on Matthews, not Justice Stephen. The latter had denied Hayward's version of the interview, and the *Times* that morning had reported it was "authorized to state that, whatever reports to the contrary may be circulated, Mr. Justice Stephen is not in the least degree dissatisfied either with the verdict of the jury or with the decision of the Secretary of State in Lipski's case." Stead was unperturbed, since he expected a denial. "No two persons," he observed, "ever agreed in giving the same version of an interview between them." Stephen had confirmed "the only essential point involved," since it had not been claimed that Stephen had thought Lipski innocent, only that he had some doubts. Stephen's actual words to the Home Secretary had been, "I did not feel so clear and strong in my opinion as you did," and Stead was quick to remind his readers again how wrong Matthews had been in the Cass case. The week's respite was meaningless, for unless Hayward could prove his client innocent he would hang anyway, and Stead warned that the whole system of capital punishment would break down "if criminals are to be hanged 'on spec.'"

The underlying problem in this latest campaign was one which has plagued the relations of the press and society to the present day. Stead tacitly acknowledged it with a heading which appeared over the press summaries on August 15: "Trial by Journalism." The *Birmingham Post* expressed itself succinctly on the point. In attacking Matthews's "pliancy and vacillation" it argued that "unless trial by jury is to give place to trial by journalism, . . . it is difficult to discover the grounds of this sudden change of resolution on the part of the Home Secretary." The *Glasgow Herald* also believed that Matthews had been frightened by the *PMG* into taking "another step in the direction of government by journalism." By now some of the other London papers had begun to take up Hayward's and Lipski's cause. The *Standard* felt that Matthews's "consenting to the merciful course" was wise, but wondered what had changed his mind if a two-hour interview with Stephen had left, as he said, "no substantial doubt in the mind of either." The *Daily News* took the same view as the *PMG*—that it was wrong to

put the burden of proof and additional evidence on Hayward—
while the *Morning Post,* the *Telegraph,* the *Globe,* and the *Echo*
all saw the case as providing a good argument for change in appeal
procedure. The *Echo,* like the *PMG,* also assailed Matthews
personally as a man from whom no mercy could be expected and
recounted his many mistakes and general unpopularity (August
15).

On August 16 the *PMG* printed a very subjectively written article
on an inside news page, headed

The Race for Lipski's Life
A Fresh Batch of Fresh Evidence
The Bottle, the Sovereign and a "Strange Man"

The evidence included the statements that the nitric acid bottle
had been tampered with, that a witness had forgotten to tell that
she had seen a strange man leave the victim's house, and that the
landlady of the house now said her jewel box had been rifled.
(Stead's point here was that Judge Stephen had ruled that lust,
rather than avarice, had been the motive for the crime.) In the
same issue the *PMG* asked in headlines over another article, "Will
Lipski or the Home Secretary Survive?" and repeated a rumor that
Matthews would resign during the recess.

For the remainder of the week the *PMG* labored mightily to
secure a further reprieve, if not a pardon. Day by day, often under
the heading "The Race for Lipski's Life," the attempts to run down
clues were described, as the *PMG* acted as its own detective force.
Scotland Yard was reviled for trying to cover up evidence; strange
men who might be involved in the crime were discussed but never
brought forth; a juror from the Lipski trial was produced who was
quoted as saying, "Spare the man." On Saturday, August 20, in a
follower, Stead declared that Matthews was determined to hang
Lipski on Monday "as a gallows offering to the offended *amour
propre* of a weak and angry Home Secretary." He admitted that
"eminent and influential barristers and judges, scandalized at the
intervention of newspapers in the administration of justice," were
supporting Matthews. "The press has taken up the cause of LIPSKI,
therefore LIPSKI must die," not because his guilt was certain, "but
because there is no doubt that the press in general, and the *Pall
Mall Gazette* in particular, have pleaded strongly that the man

should be allowed to have the benefit of the doubt." Numerous other articles and notes on the matter were scattered throughout this issue: the weakness of the prosecution's case was rehashed; mysterious clues were mentioned and the police chided for not following them; Justice Stephen was belittled as well as Matthews; a letter was printed from a correspondent who claimed to have talked to the Lipski juror who had said, "Spare the man." All told, including press summaries, the *PMG* devoted about three pages to Lipski.

As the critical weekend began, the crusade seemed to be a typical Steadian effort to save an innocent man from being outrageously wronged by callous officialdom. On Sunday something happened to change all this: Lipski sat down in his cell and wrote out a detailed confession of the murder.[16] One can only imagine what thoughts must have tumbled through Stead's mind when he heard the news, but if his reaction was one of consternation there was nothing in Monday's paper to show it. The heading for his August 22 follower read: "All's Well That Ends Well." It began blandly, "Lipski's confession fortunately removes all doubt that he has been justly accused, justly convicted, and justly executed. He has been hanged, and few criminals ever went to the gallows who better deserved their fate." Stead insisted that the *PMG* had to act as it did once the statement of Lipski's solicitor had been given, and denied that the paper had attempted to usurp the functions of a "Supreme Court of Criminal Appeal." He maintained that he had at first rejected Hayward's pleas, but changed his mind with the solitor's assurance that Justice Stephen was mentally distressed with the verdict, particularly since the life of a man was now in the hands of a "discredited Minister." Stephen's later disclaimer in the *Times* was described as not "clear and explicit," and Stead was driven to defend Stephen's doubts "against the cocksureness of the Home Secretary." Lipski's confession "releases us from the great doubt which we felt and expressed," but it also confirmed some of the criticisms leveled against the prosecution's case by the *PMG*. The right man had been convicted, but, so Stead assured his readers, on the wrong evidence. Conveniently forgetting the hue and cry raised in the *PMG* after the "real" culprits, Stead said he

16. The *Telegraph* reported that Lipski was writing a confession when, much to his surprise, he was temporarily reprieved, and also that there were officials who knew of the first confession (August 22, 1886).

was relieved that the confession had exonerated everyone else of complicity in the crime.

He also made it clear that his campaign against the Home Secretary would in no way be abated. "Mr. Matthews," he wrote, "has reason to rejoice that he has achieved the solitary success of a ministerial career now fast drawing to a close." The follower gave no hint that for a week the *PMG* had been at least implicitly proclaiming Lipski's innocence, and concluded, "The confession at once vindicates the verdict and condemns the hypothesis on which it was obtained." An article, on page 2, on the Lipski confession, "By a Compatriot Who Laboured on His Behalf," insisted that many points were still unclear and suggested that the confession did not reveal the whole story. But "it justifies most absolutely those who since Lipski's condemnation have been arguing for a reprieve. For no one—except, perhaps, Mr. Hayward . . . said Lipski was innocent." Rather, the argument had been simply that the sentence should not be passed on the basis of evidence presented at court. Once again the weaknesses of the prosecution's case were reviewed and the various still unsolved problems recited. "The Whitechapel mystery," the article concluded, "will remain a mystery. Lipski's confession if anything has but deepened it." The news story of the execution, on page 7, was given bold headlines and well over a column of space. It told of the cheers which rose from the crowd outside the prison when the black flag was hoisted, and reported that in addition to his written confession on Sunday afternoon, Lipski admitted his guilt on the scaffold on Monday.

If the reaction of the *PMG* to Lipski's confession was calm, that of its contemporaries was predictably vociferous. The *Daily News* in its story on Monday concluded that newspapers were not good courts of law. "Anything seems better," it observed, "than this system of trial by penny-a-liner, with its daily headline." The *Standard* for the day speculated on how painful "might have been the consequences had the Home Secretary permitted his judgment to be swayed by the sensational outcry which was got up for Lipski's release." The *Morning Post* respected the motive of those trying to save a man's life, but found it difficult to justify the recklessness with which the judgment of the courts was defied. The *Daily Chronicle* did not blame Matthews for delaying the sentence "in the face of the furious outcry in certain quarters," but felt the reprieve only added to the mental suffering of the prisoner.

The evening papers were more specific and more vitriolic. Thus, the *St. James's Gazette* berated its rival as a "catchpenny print, with a well-known and special animus" against Matthews, which saw in the case the double opportunity of embarrassing a political rival and doing "a good stroke of business . . . in the gutter." It ended its diatribe with the familiar reference to the "Maiden Tribute" campaign: "That this was done is perhaps the greatest disgrace that has ever happened to English journalism, hardly excepting even the deliberate commission of abominable offenses for the purpose of founding upon the experience so acquired a romance of obscene falsehood." The *Evening News* (which itself had written sympathetically about Lipski's cause) was equally appalled. Recalling Stead's fondness for insisting upon the power of the press, it maintained, "He has during the last few years done more to degrade the press than any man living; but in his efforts over the Lipski case he has surely touched low-water mark." The *Globe,* which early in the game had voiced its misgivings about Stead's actions (August 13), could see some good arising from the affair: "We trust that the system of appealing to a clamour from the verdicts of juries and the sentences of judges has received a check, and that a great many people, who cannot in every case be regarded as well intentioned, have learned a useful lesson."

Among the weeklies, the *Saturday Review* couched its criticism in general terms, but undoubtedly was referring primarily to the *PMG* in an article called "Trial by Newspaper." It began, "If the practice of endeavouring to retry convicted criminals in the columns of newspapers never recovers from the crushing blow it received at the beginning of this week, the late ISRAEL LIPSKI will not have sinned altogether in vain." The article praised the self-control shown in the case by "the respectable and moderately respectable press," but castigated "the black sheep in the journalistic flock." It termed the attack on Matthews a "hideous exhibition of party spite, combined with personal vanity," and concluded that "all this shows, dramatically enough, what newspaper investigation of contemporary crime is worth." [17]

On Tuesday, August 23, the day after it reported Lipski's death and confession, the *PMG* renewed its assault on Matthews in a leading article, "Our Minister of the Interior." In this latest exposition of the Home Secretary's inadequacy Stead not only brought up the Cass case and other incidents in which he had displayed

17. "Trial by Newspaper," *Saturday Review,* August 27, 1887, pp. 276-77.

ineptness, but also that of Israel Lipski, who was described as the man "for whom the respite necessary to clear up the judge's doubts had literally to be extorted at the eleventh hour." He hoped that Salisbury would appoint a better man as his successor—that there would soon be a successor there seemed to be no doubt. On the next day, August 24, the *PMG* took a new tack in an Occasional Note which spoke of "yet another instance of the blank ignorance of the Home Office and the police!" This time the officials involved were charged with not knowing that English girls were being engaged as singers in cafes on the Continent and forced into prostitution. In succeeding issues the *PMG* had a follow-up on this story, plus additional news articles and editorial comment on Matthews and his failures.

In respect to the Lipski case, for a time the *PMG* gave some attention to the question of whether or not the condemned man's confession was genuine and published a number of articles dealing with an alleged earlier confession and the possibility that certain officials had known of it right along. However, understandably, Lipski dropped more completely and quickly from the *PMG* pages than the other subjects of its editor's crusades. Even among the usual coterie of *PMG* supporters, there were few who could find words of praise for Stead's efforts. Despite the rancor and over-statements of some of Stead's London rivals, their basic premise— that he was in effect trying to administer justice by journalism— could not be lightly dismissed. His motives might have been laudable, and there were indeed some unusual features of this case, but the precedent was a dangerous one nevertheless. The *Freeman's Journal* perhaps best summed up the argument in Stead's defense: although it would be said that the *PMG*'s interference was unjusti-fiable, "and all the witlings of the London press will have a good time," the editor was right to act on the theory that it is better to have a guilty man go free than to hang an innocent one (August 23). Be that as it may, for the remainder of his editorial career at Northumberland Street, Stead, while not diminishing his criticism of legal officialdom, was more circumspect in his treatment of trial verdicts and appeals.

II

The major continuing news story of 1887 was undoubtedly Ireland and all of the problems related to that unhappy island. The *PMG*'s position was put forward in a series of four articles by Stead which ran from January 18 through January 26 under the general heading "What Should Be Done in Ireland?" In the first installment he explained that the answer to the question was, in essence, "that which the Irish wish to be done in Ireland." Typically, Stead put the Irish troubles in a very personalized framework: his own term in prison. "Until you have been sent to gaol in what you believe to be a good cause," he opined, "you find it difficult to understand the Irish question or entirely to sympathize with the Irish people." In the second and third installments, published on January 20 and 22, he stressed that the old system of subjugation employed since the English conquest could no longer work, and that Ireland was not India and could not be made a crown colony. His own imprecise solution was summed up in the last sentence of the fourth and final installment: give Ireland "as much Home Rule as is compatible with retaining the advantages of credit, the services, and the capital of the richest Empire in the world."

This was the year of "Parnellism and Crime" during which the *Times* printed facsimiles of letters linking Charles Parnell to the outrages in Ireland and indicating his approval of the murder of Lord Frederick Cavendish, new Chief Secretary for Ireland, and Thomas Park, permanent Undersecretary, in Phoenix Park, Dublin, on May 6, 1882. The letters ultimately proved to be spurious, although the *Times* had published them in good faith. The *PMG* disputed their authenticity from the beginning, and in its campaign against "The Forger of the 'Times' " included a detailed analysis of the facsimile signatures to prove that they could not be genuine. Thus it was particularly satisfying to Stead when the forger of the letters, Richard Pigott, confessed to the crime in February, 1889.

Another theme which emerged from the pages of the *PMG* during 1887 was hostility toward London policemen and principal law enforcement officials. As we have seen, the Cass [18] and Lipski cases gave Stead a platform for denunciation of Home Office officials and the police; in addition the *PMG* frequently carried news stories which highlighted their dishonesty, incompetence, or brutality. The index for 1887 lists numerous stories under the headings "Assaults on Women by Policemen" and "Other Assaults by Policemen." The *PMG* also directed some bitter attacks at the

18. The policeman involved in the Cass affair was charged with wrongful arrest; his acquittal was bitterly assailed in the *PMG*.

police harassment of meetings and demonstrations staged by socialists, radicals, workingmen's groups, and others determined to protest existing conditions or governmental policy. Unemployment was the principal catalyst in fomenting discontent in 1887, but low wages, poor housing, and coercion in Ireland also helped in bringing about a series of confrontations between demonstrators and police. When the climax came in the autumn it added a new dimension to Stead's campaign against officialdom, and brought about a closer friendship between him and Mrs. Annie Besant, the well-known Victorian socialist, reformer, and freethinker.[19]

As organized protests became more frequent and more bitter, Sir Charles Warren, the chief commissioner of the London Metropolitan Police,[20] saw them as menacing the public order. Beginning in October he followed a rather confusing policy of alternately permitting, prohibiting, and dispersing mass meetings in Trafalgar Square. Organizers often did not know what fate to expect for their gatherings; and on one occasion—November 6—a morning rally in the Square was dispersed by the police, yet an afternoon one was permitted. Home Secretary Matthews, other leading government officials, and most of the London press defended Warren's policies, but Stead viewed them as a further example of the violation of the rights and liberties of the citizens of London. As early as October 21 he warned in a leader that Warren was "heading fast and straight for riots."

On November 8 Warren apparently ended his policy of vacillation by issuing a proclamation which flatly banned public meetings at Trafalgar Square. Stead's reply was a leader, "Sir Charles Warren: Usurper," in which he claimed that if Trafalgar Square was to be closed, it was up to Parliament, not a policeman, to do it. He said that Warren's challenge should be met, and called for a conference of delegates from "all bodies which represent the masses." A meeting of radical and socialist groups was held that night and it was decided to go ahead with a rally planned for Sunday, November 13, to protest the detention of William O'Brien, the Irish M.P. who had been arrested under the provisions of the Irish Coercion Act

19. It was after this time that Mrs. Besant was introduced to theosophy through a book Stead gave her to review.
20. Sir Charles Warren (1840-1927) had held the post since the previous year. Before that time he had established a reputation as both a military leader and archeologist.

earlier in the year. In his November 10 leader Stead declared that the decision to defy Warren's illegal proclamation gave the original rally a wider significance. "Sunday afternoon, therefore," he wrote, "will witness a scene that will make history" by vindicating the right of public meetings. He also called for the formation of a "League for the Defence of Liberty and Law in London" to provide bail and legal aid for anyone arrested for taking part in a public gathering. It would hold meetings where police had arbitrarily prohibited them, and, as a long-range goal, agitate for "Home Rule for London."

On Friday, November 11, Matthews, speaking informally to a deputation of London shopkeepers, seemed to reverse Warren's proclamation by stating that bona fide political meetings would be permitted, but on November 12, perhaps under pressure from his police commissioner, he shifted his ground and declared that all processions were banned in certain designated areas of London, including Trafalgar Square. That evening representatives from various radical clubs, the Fabian Society, the Social Democratic Federation, and the Socialist League met together, and, with Mrs. Besant playing a prominent role, decided to carry on with the demonstration. The next day the protesters started in four separate groups, planning to converge on Trafalgar Square from different directions. The unarmed marchers were met by truncheon-wielding policemen, who were later reinforced by detachments of the Life Guards and the Scots Guards. No shots were fired during the melee, but scores of marchers were hurt, some seriously, and two men died later of injuries. Many were also arrested, the two best known being R. B. Cunninghame Graham, M.P., and the labor leader John Burns, who was still in the radical phase of his career. The bloodiness of "Bloody Sunday" was somewhat overstated, but as in St. Peter's Field in 1819—or Boston in 1770—the symbolic, emotional aspect of the clash between workers and police was what really mattered. Although a trade upswing helped to avert any repetition of the riot, "Bloody Sunday" remained a working-class, antigovernment rallying cry for a generation.

Stead's long-time dedication to the cause of free speech, his opposition to the policy of coercion in Ireland, and his identification with the working classes would have dictated his course even if "Bloody Sunday" had not represented yet another case of police bungling and repression. As it was, he now immediately launched

a new campaign against police officialdom. On Monday, November
14, the first eight and one-half pages of the *PMG* were given over to
the previous day's disorders, and articles, leaders, and letters on
some aspect of "Bloody Sunday" continued to be featured on into
the next year. In the weeks to come the paper frequently urged
workers to defy "illegal" proclamations which violated their rights,
as well as issuing a pamphlet, *Remember Trafalgar Square,* and
establishing a defense fund.

Stead also began a period of closer relationship with Mrs. Annie
Besant, whom he already knew slightly and had long admired. She
had earlier organized a Socialist Defense Association comprised of
a group of well-to-do men pledged to help persons arrested for
exercising the rights of free speech or assembly, and she spent the
day after "Bloody Sunday" bustling about London, arranging bail
for as many men as possible. The Law and Liberty League proposed by Stead on November 10 had called for similar measures,
and he had received numerous letters supporting the idea. On
November 18 the league was formally organized at a meeting
presided over by Mrs. Besant and addressed by Stead, H. M.
Hyndman, and John Burns, among others.

Mrs. Besant also seems to have been the one who devised the
plan to confer martyrdom on an innocent bystander named Linnell
who died of injuries received at Trafalgar Square. "London has
not seen in a generation a public funeral given to a poor man
killed by violence of the police," she wrote;[21] and London was
given one. Stead reported the death of Linnell, "guilty of the
heinous crime of hooting the police," on December 5 in a follower
headed "Killed by the Police!" The funeral was announced the next
day and publicized in succeeding issues in notices bordered in black
and under the same heading. On Sunday, December 18, the funeral
procession, called by the *PMG* (December 19) the greatest since
the Duke of Wellington's, took place with Stead and other leading
reformers marching at its head.[22]

Meanwhile, the friendship between Stead and Mrs. Besant was

21. Arthur Nethercot, *The First Five Lives of Annie Besant* (Chicago:
University of Chicago Press, 1960), p. 249.
22. The other man who died on "Bloody Sunday" was also given a public
funeral, but it did not gain the same publicity or support as Linnell's. A few
months later when a letter to the *Star* complained that Linnell's grave was
poorly marked, Mrs. Besant replied that the Law and Liberty League had
other uses for its money (ibid., p. 251).

deepening as the Puritan journalist and the atheist social reformer found that they shared many common ideals, including "faith and love for man." For some time Mrs. Besant had been considering the possibility that a new brotherhood might be formed of people of different religious beliefs (or none), based on a common dedication to serving mankind. Discovering that her new friend had been mulling over similar ideas, she suggested that a "Church of the future" be organized, to make men happy in this world rather than in eternity, and with the aims of "teaching of social duty, the upholding of social righteousness, the building up of a true commonwealth." [23] Encouraged by the success of the Law and Liberty League in the aftermath of "Bloody Sunday," and as a step toward bringing about their new brotherhood, Stead and Mrs. Besant founded a halfpenny weekly journal called the *Link*. It was to be the voice of the league, and to bear the subtitle *A Journal for the Servants of Man*. For the first four months of 1888 these two reformers edited their newspaper in remarkable harmony, despite their difference over religion. A flood of messages addressed to Stead by his coeditor attest to the affection between them. [24]

While the *Link* enthusiastically embraced the radical and reform causes of the day, it had certain unfortunate features—somewhat reminiscent of Stead's scheme for the journalism of the future—[25] which alienated others in sympathy with its ideas. Among the journal's special departments was one for receiving anonymous complaints; another, called "The People's Pillory," for naming public malefactors; and one which tersely proclaimed, "To Be Done, By Order of the Executive. Law and Liberty League." As Mrs. Besant's biographer, Arthur Nethercot, has written of these departments, "They looked innocent at first, but sharp-sighted critics like Bradlaugh and Hyndman quickly saw their potential dangers of totalitarianism and dictatorship, . . . of misuse by anonymous and unproved accusation." [26] However, Mrs. Besant was like Stead in that her firm, self-righteous convictions would not let her appreciate such possibilities of error or injustice. The *Link* also resembled

23. Annie Besant, *An Autobiography*, 2d ed. (London: T. Fisher Unwin, 1893), pp. 329-30. Mrs. Besant had earlier spoken of the *PMG* under Stead as "falling into a slough of 'mawkish religious sentimentality' and even imbecility" (Nethercot, *First Five Lives*, p. 260).

24. Whyte, *Life*, 1:251-53.

25. See p. 207 ff.

26. Nethercot, *First Five Lives*, p. 253.

Stead's newspaper of the future in that it was meant to be the
vehicle for a league organized in "Centers" and "Circles." Each
center would have 240 members and would be subdivided into
twenty groups of 12 members. The smaller units, each headed by
a "Captain" with authoritarian powers, were called at first
"Vigilance Circles," and later, significantly, "Ironside Circles." Each
member, rather like Stead's volunteers, was to be alert for incidents
involving exploitation of the poor, police brutality, or political
corruption, and to make reports through the hierarchy. The plan
was to have circles in every parliamentary borough, but they never
spread much beyond the metropolitan area and existed on only a
limited basis there. The undemocratic overtones of the revamped
league caused a number of the radical and socialist organizations
which had sent delegates to its first general meeting to withdraw
soon after.[27]

In April, 1888, Stead left London to travel through Europe as a
special correspondent for the *PMG* [28] and withdrew from his active
association with the *Link,* which never became one of his major
journalistic enterprises. However, his relationship with Annie Besant
remained as warm, if not as close, for the rest of his life. In a
glowing eulogy after Stead's death she wrote that he was "the ideal
Friend," and she described him professionally as "the ablest
journalist that England had produced, the man with that strong
flair for to-morrow's events and opinions which is the essence of
journalistic genius." [29]

27. Ibid., p. 254.
28. See p. 239 ff.
29. Whyte, *Life,* 1:253-54.

CHAPTER NINE

Farewell to Northumberland Street

In comparison with the dazzle and excitement of the previous years of Stead's editorial tenure, his last two years on the *Pall Mall Gazette* had an anticlimactic character, like the descent of a skyrocket. During this period the breach between the *PMG's* editor and its proprietor continued to widen, and Stead's departure from the paper could be foretold long before his official exit on the first day of 1890. Thompson's disenchantment with his erratic subordinate had begun at least as far back as the days of "The Maiden Tribute," when the unfavorable publicity and ridicule following in its wake and the ensuing slump in circulation and advertising had created a crisis between the two men. Matters had been patched up, but despite Stead's promise to forego any more "Maiden Tributing," the tension never really disappeared. Late in 1887 the *PMG's* stand on the Trafalgar Square demonstration again cost the paper readers and advertisers,[1] and Thompson could be forgiven if he felt that Stead was willing to back his own convictions down to his proprietor's last penny. Along with other new problems and new strains, the year 1888 brought a new rival evening paper, the *Star*.

I

As far back as July 22, 1887, the *PMG* had reported completion of the arrangements for the publication of a halfpenny evening paper. The political policy of this new journal would be "very advanced Gladstonian Liberalism," and its editor would be the

1. Scott, *Life and Death*, pp. 148-49. See p. 228 ff.

Irish member of Parliament T. P. O'Connor. Stead predicted that it
would provide necessary representation for London Radicalism,
which the *Echo* had failed to do; and since O'Connor was an
avowed disciple of the New Journalism, the new paper could be
expected to "treat from an advanced standpoint and with much
sympathy the great social questions which are coming more and
more to the front alongside matters of purely political interest."
Stead was correct in his preliminary assessment of the style of the
new paper; in fact, O'Connor's venture was going to make 1888
an important year in the history of popular journalism.

"Tay Pay," as O'Connor was popularly known, had come to
London in 1870 at the age of twenty-two, a refugee from Irish
poverty. For the next decade he had pursued a somewhat erratic
career as a free-lance journalist, writing a scathing biography of
Lord Beaconsfield which brought him much attention; then in 1880
he entered the political arena as an Irish Nationalist. He became a
valued aid to Charles Parnell, serving as the chief of the Irish News
Agency, which was essentially a public relations office for Home
Rulers, and as the head of the National League in Great Britain,
which directed Irish votes in English constituencies to one or the
other of the major parties. At the same time, he continued his
newspaper work (it included a stint as a parliamentary reporter
for the *PMG*), and some believe that dividing his energies between
politics and journalism kept him from achieving greater success.
In 1887 a combination of circumstances allowed O'Connor to follow
his career in journalism on a more regular and profitable basis. He
was anxious to augment his modest income (the Payment of Members Act was still twenty-four years away), and the split in the
Liberal party over home rule had further diminished the ranks of
Gladstonian newspapers. With the help and encouragement of
Henry LaBouchere, M.P., editor of *Truth* and staunch political
progressive, Tay Pay persuaded a number of wealthy Liberals to
put up the necessary money for founding a London evening paper.

On January 16, 1888, the day before the *Star* began publication,
the *PMG* welcomed the new paper by printing an interview with
O'Connor in its follower. It occupied more than a page, including
an introductory note on O'Connor's political and journalistic activities. After a description of the difficulties of interviewing the new
editor at the *Star* building amid the confusion and uproar attendant
on getting out the first issue, the body of the interview was
presented under the heading "The Confession of Faith." O'Connor

began by declaring his belief in Radicalism, the cause of the poor and oppressed, and such journalistic devices as interviews, short stories, and pictures. In what was regarded as a swipe at some existing papers, he said that he would do his best "to avoid the prolix and verbose" and that he hoped to make his columns "as readable and as humorous and as full of human interest as possible." In his reply to the question of whether or not he intended to imitate the style of American newspapers, O'Connor was somewhat equivocal. "No," he said, "I am not a believer in half a column of headlines, because I think they are merely a waste of space, but in many respects the American papers will be my model." In fact, although they did not often occupy half a column, Tay Pay's use of long, informative headlines became one of the hallmarks of the *Star*.

Tuesday, January 17, saw the long-awaited advent of the new paper. The *Star* was a four-page paper, 24″ x 18″, with six columns to the page. According to the normal practice of the day, the first three columns of the first page were filled with "small ads." Comprising the next two and one-third columns was "Our Confession of Faith," a much expanded version of the statement in the *PMG*. O'Connor pledged that he would judge all policy from a Radical standpoint, meaning that it would be "esteemed by us good or bad as it influences for good or evil the lot of the masses of the people." The rich needed no champion, but the poor did; and the *Star* would support any government that "does no more than enable the charwoman to put two pieces of sugar in her cup of tea instead of one [an expression that became famous and was popularly considered the *Star*'s prime slogan]; and that adds one farthing a day to the wage of the seamstress or the labourer." In its war against privilege, the *Star* would neither accept nor reject socialistic remedies just because they bore that label. As an Irish Nationalist, O'Connor called for the right of the Irish to choose their own government, noting in passing that the citizens of London also needed Home Rule, being governed at the time "by one of the worst and most corrupt oligarchies that ever disgraced and robbed a city." Since he did not believe that the newspaper reader lived by politics alone, he promised lively, anecdotal, nonpolitical features. The paper's ideal was "to be the earliest in the field with every item of news; . . . to be animated, readable and stirring." Ending his first leader with a confident appraisal of the *Star*'s chances for success, O'Connor pointed out that there was no other halfpenny Radical newspaper in London and excoriated "the malignant and treacherous desertion of the Liberal cause by so-called Liberal papers."

A feature of the first issue which attracted attention and drew fire from some of the more conservative journals was a first-page column, "Mainly about People." It became one of the paper's best-known and best-liked features, and later on, when he left the *Star*, O'Connor developed the idea into a full-fledged periodical called by the same name. Basically a gossip column, it dealt in anecdotal style with the doings of well-known persons—mostly their non-political activities, although political leaders often figured in it. Many of the *Star's* news items were characterized by a personal approach, and political stories frequently were written in a partisan vein. There was a sprinkling of stories about crime and violence, but in comparison with most of the other evening papers, especially the *Evening News,* their number was not excessive. The *Star* offered little in the way of foreign news and most of the purely political items stressed the Irish problem. In most of the news stories the emphasis in general was on the unusual, the unique, and what had been termed the "condition of England" question. There were feature articles, including interviews, in each issue, and as in some other evening papers (though not the *PMG*) a good percentage of space was devoted to sports news—about two and one-half columns. The *Star* carried numerous headlines and used crossheads in the longer news stories, although at first no more, proportionately, than the *PMG*. In this respect its "Americanization" came later on.

All in all, the *Star* was a worthy entry in the ranks of the New Journalism. As Tay Pay had promised, it was bright, breezy, and readable, and these qualities as much as a political philosophy designed to appeal to the masses made it an overnight success. Despite the sneers and attacks of such journals as the *Saturday Review* and the *Spectator,*[2] the *Star* began breaking circulation records with its first issue.[3] During its first month there were minor changes, but its format, style, and political philosophy remained

2. "Parnellium Sidus," *Saturday Review,* January 21, 1888, pp. 70-71; "The 'Star,'" *Spectator,* January 21, 1888, pp. 82-83.
3. Of the first day's issue the *Star* announced, "The World's Record Beaten. 142,600 Copies Sold" (January 18). Less than two months later it recorded a sale of 191,000 and boasted that its circulation was "larger for the length of its existence than that of any journal in any other time or in any other country in the world" (March 10). Other sales records were publicized throughout the year.

constant so long as O'Connor was editor. One key to the paper's success was the constellation of talent which he gathered about him. Among the very able assistant editors, sub-editors, reporters, and feature writers who contributed to the *Star* during its first years were many who achieved distinction in journalism and other fields.[4] The brightness of the first issue was furbished in succeeding issues by the introduction of illustrations and an occasional political cartoon; the journal also became noted for its headlines—some were lighthearted and entertaining; others told in capsule form the content of the article. But the *Star* did not live by sparkle and originality alone: the excellence of its news service won it many readers who might have been put off by its politics.

To begin with, the *Star* and the *PMG* could be considered as political allies and at times they launched crusades on the same issues. The *Star*, for example, campaigned against Police Commissioner Warren and Home Secretary Matthews even more vigorously than did the *PMG*. Both papers were Gladstonian, favored home rule, and defended the interests of lower classes against the rich and powerful. However, Tay Pay's Radicalism and Irish Nationalism were more advanced and more determined than Stead's, and this difference ultimately led to strained relations between their two papers. O'Connor had made Balfour his particular whipping boy, and he unfairly accused Stead of being an apologist for the Irish Secretary. The *Star* also sniped at the weakness of the *PMG*'s commitment to Radicalism and Progressivism.

The *Star*'s use of the techniques of the New Journalism led some observers to stress O'Connor's contributions to the New Journalism at the expense of Stead's. Hamilton Fyfe, for example, was correct in calling O'Connor "a pioneer of the new journalism," but when he described the *Star*'s emphasis on the human side and the personal note in the news as "the earliest stone flung at Old Journalism," he implicitly overlooked Stead's whole career on the *PMG*.[5] And Lincoln Springfield, who wrote one of the more entertaining

4. They included Robert Donald, editor of the *Daily Chronicle*, 1902-08; Ernest Parke, editor of the *Star*, 1891-1908; A. W. Massingham, editor of the *Star*, 1890, the *Chronicle*, 1892-95, and the *Nation*, 1907-23; W. J. Evans, editor of the *Evening News*, 1894-1918; Wilson Pope, editor of the *Star*, 1920-30; Thomas Marlow, managing editor of the *Daily Mail*, 1899-1926; Lincoln Springfield, Harmsworth's first news editor on the *Daily Mail*; James Douglas, editor of the *Sunday Express*, 1920-31; Sidney Webb; H. M. Hyndman; and Bernard Shaw.

5. Hamilton Fyfe, *T. P. O'Connor* (London: George Allen and Unwin, 1934), pp. 138, 140.

journalistic memoirs of the period, credited O'Connor with being one of the first to use the "new-fangled importation" of the interview, but failed to mention who was the first.[6] Although the *Star* borrowed many of its features and techniques—human-interest stories, personalized reporting, interviews, and crusades—from the *PMG* and elsewhere, it added few innovations of its own. Its importance was less in its inventiveness than in the way it adapted, distilled, and refined the practices of the New Journalism from existing models.

This is not to belittle the significance of the *Star*'s contribution to journalistic development in England. Stead had pioneered in the more imaginative use of headlines and crossheads; O'Connor with his long, informative "talking" heads went much further. All the evening newspapers had presented news stories in briefer form than the mornings; the *Star*'s were crisper and brighter. Gossip and personality sketches had long been identified with periodicals such as *Truth;* O'Connor was the first to make them an integral part of a newspaper. These were the features which led Massingham to write in 1892, "The 'Star' . . . represents the most complete adaptation to this country of the method which gives the American press its vast circulation and immense popularity." [7] The 1892 edition of *Sell's Dictionary* said much the same thing in comparing the two leading English representatives of the New Journalism: "Mr. O'Connor's bold arrangements for the 'Americanization' of English journalism far surpass anything achieved by the *Pall Mall*." [8] And Stead himself recognized Tay Pay's role. As he wrote in a character sketch a dozen years after O'Connor had left the *Star,* "He and I may fairly claim to have revolutionized English journalism. . . . We broke the old tradition and made journalism a living thing, palpitating with actuality, in touch with life at all points." [9]

The popularity of the *Star* must also be considered in assessing its significance in the growth of the New Journalism. There were, of course, fluctuations in its circulation figures, but several records

6. Lincoln Springfield, *Some Piquant People* (London: T. Fisher Unwin, 1924), p. 36.

7. H. W. Massingham, "The Great London Dailies: The Halfpenny Evening Press," *Leisure Hour,* September 1892, p. 741.

8. "Newspaper Biographies," *Sell's Dictionary, 1892* (London: Sell's Advertising Offices, 1892), pp. 80, 85.

9. Stead, "Mr. T. P. O'Connor, M.P.," *Review of Reviews,* November 1902, pp. 478-79.

were set in 1888 and by the end of the year they were at the substantial level of 120,000-150,000.[10] Despite the *PMG's* concern for the lower classes and despite occasional sensations which sent its sales skyrocketing, the *Star*, selling for only a halfpenny, was much more of a mass circulation paper. During the "Maiden Tribute" sensation Stead had shown that the New Journalism could pay; O'Connor proved that it could be made to pay on a day-to-day basis. By cleverly editing and adapting, by following eclectically the trails blazed by Stead and others, and by supporting an advanced Radicalism which captured the attention of an increasingly politically-conscious working class, O'Connor reaped some of the fruits of the Education Act of 1870. The *Star* demonstrated the potential mass appeal of the New Journalism and it only remained for Alfred Harmsworth to demonstrate the even greater triumphs that could be achieved by a morning paper.

Although its appeal was to a different constituency, the *PMG* was hurt financially—as were all of the existing evening papers—by the immediate success of the *Star*. Thus Henry Yates Thompson was even more unhappy about other difficulties which he felt Stead was causing him. In April, 1888, partly in an effort to buttress his shaky position, Stead embarked on a European tour which was to be climaxed by an interview with Czar Alexander III. His first stop was Paris, where he called on Mrs. Emily Crawford, a distinguished woman journalist who wrote for the *Daily News*. He told her that Thompson was trying to get rid of him and asked if she would help to pave the way toward some other journalistic position by arranging audiences for him with the president, the premier, the foreign secretary, and other leading statesmen of the Third Republic. On learning from his ambassador in London that Stead was notoriously indiscreet, President Sadi Carnot refused to be interviewed, but Mrs. Crawford did manage to set up a meeting with Premier Charles Floquet. Stead's years in London had not worn off his rough edges, and Mrs. Crawford was appalled by his appearance when he arrived at the premier's palace. As she described it, he wore an old sealskin cap (which he forgot to take off) and a "yellowish-brown tweed suit, ill-cut, ill-fitting and untidy." His cap

10. "London Daily Press," *Sell's Dictionary, 1888*, p. 224. The capsule descriptions of London newspapers which appeared in *Sell's* had all the earmarks of puffs written by the papers themselves, but the circulation figures seem to have been reasonably accurate.

gave him "the air of a dog-stealer" and when he smiled "he might
have been a poacher, who saw an opportunity to snare a pheasant,
for all that was craftily mischievous in his character came out in
the countenance." She conceded that when Stead warmed up in a
conversation "one saw a man of originality, not to say genius,"
and M. Floquet agreed to arrange for his visitor to have a talk with
the foreign minister, M. Goblet. Stead gave his word to Goblet
that he would not repeat their conversation or even report that
the interview had taken place. However, a few days after the
meeting Mrs. Crawford was vexed to see "a flaming article on the
international situation of France, and really an interview with the
Foreign Minister. . . . Goblet never forgave me. Floquet did." [11]
As Bernard Shaw said about the incident, "This was Stead all
over." [12]

After an uneventful German visit Stead traveled on to Saint
Petersburg. According to his own later account, he had not known
such exalted enjoyment since his days in jail. Now, he felt, he was
to be rewarded for all of the abuse he had suffered for reiterating
his faith in the Russians. In his unique position he would have
special opportunities to judge Russian policy and enjoy the
confidence of the czar. He was granted interviews with the Russian
ruler and most of his ministers, as well as other important personages, and wrote his articles "as I had never written anything since
'The Maiden Tribute.'" [13] The visit to Russia and the interview with
the czar provided the material for what became perhaps Stead's
best-known book, *The Truth about Russia* (1888). While the
portrait of the nation and its rulers was not exactly painted to show
all the warts, it was much less sycophantic than his Russophile
reputation had led most people to expect; indeed, it greatly annoyed
his old friend Mme Novikoff.

While Stead was still in Europe he sent back dispatches about
his experiences to the *PMG*, and the decisions of Cook, the acting
editor, about their positioning in the paper and their format
precipitated another crisis. On the front page of the issue of
Monday, June 18, a box at the top of column one, above the leader,
called attention to a series of articles beginning in that issue under
the heading "War or Peace?" The notice stated that the center of

    11. [Emily Crawford], "Notes from Paris: Mr. W. T. Stead," *Truth*, April
24, 1912, pp. 1029-30.
    12. Whyte, *Life*, 1:259.
    13. Scott, *Life and Death*, pp. 147-48.

power in Europe had been shifting to Saint Petersburg, in part because there was an untried monarch on the German throne, and that it was at Saint Petersburg that the issue of war or peace would be decided. The notice also referred to the unique opportunities of the *PMG* "Special Commissioner" for learning what European political leaders were thinking. The first article, like the subsequent installments on each day during the week, was carried on the bottom third of the first three pages. These bottom sections were set off from the rest of the page by a rule, were printed in six-point type, and ran in three columns instead of the usual two.

In choosing this format Cook acted in complete good faith and had no intention of playing down the importance of his chief's report, but Stead, who was convinced that his interviews with statesmen were always of great importance and that these were of special significance, took a different view of the matter. Confident that his articles were creating a sensation in London, he arrived in England on Saturday after a rough passage, expecting to find the last of them in the *Pall Mall*. His penchant for self-dramatization comes through loud and clear in his account of what followed:

> I opened the paper on the platform and discovered to my horror and confusion that the letters were being printed feuilleton-wise across the bottom of the page in small type and small snippets. The series was not half through. I felt a sinking of soul indescribable. Instantly I said to myself, "Your work on the *Pall Mall* is done. . . ." The calm ignoring of my express orders [Stead actually had not been very explicit about the way in which the articles were to be printed], the publication of my letters in a way which utterly spoilt them, and at the same time the structural alteration of the paper in such a way as to destroy the front page, which is to me the most important page, all showed that at the office they no longer cared for me or for my ideas, and that if they had their way, they would leave them out altogether. I was awfully upset.[14]

It was the understatement of the year. Stead at once resolved that he would show he was still master of the ship by insisting that the articles be run again, reset so as to make a bigger splash.

During the course of a sleepless Sunday night, he arose at

14. Ibid. This and the quotation in the following paragraph are from p. 148.

1:00 A.M. to write a leader for the next day's *PMG*. In the morning
he stormed down to Northumberland Street to detonate his
"thunderbolt" and found Cook and the staff quite unaware of
having sinned. According to Stead, "Cook said nothing about the
reprinting, but agreed in his usual nonchalant way. When the proof
of the leader came down he made no remarks." But Cook apparently
was not as nonchalant as he appeared to Stead. The entry in his
own diary for that Monday reads:

> June 25, 1888. —Crisis at "P.M.G." begins. Stead back on
> Saturday. Travelling straight through had seen nothing of the
> way we dished up his articles till he arrived at Queensborough.
> Blackguarded me strongly—disobeyed his express orders—
> equivalent to dismissing him from editorship—was he editor
> or not, etc.? He had written a leader and a statement
> explaining that the whole would be begun *de novo*.[15]

That same afternoon Cook sent a letter to Stead presenting his side
of the matter—an explanation which most likely he was not allowed
to make during the first explosion of Stead's wrath. In his letter
Cook said that Thompson had assured him he had complete
editorial discretion on the Russian letters and that this had been
arranged with Stead. Since Stead had left him no instructions
whatever, Cook hoped that the charge of bad faith would be
withdrawn. A copy of the letter was sent to Thompson in Paris for
confirmation of Cook's account of the situation.

The leader which Stead had written late on Sunday night was
published in the *PMG* for Monday, June 25, and took up almost
two columns. It began:

> We have been publishing from day to day last week more
> or less snippety installments of our Special Commissioner's
> Report from St. Petersburg upon the prospects of War or
> Peace in Europe. Our Special Commissioner arrived himself
> from the Russian capital on Saturday night, and his personal
> report as to the sources of his information and the nature of
> the communications on the strength of which his estimate of
> the future outlook in Europe was based has necessitated an
> immediate adoption of a course which although absolutely
> unprecedented in journalism, is fully justified by the unique
> nature and signal success of his Commission.

15. Mills, *Edward Cook,* pp. 101-2.

Stead then explained that the next day the *PMG* would begin
reprinting the whole series in installments lengthy enough for the
public "to follow the drift of his argument." Because of its sources
and the circumstances under which it was written, his study of
contemporary problems was one which "stands absolutely alone
in the history of Modern Journalism." Further, his mission was
important "not merely because it was crowned with the most
complete and brilliant success," but also because of its probable
effect both at home and abroad. The leader ended with one of
Stead's lectures on the responsibility of the press, deriding some of
the *PMG's* contemporaries who were interested only in "parochial
small beer," party banalities, and sporting news. Stead saw himself
as bearing the burden of the responsibility to make the press "at
once the instructor, the inspirer, and the guide of an enlightened
and serious Democracy."

If the reprinting of the articles was not actually "absolutely
unprecedented in journalism," it was at least sufficiently unusual
to raise the eyebrows of both readers and newspapermen. Frederic
Whyte is probably right when he denies the charge of Cook's
biographer, J. Saxon Mills, that Stead "inflicted a sort of public
reprimand on his lieutenant, and sacrificed the interests of his
paper and its readers for a rather petty revenge." [16] As upset as
he was, it was not in character for Stead to behave in such a fashion;
spite and petty vengeance did not appeal to him. Nevertheless, the
leader and rerunning of the series must have looked like a public
reprimand, and it is understandable that Cook was nettled.

Nor did the crisis end there. Thompson had returned from
Paris and, upon seeing the Monday *PMG* at Dover, made straight
for the newspaper office. Cook described the scene which followed:
"He was very angry and walked about the room swearing, wishing
to God he had been back—why in the world couldn't Stead have
waited, instead of being so utterly discourteous and lacking in
consideration?" [17] Then came the confrontation between proprietor
and editor, at which Thompson insisted that Stead had insulted
him, and said that he had more confidence in Cook. Thompson also
reminded his editor that because of the Trafalgar Square furor and
the new competition, sales and advertisements were both down.
The men parted with the understanding that Stead's contract with

16. Ibid., p. 103.
17. Ibid., p. 102.

the paper would come up for reconsideration sometime before October 1. On September 19 they had another meeting at which the proprietor was, in Stead's words, "somewhat brutal." When Stead suggested that Cook be made editor, with himself only an outside contributor, Thompson confessed he was puzzled as to just what he should do. He did make it clear, however, that if Stead remained on the *PMG* after October 1 it would be at a salary reduced from twelve hundred to one thousand pounds, and with the understanding that when matters likely to cause trouble arose, he must consult with Cook and Thompson before following any course of action. After the conversation Thompson sent Stead a letter confirming these two provisos. When Stead responded by suggesting that the *PMG* might profit by an improved distribution system, Thompson wrote that the main need of the moment was for Stead to run the paper as he had between 1882 and 1885. During those years circulation had risen from an average of 8,360 daily to 12,250, and the distribution system was no better then. Only through "vigorous but steady conduct of the paper" could the circulation be increased. The vital necessity was to regain the confidence of the *PMG*'s old penny public—both advertisers and readers. Thompson believed that people's memories were short "and that the position is recoverable with care, but only with care."

He also wrote that to show that his action in cutting Stead's salary was due to genuine alarm and distress at past risks, he would restore the two hundred pounds at the end of 1889 if during the year Stead had fulfilled the conditions of caution imposed on him. Although Stead continued as editor, one can readily understand his feelings when he wrote in his diary on September 25 that after his exaltation in June, he had been humiliated into despair. "From the very pinnacle of success," he wrote, "I have been hurled into the abyss of failure." [18] Stead's mercurial temperament did not permit this black mood to last, but it was obvious that things would never again be the same for him at the *Pall Mall Gazette*. From this time forward, despite the extension of his contract he was convinced that his days on the paper were numbered. It was a question only of how many there were to be and to what service God would call him next.

While these upheavals were taking place, the *PMG* showed little visible change in direction, emphasis, and format. Perhaps because

18. Scott, *Life and Death*, pp. 149-50.

of the *Star* it increased its sports coverage somewhat, but in a selective way: cricket and university rowing commanded more space than more plebeian activities. Prize fights were covered, but usually in a derogatory fashion, and rival papers were chided for their longer descriptive accounts. Almost certainly the *PMG* was following the *Star*'s lead when it introduced its own gossip column. On several occasions in the past Stead had defended what he called "tittle-tattle" in the press, and in November, 1888, he introduced "Tittle-tattle for the Tea Table." It became a daily feature and, like O'Connor's "Mainly about People," it frequently treated the upper classes irreverently.

The *PMG* continued to give other newspapers the benefit of its unsolicited observations and advice. When the *Morning Post* began to break up its long reports of parliamentary speeches with cross-heads, an Occasional Note of March 27 rejoiced in another victory for the techniques of the New Journalism. Between August and November the so-called Jack-the-Ripper murders received extensive coverage from all London newspapers, including the *PMG*, but Stead felt that many of his rivals were guilty of the wrong kind of sensationalism, giving excessive attention to bloodthirsty details and deliberately prolonging the story. In the front-page leader of October 9 he called for a "court of conscience" (the details of which remained completely vague) to provide guidance for the "puzzle-headed millions" in the modern state. (For all of his democratic idealism, Stead often betrayed a lack of faith in the taste and judgment of the masses.) The closest thing to such a court then in existence was the press, but the newspapers needed a court of conscience to decide, for instance, how to treat murders. The profitable approach was "to bring out a sheet which drips in gore or is almost as 'creepy' and revolting as the gashed and mangled corpses of the murderer's victims." Building up the sensation by using every journalistic resource—reporters, interviewers, artists, specialists in typography—to bring out the special murder editions was "the plain path set before the journal by considerations of profit and loss."

Whatever Stead's views on the newspaper coverage of the Whitechapel tragedies, those brutal unsolved murders did provide him with more ammunition for his war on the police, Home Secretary Matthews, and Police Commissioner Warren. For one thing, the failure of the police to solve the murders could be

effectively contrasted with their efficiency in abridging civil liberties
at popular meetings and demonstrations. On October 8 the *PMG*
leader, "Who Is Responsible?," [19] introduced a new series, "The
Police and the Criminals of London." While the leader denied any
prejudice against Warren and acknowledged that he had not been
responsible for giving the orders for the charge at Trafalgar Square,
it held him accountable for the failure to deal with current criminal
activities. In its six installments, which ran through October 13, the
series pointed out the low ratio of policemen to population, weaknesses in administration and personnel, the high incidence of
unsolved crimes, and discontent in the ranks. It ended, unsur-
prisingly, by blaming Warren for the shortcomings of the police.
Accompanying the series were numerous news stories and leaders
which condemned or ridiculed the police commissioner. Most of the
press took up the hue and cry, and on November 12 that much
abused official resigned.

The next morning most of the London papers applauded his
departure; only the *Standard* took a completely pro-Warren point
of view. The *Standard* particularly regretted his resignation because
it appeared to be the result of "one of the most violent and
unjustifiable agitations which ever disgraced the less reputable
portion of the London press." The *Times* and the *Telegraph* saw
the removal of Matthews as the next necessary step, and the *PMG*
took the same line. In fact, Warren, whose resignation had been
triggered by a quarrel with the Home Secretary, now became almost
a sympathetic figure in its pages. According to its November 13
leader, "Who Must Succeed Mr. Matthews?," the *PMG*'s unswerving
hostility during the past year had been directed not at Warren but
at "the system of repression which he established." It took the
lion's share of the credit for the commissioner's departure, ignoring
a similar early stand taken by the *Star*, and observed piously that
"although as the *Standard* frankly admits, [Warren's] resignation
is largely due to our action and that of the others who followed in
our wake, we feel no inclination to exult over the fallen chief." It
predicted that the popularity Matthews had gained by firing
Warren would be short-lived, and asserted that newspaper discussion about who would succeed Warren was less important than
the question of who would succeed Matthews. Whether or not the

19. The leader may have been Cook's; Stead was absent from the paper a
great deal during his last months as editor.

PMG was on the side of the angels in advocating the removal of Matthews,[20] the campaign against him was destined to fail. His tenure at the Home Office outlasted Stead's at the *Pall Mall Gazette*.

II

Stead introduced his last major change in the *PMG* on the first day of his last year as its editor. Beginning with the issue of January 1, 1889, the size of the paper was increased from 14½" x 10" to 19½" x 14", with a three-column page.[21] In style and content, however, there was no reflection of Stead's changing relationship with Cook and Thompson. Certain new features appeared and others vanished, but none of the changes were pronounced. There were no attention-rousing crusades, although there were articles on such long-standing concerns as the strength of the navy and the problem of housing for the working classes. Stead also persisted in what many considered his personal vendettas against Dilke and Matthews. The report of the Parnell Commission, appointed to investigate charges made by the *Times* against the Irish leader, brought forth one of the biggest headline displays in the paper's history on February 26,[22] and the *PMG* gave extensive coverage to the famous Dockers' Strike of 1889. T. P. O'Connor's strictures on Stead's lukewarm Radicalism notwithstanding, he warmly supported the workers' cause throughout, with emphasis on the labors of his good friend Cardinal Manning.

In April, Stead, the imperial dreamer, met Cecil Rhodes, the empire builder, and for a time he believed that this meeting was going to be another major turning point in his career. Swift MacNeill, an Irish M.P., had informed Stead that Rhodes, who thought highly of his work on the *PMG*, was looking for a way to exercise political power. The editor suggested that he start a newspaper and MacNeill sent the suggestion to Rhodes, with a copy of Stead's *Contemporary Review* article "Government by

20. R.C.K. Ensor says of Matthews that "he did more, perhaps, to render the government unpopular than any other minister" (*England*, p. 173).

21. The bottom third of the front page was ruled off, as it had been when Stead objected to the presentation of his articles from Europe in 1888, and usually had a feature article. Other feature articles and gossip or chitchat columns also appeared above the line, along with the traditional leader and follower.

22. The Parnell Commission story that day featured the flight of the forger Pigott, and his confession. The headline over it was fourteen lines of eighteen-point type, taking up almost half of the column.

Journalism." The two men met on April 3 [23] at a luncheon which
Stead left full of admiration for his new friend. Rhodes had been
taken aback to learn that it would take £250,000 to start a newspaper, and explained that his current obligations would prevent
him from raising that much money at the time. As a first step,
however, he offered Stead a gift of £20,000 to make a down
payment on the *Pall Mall Gazette*.[24] Stead declined the gift, but the
very next day he asked Rhodes to help him out of another uncomfortable situation with Thompson. On April 4 a libel suit was
decided against the *PMG*, and the judge, who "commented strongly
on the style of the libel as sensational journalism," [25] awarded the
plaintiffs, a Mrs. Irwin and a Mr. Layard, a total of £1,500 in
damages. Stead considered this a debt for which he was personally
responsible. Immediately upon learning the verdict he wrote a note
to Rhodes asking for £2,000 to cover damages and costs. His new
friend complied and Stead was able to tell Thompson that the
case "will not cost you a farthing." Well aware that his position on
the *PMG* was precarious, Stead wrote in his journal, "The
importance of this is that it clinches me with Rhodes." [26]

In the same journal entry Stead predicted that he would be
leaving the *PMG* by June 30 and starting a new venture by January,
1890. Caught up in a new enthusiasm, he wrote exultantly, "I
now see that I am called to found for the Nineteenth Century a
city of God which will be to the age of the printing press and the
steam engine what the Catholic Church was to Europe of the 10th
century." What he envisioned was more a worldwide university
than a newspaper, with fellowships, scholarships, missionaries, and
endowed correspondences. "It will be father confessor, spiritual
director, moral teacher, political conscience. . . . It will be the
mother of mankind." In order to prepare himself to edit a newspaper

23. Whyte gives this meeting the erroneous date of April 4. He quotes
from the letter arranging it for Wednesday, which was April 3 (*Life*, 1:270).
In his diary Stead mentions that the judgment against him in a libel suit,
which was reached on April 4, came the day after his luncheon with Rhodes
(Scott, *Life and Death*, p. 151).

24. Whyte, *Life*, 1:270.

25. *Times*, April 5, 1889. On July 11, 1888, the *PMG*, in an Occasional Note
about a divorce case, claimed that the husband had been drugged by Mrs.
Irwin and unjustly committed to an insane asylum while she was having an
affair with his solicitor, Mr. Layard. The judge ruled against the *PMG's*
contention that this was a fair comment on the facts which had come out of the
trial.

26. Scott, *Life and Death*, pp. 151-52.

for the world, Stead planned to use some of Rhodes's money for a trip around the globe with his good friend Reginald Brett, his son Willie, and a shorthand clerk. Unfortunately, because of Rhodes's other commitments he was never able to provide the money for either the newspaper or the trip, and Stead recorded his disappointment as he waited in vain for another sign from God.[27] But despite the collapse of his plans he remained a close friend of Rhodes.[28]

In August he clashed again with Cook, this time over the Infectious Disease Bill, long anathema to Stead, which was then being considered in Parliament. After careful study Cook decided that he favored the legislation and wrote to his chief, "If this bill is to be slain, you must slay it." Cook had meant only that since he did not share Stead's feelings, it would be better if the editor wrote the article attacking the bill, but Stead was exasperated and depressed by the letter. He noted on the first page, "Replied that in my altered position on the paper, I could only ask him to be silent on a subject on which for fifteen years I have held strongest views." Cook's stand seemed to him "another nail in my *P. M. G.* coffin."[29]

On October 31 the *PMG* began a series entitled "Letters from the Vatican: The Pope and the New World," with Stead serving as special correspondent for the last time. The first article asked what the papacy could or would do to meet the challenge of three great developments of the modern era: the growing domination of English-speaking people, the growth of a socialist basis for society, and the movement toward women's equality. The articles appeared in ten installments through December 16, and were collected in a book which enjoyed a good sale. The writing was in the best Steadian tradition—lively and perceptive, if not profound. After its publication Stead was attacked both for being pro-Catholic and for showing an antipapal bias, which perhaps suggests an overall objectivity. At any rate, the Puritan Stead had often shown that he was fascinated by the Church of Rome. It may be that Stead

27. Ibid., pp. 152-53.
28. Stead was either beneficiary or executor in Rhodes's famous wills until written out by a 1901 codicil, which read, "On account of the extraordinary eccentricity of Mr. Stead, though always having a great respect for him, but feeling the objects of my will would be embarrassed by his views, I hereby revoke his appointment as one of my executors" (ibid., p. 174). The "eccentricity" might have referred to Stead's opposition to the Boer War or to his belief in spiritualism, which by then had become well established.
29. Whyte, *Life,* 1:287.

undertook the series for the same reason that he made the trip to
Russia—to bolster his faltering position on the *PMG*—but it is more
likely that by October of 1889 he realized he had passed the point
of no return with Henry Yates Thompson.

During his last two months as editor Stead continued to comment
on the journalistic scene, adding to his tongue-in-cheek commendations of rivals who adopted his innovative techniques. On November
8 an Occasional Note congratulated the *St. James's Gazette* for
introducing crossheads, maps, and illustrations, and publishing an
illustrated extra. If it kept up the good work, said the *PMG*, "we
shall make a creditable paper of it yet." Six days later a short
paragraph in the "Tittle-tattle" column reported the appearance of
interviews in both the *St. James's Gazette* and the *Globe,* and
predicted that "we shall level them all up in time." Two longer
articles on the press in November gave a glimpse of paths that
English journalism would follow in the future. The leader for
November 6, "The Age of Advertisement," was occasioned by a
banquet given by Sir Algernon Borthwick of the *Morning Post* for
the managing director of the Pears' Soap Company, and portrayed
in laudatory terms the role of the advertiser in the growth of the
popular press. It pointed out that many newspapers were able to
survive only because of advertising revenue, and went so far as to
maintain that as important as an editor was to a newspaper, he
was "far less indispensable than the Enterprising Advertiser. For
good or evil this is the age of the Press; but the Press would be
powerless if the age were not also the age of Advertisement." (A
news article on the banquet the next day mentioned that Pears'
Soap spent a hundred thousand pounds annually on advertising.)
The second piece was an interview with W. L. Thomas, director of
the *Graphic,* who told of plans to publish a daily edition of that
successful illustrated weekly, beginning in January, 1890. Thus
Stead's pioneering use of news pictures was to reach fruition with
the appearance of a full-scale illustrated daily.

In December came Stead's final break with the *Pall Mall
Gazette.* George Newnes, whose journalistic fame and fortune had
continued to increase, had proposed that Stead edit a new monthly
review which he planned to publish. It would include a digest of
notable articles from other periodicals, an index of the periodicals
surveyed, a lengthy character sketch, a summary of the news of the
month, editorial opinion, and other original material. The final

decision to go ahead with this magazine, eventually called the *Review of Reviews,* was made on December 7; three days later Stead wrote to Thompson, informing him that he intended to edit a new publication for Mr. Newnes. Thompson replied immediately "in acknowledgement of *an accomplished fact.* . . . I very much wish you had consulted me first. I should certainly have said what I say now, that the editing of Mr. Newnes' magazine is quite incompatible with editing the *P. M. G.* . . . I don't, as at present advised, see the least prospect of seeing my way to going shares in the Editor." [30] At a December 13 meeting the editor and the proprietor agreed that Stead would leave the *Pall Mall* either January 1 or April 1, 1890. Stead indicated a preference for the earlier date, and Thompson wrote to him on December 14 assuring him that if he should change his mind or if the deal fell through, both Thompson and Cook would be happy to have him stay till April.

Ironically, Stead's last major *PMG* story on his favorite topic, Ireland, concerned the O'Shea divorce case in which Parnell was named corespondent.[31] (Stead could not know, of course, that he was really commenting on the end of the dream of home rule.) On December 28 the *PMG* ran a modest three-inch item on the case and Stead's last leader on the subject appeared December 29. "Mr. Parnell," he declared, "is not quite the man to sacrifice a great cause to a guilty passion." At least, he never had to record his eventual disillusionment in the pages of the *Pall Mall.*

No mention was made in the *PMG* of Stead's departure, just as none had been made of Morley's, in accordance with a directive from Thompson.[32] The first issue of the *Review of Reviews* appeared on January 15, 1890, and despite the haste with which it had been put together, this monthly magazine, unique for its day,

30. Scott, *Life and Death,* p. 154.

31. Parnell and Kitty O'Shea had been living together since 1881, with Captain O'Shea's knowledge. However, in December, 1889, for political or financial reasons—or both—O'Shea sued his wife for divorce, naming Parnell as corespondent, and the suit was not contested. This not only cost Parnell the support of Gladstone's Liberal party, with its strong Nonconformist element; after a long debate only twenty-six of seventy Irish M.P.'s agreed to remain under Parnell's leadership. Stead, in the *Review of Reviews,* campaigned against the Irish leader who, like himself, had violated the Victorian moral code.

32. Stead's attempt in 1904 to found a new, typically idealistic journal, the *Daily Paper,* resulted in complete and almost instant disaster; thus for all practical purposes he left London daily journalism for good on January 1, 1890.

was well received. Denied the opportunity to edit a paper backed by Rhodes, the ever resilient Stead transferred his lofty visions of the future to the new venture. Although the general feeling in the *PMG* office was that he had been even madder than usual to make the move, Stead as always was sublimely confident about the wisdom of his course. He saw in the *Review* "boundless possibilities, the unexpected first step to a world-wide journalistic, civil church, with a faith and religious orders and endowments and all the rest of the paraphernalia of the Church Militant." [33]

Within three months he bought out Newnes,[34] and the *Review of Reviews* remained his central concern for the rest of his life. There were occasional financial crises, brought on by his haphazard business methods as much as anything, but the journal was a good property. From his new editorial chair Stead continued to carry out crusades and to give unsolicited advice to the London press. He also continued to promulgate his views on a wide variety of subjects in tracts, pamphlets, and books. His death while still in harness, on April 15, 1912—he was lost in the *Titanic* disaster —evoked an extraordinary number of tributes from all manner of people. He would have been especially gratified by the letter Lord Fisher wrote to Lord Esher on April 22, when word of the tragedy reached him:

> The loss of dear old Stead numbs me! Cromwell and Martin Luther rolled into one. The telegrams here say he was to the forefront with the women and children, putting them in the boats! *I can see him!* and probably singing "Hallelujah," encouraging the ship band to play cheerfully. He told me he would die in his boots. So he has. *And a fine death.*[35]

III

It is a mark of what Stead meant to his times that assessments of his character and contributions were so often contradictory. A man who accomplishes much will be damned as well as praised. Wemyss Reid in an 1893 article in the *Speaker* summed

33. Scott, *Life and Death*, p. 155.
34. The two men remained on good terms but Stead's volatile approach to sensitive topics as well as his failure to master sound business methods had worn Newnes down rather quickly.
35. John A. [Lord] Fisher, *Memories* (London: Hodder & Stoughton, 1919), pp. 264-65.

it up very well: "Mr. Stead is a gentleman regarding whom most men find it impossible to entertain a neutral or even a judicial mind. . . . The one class believes him to be a hero, apostle, prophet and martyr, the man to whom the world may be indebted for its deliverance from the intolerable load of sin and misery it has to bear upon its weary shoulders. To the other class he is an imposter, a charlatan, a hypocrite, and an adventurer."[36] The variations in opinion about Stead can be ascribed, at least in great part, not only to the eagerness with which he thrust himself into controversy—or, frequently, created it—but to the fact that his stands on controversial issues often seemed contradictory. Stead was an ardent pacifist and known for his work in peace groups, but he was also a champion of naval armament in England. An active imperialist, he was a friend and admirer of Cecil Rhodes, but he was to be as pro-Boer as any Little Englander. His being a firm believer in liberty and freedom did not stop him from speaking out in defense of czarist Russia. He thought of himself as a hardheaded journalist and never tired of stressing the journalist's obligation to ascertain all the facts, but in the later years of his life he tarnished his reputation by promoting spiritualism.

Still, there is general accord, if not unanimity, about certain elements of Stead's character and personality—for example, his supreme self-confidence, so often indistinguishable from arrogance. One observer noted that "his egotism was wonderful and almost touching in its naiveté."[37] As a corollary, he was at times almost pathetically eager to be noticed, to receive recognition and acclaim. Aaron Watson, once a *PMG* staff member, saw this trait in Stead's well-known eccentricities in dress and behavior: "He was insensible to ridicule, except, perhaps in the sense that it pleased him more to be laughed at than not to be noticed at all."[38] And he *was* noticed: the very debates over his role in the various controversies attest to it. "It was easy to scoff at William Stead," said an old friend, A. G. Gardiner, "it was easy to distrust his judgment. But it was impossible to forget or ignore him."[39] Most of those who knew him were agreed, too, on his almost quixotic idealism, his

36. "The Modern Press: IV—'The Review of Reviews,'" p. 99.
37. E. T. Raymond, *Portraits of the Nineties* (London: T. Fisher Unwin, 1921), p. 178.
38. Watson, *Memories*, p. 67.
39. A. G. Gardiner, "The Book of the Month: William T. Stead," *Review of Reviews*, October 1913, p. 305.

dedicated sense of mission, and the courage with which he undertook his crusades. As Watson conceded, although he was a
"sensational journalist in grain," Stead had high aspirations and
"was capable of making the greatest sacrifices for causes in which he
believed." [40] His long-time friend Lord Fisher stressed this quality
in a letter to Lord Esher. Recalling that Morley had described Stead
as a man of absolute integrity, who feared no one, Fisher declared:
"I myself had heard him tackle a Prime Minister like a terrier with
a rat. I have known him to go to a packed meeting and scathe the
whole mob of them. He might have been a rich man if he hadn't
told the truth, I know it." [41]

Stead, the hardheaded journalist, often let his emotions lead him
into battle. Others might object and ridicule him, or recoil in horror
or contempt, but Stead, endowed with a strong sense of spiritual
righteousness, marched on undeterred on the course upon which he
had set himself. He never wavered from the conviction that like
his hero, Oliver Cromwell, he had a great role to play as God's
servant. It is perhaps the religious element in Stead's personality
that distorts the image of the man and makes him appear to some
the relict of an earlier age. Hugh Kingsmill has depicted him as "a
Puritan born too late to simplify the modern world," continuously
involved in a struggle to reconcile his Old Testament background
to the complexities of life in the late nineteenth century.[42] But is
this really an accurate analysis of the career of William T. Stead?
There is much evidence to the contrary. If a man as complicated
and as paradoxical as Stead can be categorized, he was a harbinger
of the future more than a throwback to the dead past.

Through his contributions to the development of the New
Journalism, this North Country Puritan did as much as any man to
lay the foundations of modern British journalism; more, in fact, than
many others who have received the credit—or blame. Stead left
behind him the seeds of journalistic revolution, though they had not
all sprouted when he left the _PMG._ Even the outward appearance
of the London press had changed between 1880 and 1890. Not that
the changes were radical or universally accepted; it would take
more than a decade of Steadian example to alter the format of the
good, gray _Times._ Yet a survey of London newspapers when Stead
moved on from Northumberland Street showed more use of head-

40. Watson, _Memories,_ p. 68.
41. Fisher, _Memories,_ p. 262.
42. Kingsmill, _After Puritanism,_ pp. 171-72.

lines and crossheads, more paragraphing, more illustrations. The once despised interview was a regular feature in many of the metropolitan papers, and if Stead liked to rib his rivals as they reluctantly bowed to the inevitable, he surely can be forgiven. He not only teased them, he praised them, lectured them, scolded them, cajoled them; in short, he *noticed* them—and that in itself was an innovation. Moreover, he compelled them to notice the *Pall Mall Gazette*.

George Newnes is generally credited with being the first English journalist to tap the new market nurtured by the Education Act of 1870, although it is quite unlikely that he did so consciously. By founding a weekly tailored to his own tastes, he reached a vast audience uninterested in—or unable to cope with—the starchy, somber pages of the old, established journals. The gibe that *Tit-Bits* appealed to people whose lips moved when they read was not altogether unjustified. Stead had shown that such an audience existed, even if he never came close to capturing it. In fact, the *PMG* was aimed at the people who counted, at the class that set standards and made political decisions, and this was reflected in the paper's style as well as its price. Yet it was Stead, the founder of the New Journalism, who aligned it with the New Democracy. The enactment of two measures—the Franchise Act of 1867, which gave the working classes some reason to want to read newspapers, and the Education Act of 1870, which enabled them to do so—created a new readership. When Stead felt impelled to reach this wider audience—for purity, not for profit—he showed the world of journalism how to do it. Crusading journalism had been known before, but never had it been so closely identified with the interests and aspirations of the masses. Crusades and campaigns became an integral part of the New Journalism, and they remained so even after it was no longer new. Later practitioners of the newspaper crusade may have been motivated by less exalted considerations than Stead, but they were following in his path.

The adjective *dynamic* is worn from use, but no other suits Stead so well. A flamboyant, eccentric egotist who humbly served a Puritan God, he had a flair, a style, and an intuitive journalistic sense that far outweighed his carelessness in some matters and his limited intellectual horizons. By virtue of his crusades and innovations and by demonstrating that a newspaper could affect a nation's policy, William T. Stead stands as a maker of modern journalism.

Bibliography

The only full-scale biography of Stead—Frederic Whyte's *The Life of W. T. Stead* (2 vols.; London: Jonathan Cape, 1925)—was a major source for this study, particularly volume one, which covers his years on the *Pall Mall Gazette*. Whyte, however, while not completely uncritical, was generally determined to show his subject in a favorable light, and his work cannot be called completely objective. Whyte devotes a good portion of the first volume to Stead's crusades and other examples of his New Journalism, but he makes scant use of the files of the *PMG* or its contemporaries.

J. W. Robertson Scott wrote a number of partly autobiographical works on the British press which contain valuable information about Stead and the *Pall Mall Gazette*. The most important of these for this work was *The Life and Death of a Newspaper* (London: Methuen, 1952), a history of the *PMG* which gives considerable attention to the 1880-89 period. The numerous and lengthy extracts from Stead's journals give *Life and Death* added value, but it is flawed by occasional errors of fact and faulty recollections.

Hugh Kingsmill devoted a long chapter of his *After Puritanism* (London: Duckworth, 1929), to Stead and provided some interesting and perceptive insights into the character and temperament of the editor. However, the limitations imposed by the major theme of showing a seventeenth-century Puritan frustrated by the complexities of nineteenth-century society precluded a very comprehensive study. Biographies of other journalists of the period were also useful, particularly *Sir Edward Cook, K.B.E.* (London: Constable, 1921) by J. Saxon Mills, which explores the relationship between Stead and his successor on the *PMG* in some detail.

Of several contemporary works dealing with the actual operation of an English newspaper in the 1880s, John Dawson's *Practical Journalism* (London: L. Upcott Gill, 1885) was probably the most thorough and illuminating. Stanley Morrison, whose contributions to journalistic history include the monumental official history of the *Times*, also produced the definitive study of British newspaper typography with his *The English Newspaper* (Cambridge: Cambridge University Press, 1932). In it he gives due recognition to the developments on the *Pall Mall Gazette* under Stead.

The files of the major London morning and evening newspapers of the period provided the major primary source for this study. They included:

257

Daily Chronicle, 1880-89
Daily News, 1880-89
Daily Telegraph, 1880-89
Echo, 1889
Evening News, 1881-89
Evening Standard, 1880-89
Globe, 1880-89
Morning Post, 1880-89
Pall Mall Gazette, 1880-89
St. James's Gazette, 1880-89
Standard, 1880-89
Star, 1888-89
Times, 1880-89
Periodicals which were of particular use as source materials were:
Review of Reviews, 1890-1912
Saturday Review, 1880-89
Spectator, 1880-89
Extensive use also was made of *Hansard's Parliamentary Debates,* 3d ser. (1880-89) and journalistic trade publications such as *Deacon's Newspaper Handbook* (London: Samuel Deacon, 1880-89) and *Sell's Dictionary of the World's Press* (London: Sell's Advertising Offices), 1883-89.
In addition the following books and periodical articles were of value.

BOOKS
Altick, Richard D. *The English Common Reader: A Social History of the Mass Reading Public, 1800-1900.* Chicago: University of Chicago Press, 1957.
B., H. A. *About Newspapers.* Edinburgh: St. Giles, 1888.
Bell, E. Moberly. *Josephine Butler, Flame of Fire.* London: Constable, 1962.
Besant, Annie. *An Autobiography.* 2nd ed. London: T. Fisher Unwin, 1893.
Blumenfeld, R. D. *R.D.B.'s Diary, 1887-1914.* London: Wm. Heinemann, 1930.
Blunt, Wilfrid Scawen. *Gordon at Khartoum.* London: Stephen Swift, 1911.
———. *My Diaries.* 2 vols. London: Martin Secker, 1919-20.
Boon, John. *Victorians, Edwardians and Georgians.* Vol. 1. London: Hutchinson, [1928].
Bourne, H. R. Fox. *English Newspapers.* 2 vols. London: Chatto and Windus, 1887.
Brett, Maurice V. *Journals and Letters of Reginald Viscount Esher.* Vol. 1, 1870-1903. London: Ivor Nicholson and Watson, 1934.
Briggs, Sir John Henry. *Naval Administrations, 1827-1892.* Edited by Lady Briggs. London: Sampson, Low, Marston, 1897.
Butler, Josephine E. *Rebecca Jarrett.* London: Morgan and Scott, [1885].
Cook, Edward T. *Edmund Garrett, a Memoir.* London: Edward Arnold, 1909.
Cook, Sir Edward. *Literary Recreations.* London: Macmillan, 1918.
Cromer, Earl of [Evelyn Baring]. *Modern Egypt.* London: Macmillan, 1911.
Dawson, John. *Practical Journalism.* London: L. Upcott Gill, 1885.
Dodwell, H. H. *Cambridge History of the British Empire.* Vol. 5, *The Indian Empire.* Chapter 23, "Central Asia, 1858-1918." Cambridge: Cambridge University Press, 1932.
Ensor, R.C.K. *England, 1870-1914.* London: Oxford University Press, 1963.
Escott, T.H.S. *England: Its People, Polity and Pursuits.* 2d ed. London: Cassell, 1881.
———. *Masters of English Journalism.* T. Fisher Unwin, 1911.

Fawcett, Millicent, and Turner, E. M. *Josephine Butler*. London: Association for Moral and Social Hygiene, 1927.
Fisher, John A. [Lord]. *Memories*. London: Hodder and Stoughton, 1919.
Fraser-Tytler, W. K. *Afghanistan*. London: Oxford University Press, 1953.
Friederichs, Hulda. *Life of Sir George Newnes*. London: Hodder and Stoughton, 1911.
Fyfe, Hamilton. *Sixty Years of Fleet Street*. London: W. H. Allen, 1949.
———. *T. P. O'Connor*. London: George Allen and Unwin, 1934.
Gretton, R. H. *A Modern History of the English People, 1880-1922*. London: Martin Secker, 1930.
Harris, Frank. *My Life and Loves*. New York: Grove Press, 1963.
Hatton, Joseph. *Journalistic London*. London: Sampson, Low, Marston, Searle and Rivington, 1882.
Herd, Harold. *The Making of Modern Journalism*. London: Allen and Unwin, 1927.
———. *The March of Journalism*. London: Allen and Unwin, 1952.
Hirst, F. W. *Early Life and Letters of John Morley*. 2 vols. London: Macmillan, 1927.
———. *The Six Panics and Other Essays*. London: Methuen, 1913.
Hyndman, Henry Mayers. *The Record of an Adventurous Life*. London: Macmillan, 1911.
Jenkins, Roy. *Sir Charles Dilke: A Victorian Tragedy*. London: Collins, 1958.
Johnson, George W. and Lucy. *Josephine Butler: An Autobiographical Memoir*. Rev. ed. London: J. W. Arrowsmith, 1909.
Jones, Kennedy. *Fleet Street and Downing Street*. London: Hutchinson, 1919.
Kingsmill, Hugh. *After Puritanism*. London: Duckworth, 1929.
Lynd, Helen Merrell. *England in the Eighteen-Eighties*. London: Oxford University Press, 1945.
Magnus, Philip. *Gladstone*. New York: E. P. Dutton, 1954.
Maitland, Frederic William. *The Life and Letters of Leslie Stephen*. London: Duckworth, 1960.
Marlowe, John. *Mission to Khartum*. London: Victor Gollancz, 1969.
Matthews, T. S. *The Sugar Pill*. London: Victor Gollancz, 1957.
Mills, J. Saxon. *Sir Edward Cook, K.B.E.* London: Constable, 1921.
Milne, James. *A Window in Fleet Street*. London: John Murray, 1931.
Morison, Stanley. *The English Newspaper*. Cambridge: Cambridge University Press, 1932.
[———]. *The History of "The Times."* Vol. 3, *The Twentieth Century Test, 1884-1912*. London: Times Publishing Company, 1947.
Morley, Charles. *Travels in London*. London: Smith, Elder, 1916.
Morley, John, Viscount. *Recollections*. Vol. 1. London: Macmillan, 1917.
Nethercot, Arthur H. *The First Five Lives of Annie Besant*. Chicago: University of Chicago Press, 1960.
Nutting, Anthony. *Gordon, Martyr and Misfit*. London: Constable, 1966.
O'Connor, T. P. *Gladstone's House of Commons*. London: Ward and Downey, 1885.
Pendleton, John. *Newspaper Reporting*. London: Elliot Stock, 1890.
Pope, Wilson. *The Story of the Star, 1888-1938*. London: the *Star*, 1938.
Pound, Reginald. *Mirror of the Century: The Strand Magazine*. New York: A. G. Barnes, 1967.
Progress of the British Newspapers in the 19th Century. London: Swan Electric Engraving Company, 1903.

Railton, G. S. *The Truth about the Armstrong Case and the Salvation Army.* London: Salvation Army Bookstores, [1885].

Raymond, E. T. *Portraits of the Nineties.* London: T. Fisher Unwin, 1921.

Reid, T. Wemyss. *The Life of the Right Honourable William Edward Forster.* Vol. 2. London: Chapman and Hall, 1888.

———. *Memoirs.* Edited by Stuart J. Reid. London: Cassell, 1905.

Scott, Benjamin. *A State of Iniquity: Its Rise, Extension and Overthrow.* London: Kegan Paul, Trench, Trübner, 1890.

Scott, J. W. Robertson. *The Day Before Yesterday.* London: Methuen, 1951.

———. *The Life and Death of a Newspaper.* London: Methuen, 1952.

———. *The story of the Pall Mall Gazette.* London: Oxford University Press, 1950.

———. *'We' and Me.* London: W. H. Allen, 1956.

Shannon, Richard Thomas. *Gladstone and the Bulgarian Agitation, 1876.* London: Thomas Nelson and Sons, 1963.

Snell, Harry [Lord]. *Men, Movements, and Myself.* London: J. M. Dent, 1938.

Spender, J. A. *Life, Journalism and Politics.* 2 vols. London: Cassell, 1928.

Springfield, Lincoln. *Some Piquant People.* London: T. Fisher Unwin, 1924.

Stark, Malcolm. *The Pulse of the World: Fleet Street Memories.* London: Skeffington and Son, 1915.

Stead, Estelle W. *My Father.* London: Wm. Heinemann, 1913.

Stead, William T. *Josephine Butler: A Life Sketch.* London: Morgan and Scott, [1888].

———. *The M.P. for Russia.* 2 vols. London: Andrew Melrose, 1909.

Strachey, Lytton. *Eminent Victorians.* London: Chatto and Windus, 1918.

Symon, J. D. *The Press and Its Story.* London: Seeley, Service, 1914.

Taylor, A.J.P. *The Trouble Makers: Dissent over Foreign Policy, 1792-1939.* London: Hamish Hamilton, 1957.

Terrot, Charles. *The Maiden Tribute.* London: Frederick Muller, 1959.

The *Times.* *The Times, a Newspaper History, 1785-1935.* London: Printing House Square, 1935.

Watson, Aaron. *A Newspaper Man's Memories.* London: Hutchinson, [1925].

Waugh, Benjamin. *William Stead: A Life for the People.* London: H. Vickers, 1885.

Whyte, Frederic. *The Life of W. T. Stead.* 2 vols. London: Jonathan Cape, 1925.

Williams, Francis. *Dangerous Estate.* London: Longmans, Green, 1957.

Wrench, John Evelyn. *Alfred Lord Milner.* London: Eyre and Spottiswoode, 1958.

Yeo, H. *Newspaper Management.* Manchester: John Heywood, 1891.

ARTICLES

Arnold, Matthew. "Up to Easter." *Nineteenth Century,* May 1887, pp. 629-43.

Arnold-Forster, H. O. "Our Position as a Naval Power." *Nineteenth Century,* January 1883, pp. 1-3.

———. "The People of England *versus* Their Naval Officials." *Nineteenth Century,* November 1884, pp. 702-14.

Blackburn, Henry. "The Illustration of Books and Newspapers." *Ninteenth Century,* February 1890, pp. 213-24.

Blackith, C.H.F. "Fleet Street in Paris: VIII—The Pall Mall Gazette." *Journalist,* January 14, 1887, p. 222.

Blathwayt, Raymond. "Lions in Their Dens: III—George Newnes at Putney." *Idler,* March 1893, pp. 161-73.

————. "Literature in Journalism: A Talk with Sir Wemyss Reid." *Great Thoughts,* April 5, 1902, pp. 217-18.

————. "The Press and the Democracy: A Talk with Mr. Ernest Parke of 'The Star.'" *Great Thoughts,* May 27, 1893, 170-72.

C., S. "A Few Remarks on the 'Fourth Estate.'" *Welsh Review,* July 1892, pp. 932-36.

Chamberlain, Joseph. "Labourers' and Artisans' Dwellings." *Fortnightly Review,* December 1, 1883, pp. 761-76.

Conservative Journalist. "The Establishment of Newspapers." *National Review,* August 1885, pp. 818-28.

"Contemporary Literature: VIII. Newspaper Offices." *Blackwood's Magazine,* October 1879, pp. 472-93.

[Crawford, Emily.] "Notes from Paris: Mr. W. T. Stead." *Truth,* April 24, 1912, pp. 1029-30.

Dawson, Albert. "An Interview with Sir George Newnes, Bart." *Bookman,* May 1899, pp. 38-40.

Demos [pseud.] "To the Metropolitan Editors." *Journalist,* October 22, 1886, p. 30.

Dennis, Robert. "'The Future of Journalism': A Reply to Mr. Stead." *Journalist,* November 26, 1886, pp. 101-2.

Fawcett, Millicent Garrett; Holland, Henry Scott; and Cook, E. T. "W. T. Stead." *Contemporary Review,* May 1912, pp. 609-17.

Gardner, FitzRoy; Cust, Henry; Pollock, Walter Herries; Henley, W. E.; and Low, Sidney J. "The Tory Press and the Tory Party." *National Review,* May 1893, pp. 357-74.

Hurd, Archibald. "Our Panic-Built Navy: Before and after the War." *Fortnightly Review,* October 1, 1915, pp. 644-58.

"The Law and the Lawyers." *Law Times,* May 28, 1887, p. 55.

A London Sub-Editor: "Sub-Editing a London Newspaper." *Chambers's Journal,* October 18, 1879, pp. 663-64.

[Massingham, H. W.] "A Great Journalist." *Nation,* April 20, 1912, p. 83.

————. "The Great London Dailies: The Halfpenny Evening Press." *Leisure Hour,* September 1892, pp. 740-43.

————. "The Great London Dailies: The Penny Evening Papers.—The 'Pall Mall Gazette.'" *Leisure Hour,* July 1892, pp. 607-10.

"The Modern Newspaper." *British Quarterly Review,* April 1872, pp. 348-80.

Morland, C. E. "The Art of Interviewing." *Great Thoughts,* June 11, 1892, pp. 373-74.

"Notes." *Tablet,* May 7, 1887, pp. 727-28.

"Notes of Current Events." *Methodist Times,* October 1, 1885, p. 656; May 19, 1887, p. 317; August 18, 1887, pp. 548-49.

O'Connor, T. P. "The New Journalism." *New Review,* October 1889, pp. 423-34.

Pennell, Joseph. "Art and the Daily Paper." *Nineteenth Century,* October 1897, pp. 653-62.

Phillips, Evelyn March. "The New Journalism." *New Review,* August 1895, pp. 182-89.

Phillips, H.A.D. "Offenses against Marriage and the Relations of the Sexes." *Law Quarterly Review,* October 1885, pp. 471-84.

Reed, H. Bryon. "The Conservative Provincial Press." *National Review,* August 1885, pp. 866-68.

Reid, Arnot. "The English and the American Press." *Nineteenth Century,* August 1887, pp. 219-33.

————. "Twenty-Four Hours in a Newspaper Office." *Nineteenth Century*, March 1887, pp. 452-59.

[Reid, Wemyss]. "The Modern Press: IV.–'The Review of Reviews.'" *Speaker*, January 28, 1893, pp. 99-100.

Roberts, W. "Leading London Papers and Their Editors: No. 1–The 'Pall Mall Gazette' and Mr. Cook." *Great Thoughts*, October 22, 1892, pp. 73-74.

————. "Leading London Papers and Their Editors: the 'Review of Reviews' and Mr. Stead." *Great Thoughts*, March 18, 1893, pp. 443-44.

Rossiter, E. "The Commercial Department of a Newspaper." *Journalist*, February 18, 1887, p. 302.

Salisbury, Lord. "Labourers' and Artisans' Dwellings." *National Review*, November 1883, pp. 301-16.

Scott, J. W. Robertson. "Newspaper Head-Lines." *Journalist*, June 24, 1887, pp. 173-74.

Stead, W. T. "The Future of Journalism." *Contemporary Review*, November 1886, pp. 663-79.

————. "Government by Journalism." *Contemporary Review*, May 1886, pp. 653-74.

————. "The Press in the Twentieth Century." *Great Thoughts*, March 1895, pp. 363-64.

"Steady, Sir, Steady." *Punch*, July 11, 1885, p. 17.

Stout, Edwin H. "How an Evening Newspaper Is Produced." *Young Man*, November 1893, pp. 373-74.

"The Younger Editors of To-Day: IV.–Mr. E. T. Cook." *Young Man*, September 1893, pp. 311-14.

"The Younger Editor of To-Day: I.–Mr. T. P. O'Connor, M.P." *Young Man*, May 1893, pp. 152-54.

Index

263